Emotional Development
in Atypical Children

Emotional Development in Atypical Children

Edited by
Michael Lewis
Margaret Wolan Sullivan
Robert Wood Johnson Medical School

LEA LAWRENCE ERLBAUM ASSOCIATES, PUBLISHERS
1996   Mahwah, New Jersey

Lawrence Erlbaum Associates, Inc., Publishers
10 Industrial Avenue
Mahwah, New Jersey 07430

Cover design by Gail Silverman

Library of Congress Cataloging-in-Publication Data

Emotional development in atypical children / edited by Michael Lewis,
    Margaret Wolan Sullivan.
            p.   cm.
        "Originally presented at a conference sponsored by the Center for
    Human Development and Developmental Disabilities at University of
    Medicine and Dentistry of New Jersey-Robert Wood Johnson Medical
    School"—Pref.
        Includes bibliographical references and index.
        ISBN 0-8058-1967-3 (cl. : alk. paper).—ISBN 0-8058-1968-1 (pbk.
    : alk. paper)
        1. Exceptional children—Psychology—Congresses. 2. Handicapped
    children—Psychology—Congresses. 3. Emotions in children—
    Congresses. 4. Social skills in children—Congresses. I. Lewis,
    Michael, 1937 Jan. 10- II. Sullivan, Margaret Wolan. 1952-   .
    BF723. E9E47   1996
    155.45—dc20   95-49703
                                                    CIP

Books published by Lawrence Erlbaum Associates are printed
on acid-free paper, and their bindings are chosen for strength
and durability.

Printed in the United States of America
10 9 8 7 6 5 4 3 2 1

Contents

Preface

Since the 1970s, there has been a significant increase in interest in emotional development. Research on the emotional lives of infants and young children has been recognized as important in understanding the nature of children's development. In general, children's functioning in relation to their peers, teachers, parents, and themselves requires that we pay attention to their emotional well-being. Recently, a handbook of emotions was published (Lewis & Haviland, 1993), perhaps the best acknowledgment that the study of emotions now occupies an important place in our intellectual exploration. Although research in emotional development continues, most of our studies have involved emotional development in children without disabilities. Little research has been conducted in terms of emotional development in children with atypical needs. This is surprising for at least two reasons. To begin with, without an appreciation of atypical emotional development, any theory about emotions will be incomplete. Thus, there is much to learn from the study of children with disabilities that will bear on our general theories of emotional development. Second, and perhaps of equal importance, is the fact that without an understanding of emotional development in children with disabilities we are unlikely to either understand fully the causes of their difficulties or to ameliorate these difficulties. Imagine for example the feelings of an 8-year-old child with learning disabilities who has trouble reading or those of a child who has motor impairment and cannot run and play with other children. It is not difficult to realize that their emotional lives are affected by such disabilities. Certainly, their feelings of embarrassment and shame are bound to have profound affects on their learning, on their social adjustment, and on how they think about themselves. It is not too far fetched to argue that most disabilities cause secondary problems for these children, problems having to do with their inability to cope with the emotions associated with the stigma of the disability.

Early emotional development, emotional regulation, and the links between emotion and social or cognitive functioning in atypically developing children have not received much attention. This lack is due in part to the priorities given to the educational and therapeutic needs of these children. Yet an understanding of the basic emotional processes in the child with atypical development can only serve to promote more effective strategies for teaching and intervening in the lives of these children and their families and may contribute to our understanding of basic emotional processes.

Attention to the emotional development of the atypical child is especially timely. Infants and young children with physical and/or mental disabilities are increasingly coming to the attention of the health care and educational communities. This influx reflects, in part, social policies mandating the provision of infant intervention services and preschool education for such children, advances in medical care of the young child with disabilities, and better identification and outreach procedures. The focus of intervention and education programs for the atypically developing child, and indeed until recently, much of the research, was largely on facilitating the attainment of physical and cognitive milestones. In recent years, the focus of education and intervention efforts has moved toward an emphasis on the functional adaptation of children with disabilities within the family and their inclusion as far as possible into the mainstream of life. Emotional and social factors in the development of children with known disabilities or those who are at risk for atypical development are therefore of considerable interest. Information on emotion and its interaction with social and cognitive processes are important for assessing and predicting competence because these are likely to impact on the emerging social and functional adaptation of these children. But even more important, they are necessary for the design of appropriate intervention and educational practices.

Emotions, as we have come to understand, are affected by a variety of factors. These factors are themselves likely to be affected by disabilities. Let us consider some of these factors. To begin with, perceptual-motor skills are needed in order to perceive the expressions of others as well as to produce recognizable expressions. In addition to these skills are basic cognitive capacities, the ability to remember and to associate events that have emotional content, what is painful or not, and to remember who is familiar or strange. As the child gets older, new cognitive skills emerge and affect emotional growth. With the development of self-consciousness in the second half of the second year of life comes the ability to feel embarrassment, shame, and pride (Lewis, 1992a). Many more capacities are involved in emotional life and in each case the child with disabilities may differ on one or more of them. Consideration of how variation in these capacities impact on the emotional lives of children with disabilities affords us the opportunity to broaden our understanding of emotional development.

Before turning to the contents of this volume, it is important once again to emphasize that when we speak about "emotions," we usually mean some complex set of processes and abilities, whether or not our topic is normal or atypical development. When we use the term *emotion*, we usually mean at least three things: emotional expressions, emotional states, and emotional experiences (Lewis & Michalson, 1983). Emotional expressions represent the surface manifestation of emotion, the facial and bodily activity first described by Darwin (1872/1969) and later formalized in two facial coding systems by Izard (1979) and Ekman (1984). Emotional states represent as yet undiscovered, internal changes located in the body (soma, central nervous system, or hormones) that correspond to the expressions, although not necessarily in any simple one-to-one fashion. Finally, there are emotional experiences, those cognitive states or mental representations of our expressions and states. Thus, when someone says "I am happy," he or she means that he or she is in a state of happiness and is aware of that state. Again, experiences need not have any one-to-one correspondence with expressions or states.

These three aspects of emotional life are affected by socialization practices, maturational change, and individual biological differences including in this case differences in children as a function of disability. The nature of the disability in connection with the type of socialization can affect any one or all of these features of emotional life. In any volume on emotional development in children with disabilities, it would be enlightening to present examples from different disabilities as they affect these different features of emotional life. Unfortunately, little information is currently available that would allow us to do this. Nevertheless, this volume presents examples from several areas and provides at least a start in that direction.

Emotional expression is the most used measure of emotions, especially in infants and young children. The research on facial expression feedback and differences in facial expression between children with and without disabilities is represented in several chapters. Facial expression is above all a communicative act between two people. In children with disabilities facial communication is likely to show difficulties because it involves motor impairment in the ability to express emotion. For example, in infants with Down syndrome, the onset of smiling is known to be delayed relative to infants without the syndrome, and thus may affect early mother–infant social exchanges. In this volume, emotional expression and its interaction as a function of atypical development is considered in Field's chapter on expressivity as well as in Walden and Kniep's chapter on children's reading and responding to social signals of their mothers. It is also the center piece of the Lewis and Sullivan's chapter as well as Mundy and Willoughby's work on nonverbal communication.

At the earliest and perhaps simplest cognitive level is the ability to recognize and therefore respond to the socioemotional signals of others. Walden and Kniep examine the differences between children with and without disabilities in their ability to detect and respond to the social signaling of their mothers. Lewis and Sullivan examine the situational constraints with respect to emotional expression in early social interaction. In their work, individual differences in the mother–child interaction, as a function of context as well as disability status, point to the differences in meaning that are established through the mother–child relationship. More complex cognitive levels are addressed in Kasari and Sigman's work examining emotional understanding and responsiveness in autistic children and pointing out the potential cognitive deficits that may be associated with this disorder.

Work on attributions and on self-conscious emotions occupies a larger than usual share of space in this volume because this topic has received perhaps the least attention in the work on children with disabilities. Attributions or the beliefs in why things happen the way they do, as well as self-focused attention have to be considered in any discussion of emotional development in children with disabilities. Once past infancy, how children think of themselves is a central issue in their emotional behavior and development (Lewis, 1992b). In a series of chapters, this topic is taken up in some detail. Fox and Sobel look at how children think about themselves in terms of children's inhibited behavior. Turner and Casey, in their separate chapters, each explore the attributional attitudes of children with handicaps; in particular, how they view themselves in terms of whether they or chance determines why things happen. It is quite clear that children often view themselves as the cause of their disability and also view themselves as helpless in the face of those disabilities. As is seen here, this attributional style has critical impact on children's emotional development.

Alessandri and Lewis explore how unique social experiences affect children's emotional expressions and experiences. Observing maltreated children, they examine children's reactions to success and failure, in particular children's shame and pride when they fail or succeed. Collectively, these chapters on attributions touch on what is perhaps one of the most neglected areas in development of emotion in life, the problem of self-conscious, self-evaluative emotions. Camras, Sachs-Alter, and Ribordy pick up on the theme of emotional understanding in maltreated children as they explore how maltreatment impacts on children's emotional lives. The final chapter by Denham, Lydick, Mitchell-Copeland, and Sawyer presents an overview of the instruments available for measuring socioemotional behavior in children. This chapter allows clinician and scientist alike to consider emotional development by presenting available instruments for its measure.

The issue of socialization of emotions is addressed in nearly every chapter by considering how the social environment in conjunction with the child's growing cognitive ability impact on children's emotional development. Socialization practices, especially with children with disabilities, constitutes a feature of nearly all the chapters and provides much needed information on children with atypical development.

These chapters bring together the latest findings from a number of leading researchers in the field of emotional development as well as innovative work by a number of investigators working with children with disabilities. The chapters were originally presented at a conference sponsored by the Center for Human Development and Developmental Disabilities at University of Medicine and Dentistry of New Jersey—Robert Wood Johnson Medical School. The conference, part of a series dealing with research issues in developmental disabilities and mental retardation, is an interdisciplinary effort of the Department of Pediatrics of Robert Wood Johnson and was funded in part by the State of New Jersey, Department of Human Services, Office for Prevention of Mental Retardation and Developmental Disabilities. The volume is the second in the series and we gratefully acknowledge the continued support of David Carver, Chairman of Pediatrics, and Deborah Cohen, Director of Department of Human Services/Office for Prevention of Mental Retardation and Developmental Disabilities in our efforts to bring the conference papers to the larger community.

We hope that the volume will be informative for researchers, clinicians, and educators in a variety of disciplines and settings. Our aim is to bring into sharper focus issues in the emotional life of children with atypical development and highlight new areas of study and intervention. In addition to the participants involved in the chapters, we wish to thank Margaret Bendersky, Candice Feiring, Claire Kopp, Mary Lotze, David Mandelbaum, Robert Marvin, Janice Prontnicki, Douglas Ramsay, Kapila Seshadri, and Lawrence Taft who attended the conference and contributed to the volume through their observations, comments, and discussion of the various papers.

—Michael Lewis
—Margaret W. Sullivan

REFERENCES

Darwin, C. (1969). *The expression of emotions in man and animals.* Chicago: University of Illinois Press. (Original work published 1872)

Ekman, P. (1984). Expression and the nature of emotion. In K. R. Scherer & P. Ekman (Eds.), *Approaches to emotion* (pp. 319–344). Hillsdale, NJ: Lawrence Erlbaum Associates.

Izard, C. E. (1979). *The Maximally Discriminative Facial Movement Coding System* (MAX). Newark: Instructional Resources Center, University of Delaware.

Lewis, M. (1992a). *Shame: The exposed self.* New York: The Free Press.

Lewis, M. (1992b). Stigma. In M. Lewis, *Shame: The exposed self* (pp. 194–207). New York: The Free Press.

Lewis, M., & Haviland, J. (Eds.). (1993). *Handbook of emotions.* New York: Guilford Press.

Lewis, M., & Michalson, L. (1983). From emotional state to emotional expression: Emotional development from a person–environment interaction perspective. In D. Magnusson & V. L. Allen (Eds.), *Human development: An interactional perspective* (pp. 261–275). New York: Academic Press.

Expressivity in Physically and Emotionally Handicapped Children

Tiffany Field
University of Miami School of Medicine

Handicapped children, like nonhandicapped children, have individual differences in their expressivity. But additional constraints, both physical and social, work against the communication value of their expressivity. It is more difficult to read their emotions, harder to understand their gestures, and difficult to encourage their natural expressivity because they sometimes look and sound abnormal. In this review of our research on expressivity in physically and emotionally handicapped children, I discuss some of the constraints posed by genetic predispositions, biological or handicapping condition limitations, preschool and other environmental influences, and potential neurochemical influences.

GENETIC PREDISPOSITIONS

Individual Differences in Expressivity

Expressivity differs among individuals as early as birth. These individual differences may relate to temperament, autonomic reactivity, and neurochemical differences. Infants' expressivity and electrodermal responses to stimuli such as rats, buzzers, and bells were studied by Jones (1950). Consistent patterns of expressivity and autonomic reactivity were noted, patterns that Jones labeled *internalizer*, *externalizer*, and *generalizer* (see Fig. 1.1 for model). Internalizers had frequent galvanic responses but were not overtly expressive, whereas externalizers were overtly expressive but had

Internalizer	Generalizer	Externalizer
Low threshold	Moderate threshold	High threshold
High physiological reactivity	Moderate physiological reactivity	Low physiological reactivity
Low expressivity	Moderate expressivity	High expressivity
Rapid conditioning	Moderate conditioning	Slow conditioning

FIG. 1.1. Model for individual differences in expressivity.

infrequent physiological responses. Generalizers were both overtly and internally responsive. According to Jones (1960), infants were extraverted by nature, but later in childhood children increasingly controlled or inhibited their overt expressions, and electrodermal responses increased. This model is consistent with that of Eysenck (1967), who noted in studies on adults that facially expressive adults had low-level physiological responses. In addition, they rated themselves as more extraverted, had higher thresholds to stimulation, and were more difficult to condition. By contrast, introverted adults were less expressive facially, had lower thresholds to stimulation, showed physiological responsivity to stimulation, and were more readily conditioned.

Eysenck (1967) suggested that introverts had a lower threshold to activation of the ascending reticular activating system (ARAS) and are therefore more readily conditioned or more sensitive to socialization. During socialization, overt responses are inhibited, and a negative relationship develops between overt expression and electrodermal responding in the introverted person. The lower thresholds of the ARAS and the propensity to introversion are also seen as an innate process by Eysenck. The internalizing–externalizing mode of expressivity may be present from birth and merely reinforced or attenuated by socialization experiences.

Expressivity Differences in Newborns

In one of our studies, neonatal expressivity, thresholds to stimulation, and physiological reactivity were recorded to determine the extent to which the newborns' physiological reactivity was related to their expressivity (Field, Woodson, Greenberg, & Cohen, 1982). In this study, sleep state, activity level, facial expressions, heart rate (HR) and response to a series of pinpricks (as in the Brazelton Scale) were recorded to determine the sleeping neonates' threshold for tactile stimuli. Cry sounds were also recorded for measures of latency to cry and cry duration and a series of buzzer tones were presented to determine the infants' threshold for auditory stimulation. These procedures were followed by the Brazelton Scale and a facial discrimination/imitation procedure.

TABLE 1.1
Means for High- and Low-Expressivity Groups[a]

Measures	Expressivity of Infant	
	Low	High
Threshold		
Pinpricks to response	1.2	1.9
Expressivity (in percent)		
Accuracy of observers' guesses	48	80
Happy (mouth widens)	5	14
Sad (lip protrusion)	8	22
Surprise (mouth open)	20	44
Physiological responsivity		
Heart rate variability (beats per minute)	32	23
Habituation		
Trials to criterion	7	11
Looking time (seconds)	10	16

[a]All means significantly different at $p < .05$

The high-expressive infants (see Table 1.1) showed more frequent imitative expressions, their facial expressions were accurately guessed more often than chance, they looked longer during the later trials of the series of faces presented to them, they had a lower mean HR but higher HR variability during sleep, they received more optimal Brazelton scores on orienting, state organization, and response to stress, and they had shorter mean latency to cry during the pinprick procedure. The high-expressive infants in this study were more socially responsive during the Brazelton interaction items and were more modulated or less irritable in their responses to stimulation, particularly stressful stimulation during the Brazelton. The Brazelton data suggest that the high-expressive infants were less aroused, showed higher sensory thresholds, and showed less intense responses to stimulation.

The lower mean HR of the high-expressive infants during sleep, together with their greater HR variability, was similar to data by Garcia-Coll, Kagan, and Reznick (1984), who found that infants who were uninhibited in their expressivity had lower resting mean HR and greater HR variability. During auditory stimulation trials, the high-expressive infants also showed lower mean HR and greater HR variability. Unfortunately, because of concerns about movement artifacts neither our group nor Garcia-Coll et al. collected HR data during the actual procedure for which the data on expressive or uninhibited behaviors were collected. That HR data would have more directly assessed the hypothesized negative relationship between facial expressivity and autonomic reactivity. This negative relationship might also explain data by Lewis, Brooks, and Haviland (1978) in their cleverly titled paper "Hearts and Faces," suggesting strong facial responses in some infants and strong HR responses in other infants.

The fact that our high-expressive infants looked longer at the face stimuli during the latter trials suggests that they were less readily habituated to the face stimuli, a result that is somewhat similar to Eysenck's (1967) data on extraverted adults, all of whom were less readily conditioned. An external-izer–internalizer typology or the extraverted–introverted distinction pro-posed by Eysenck is suggested by the significant individual differences between high- and low-expressive infants on attentiveness, responsivity to social stimulation, autonomic reactivity, and accuracy of mimicry soon after birth. The expressive infants were less reactive autonomically, had higher thresholds, and were less readily habituated to face stimuli.

Monozygotic Twins are More Similar on Expressivity at Birth

To further explore individual differences in expressivity we assessed 28 monozygotic (MZ) and 28 dizygotic (DZ) twins in the same habituation-imitation procedure. The analyses in general revealed greater concordance within the MZ twin pairs than within the DZ twin pairs. With respect to the habituation data, the mean number of trials to habituation and the mean looking times per trial did not differ between the MZ and DZ twin groups. However, the difference scores between individual infants within twin dyads were greater for the DZ twins than for the MZ twins. The average difference scores for mean looking time during the happy face trials were 2.5 seconds for the MZ twins and 5.5 seconds for the DZ twins. Even greater differences were noted between MZ and DZ twins on the sad face and surprise face trials.

Similarly, for a 5-point expressivity rating, a greater difference was observed in expressivity between infants belonging to DZ twin pairs than between infants belonging to MZ twin pairs. There was a similarly greater discordance between the DZ twins for the measure of accuracy with which the model's facial expression could be guessed by looking at the expression on the neonate's face. For example, for the happy face expression trials the discordance rate for the DZ twins was 60% versus 43% for the MZ twin pairs. These data on the greater concordance of expressivity in newborn MZ twins versus DZ twins provide additional support for the observation that individual differences in expressivity occur as early as birth. Expressive neonates begin life with the advantage of being more socially responsive, as evidenced by their superior Brazelton interaction scores. This, in turn, contributes to better interactions with their parents. At the preschool stage, more expressive children are more popular and experience more positive social interactions with their peers (Buck, 1975; Field & Walden, 1982). In addition to experiencing less difficulty in interacting with their peers, expressive, externalizer children may experience less physiological arousal and less stress-related disease and may show more empathy.

BIOLOGICAL OR HANDICAPPING CONDITION LIMITATIONS

In this section, research is reviewed suggesting that the more severe the handicapping condition, the more difficult the temperament on all dimensions; expressivity or temperament differs across handicapping conditions even when the children are the same developmental age; there is some variation across situations, for example, the child interacting with the mother versus interacting in the classroom; and there is moderate agreement across observers, be they teachers, parents, or observers. We considered that temperament may be less optimal in more severe handicapping conditions because of the frustrations felt by the infant with a greater handicap, and we expected that temperament assessments might differ across parents and teachers because they were being observed in two different environments, at home and in school.

Severity of Handicapping Condition Affects Temperament

In a study exploring these questions (Greenberg & Field, 1982), 55 normal and same-developmental age, developmentally delayed, Down syndrome, cerebral palsy, and audiovisually handicapped infants (see Fig. 1.2) were observed. The infants' temperament was assessed on the Carey Infant Temperament Questionnaire by the infants' mothers, teachers, and an independent observer. In addition, a rating scale was adapted from that questionnaire for observers to rate the temperament of the infants during classroom play interactions and during dyadic play interactions with the infants' mothers and teachers. Thus, the three variables assessed were the condition of the infant, the play situation, and the person making the assessment. The handicapped infants averaged 22 months chronological age and 10 months developmental age. The amount of developmental delay assessed by the inverse of the ratio of developmental age to chronological age ranged from 1% to 90% with the developmentally delayed infants averaging significantly less delay (32%) than the Down syndrome (52%), CP (56%), and audiovisually impaired (58%) infants. The observers' ratings were based on 12 weeks of 3 hours observation per week.

The data analyses suggested that normal and Down infants had less difficult temperaments than the developmentally delayed infants who, in turn, were rated as less difficult than the Cerebral palsy and perceptually handicapped or audiovisually impaired infants (see Fig. 1.2). Mothers rated infants' temperament as less difficult than the observers who in turn rated infants as less difficult than the teachers. Greater interrater agreement

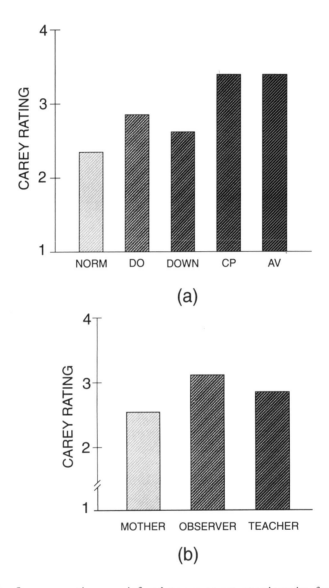

FIG. 1.2. Summary ratings on infants' temperament questionnaire for normal (NORM), developmentally delayed (DD), Down syndrome, cerebral palsied (CP), and audiovisually handicapped (AV) infants.

occurred between teachers and observers than teachers and mothers, probably because the teachers and observers had rated their child in the same environment (the classroom). A child's temperament may differ at home and school and mothers and teachers may have different expectations and different baselines for comparisons.

A step effect could be seen across developmental disability on all temperament dimensions including activity, adaptability, threshold, approach, intensity, mood, distractibility, and persistence. On the activity dimension, the audiovisually impaired infants received the most difficult ratings; not surprising because a motor handicap, blindness, or deafness significantly constrains activity. On the adaptability dimension, the Down infants were rated as the most adaptable, consistent with the stereotype that Down infants are generally accepting of novel situations and changes in routine and are generally pleasant and friendly. On the threshold dimension, the normal and developmentally delayed infants were noted to have lower thresholds to sensory stimulation. The handicapped infants reacted similarly to different people and only to moderate amounts of stimulation. This finding is consistent, at least with Cicchetti and Sroufe's (1978) finding that more stimulation is required to elicit laughter in the Down syndrome infant. On the intensity dimension, responses were more intense for normal infants than handicapped infants, for example, to hunger, new food, diaper changes, baths, sounds, strangers, and familiar people. On the mood dimension, the Down, CP, and blind–deaf infants had neutral or flat affect. On the distractibility dimension, the normal and developmentally delayed infants were more readily distracted from ongoing behaviors than were the sensory handicapped infants. This seems inconsistent with the Cicchetti and Sroufe data suggesting that once a crying response was elicited from a Down infant the examiner would have considerable difficulty "turning him off" or "distracting him" from an ongoing behavior like crying. On the persistence dimension, the handicapped infants, because of more delayed motor and cognitive development, had difficulty sustaining activities.

Ratings Differ by Interaction Context and by Observer

When temperament ratings were compared across the interaction contexts (classroom, dyadic teacher, and dyadic mother interactions) ratings were easier for the dyadic interactions with the teacher than the classroom ratings on several of the temperament dimensions. The only dimension for which the classroom rating was easier was the persistence dimension. Temperament was also rated easier in the infants' dyadic interactions with the mothers than in the classroom. Ratings of the mother and teacher interactions did not differ, except on the intensity dimension that was rated as less difficult during interactions with teachers, and on a threshold dimension on which the infants received easier ratings during interactions with their mothers. Mothers appeared to be less directive with the infants than the teachers, and the teachers usually managed to elicit better task performance. The mothers elicited more affective behavior.

Generally speaking, the developmentally delayed children were expressive and, although their temperament reflected individual differences, they generally were fairly positive. The children with moderate physical and mental handicaps who were not severely disabled seemed to exhibit more swings in expressivity and tended to be "cranky" at times and "more than content" at other times. The severely handicapped children were mostly passive and unresponsive and only occasionally cried. Generally, however, the handicapped children were passive, less actively engaged, had flat affect, and neutral responses. They became more active and expressive in dyadic play situations where they seemed to have easier temperament.

CLASSROOM ENVIRONMENT INFLUENCES

In this section, studies are reviewed on various environmental variables: (a) mainstreaming versus homogeneous grouping; (b) equal numbers of handicapped children integrated with normal children versus the handicapped being outnumbered; (c) being grouped with developmentally younger/ older children; (d) classroom versus playground setting effects; and (e) the play of handicapped children with and without friends.

Mainstreaming Versus Homogeneous Grouping

Until recently, most investigations of mainstreaming have involved children of grade-school age and the assimilation of a very small number of handicapped children into the normal classroom. Mainstreaming was considered ineffective in part because it was started too late and in part because the handicapped children were outnumbered (Bryan, 1974; Iano, Ayers, Heller, McGettingen, & Walker, 1974). In a later study conducted at the University of Miami (Field, Roseman, DeStefano, & Koewler, 1982), handicapped children were observed in a nonintegrated situation (handicapped alone in a group) and in an integrated situation (handicapped and normal children together in the same setting, the school playground). Approximately equal numbers of normal and handicapped preschool-age children were together in the integrated setting. The setting was a large playground adjacent to the school featuring a number of climbing structures, tree swings, crawling tunnels, a sand box, and a wading pool.

The behavior observations suggested the following (see Table 1.2):

1. the normal preschoolers spent more time than the handicapped preschoolers during both integrated and nonintegrated play in looking at, vocalizing to, and being physically close to the other children. In

TABLE 1.2
Mean Proportions of Time of Behavior Directed at Same-Class and
Other-Class Peers, Teachers, and Objects During Integrated and
Nonintegrated Play Session

Behavior Directed at	Normal Children				Handicapped Children			
	Nonintegrated		Integrated		Nonintegrated		Integrated	
Children								
(same class and other class)								
Looking	62.0	<	52/20*	>	46.0	<	35/32	
Vocalizing	27.0		22/2*	>	3.0		2/2	
Smiling	2.0		2/.2		.5		.2/.8	
Being close to	71.0	<	71/20*	>	48.0	<	45/36	
Touching	6.0		4.1*		4.0		5/2*	
Teacher								
Looking	25.0		24.0	<	41.0	>	34.0	
Vocalizing	6.0		2.0		11.0		8.0	
Smiling	4.0		3.0		4.0		2.0	
Being close to	23.0		22.0	<	43.0		49.0	
Touching by child	5.0		4.0		1.0	>	11.0	
Touching by teacher	.5		2.0	<	7.0	>	4.0	
Play Objects								
Looking	45.0	>	31.0		42.0		34.0	
Vocalizing	.4		1.0	<	7.0	>	0.0	
Smiling	.2		.1		.1		0.0	
Touching	59.0		67.0	>	53.0		46.0	
Self								
Looking	.1		.4		.3		.8	
Vocalizing	8.0	>	3.0		3.0		3.0	
Smiling	2.0		1.0		3.0		3.0	
Touching	1.0		4.0		1.0		2.0	

Note. < = significantly less than; > = significantly more than; * = significant differences between behavior directed at same-class or other-class children.

addition, they spent less time looking at and less time close to the teachers and were touched less often by the teachers. Their object-directed play involved less vocalizing but more manipulation of objects;

2. when playing in the nonintegrated compared to the integrated situations, the normal preschooler spent less time looking at other children and being close to them but more time looking at toys and more time talking to themselves;

3. when playing in the nonintegrated compared with the integrated situation, the handicapped preschoolers spent less time looking at other children and being close to them as well as less time touching the teachers, but more time being touched by the teachers and looking at the teachers and more time vocalizing to toys;

4. in the integrated situation, the normal and handicapped preschoolers did not differ on smiling at, vocalizing to, and touching children from the opposite classroom, but the handicapped children looked more frequently at and stayed closer to children of the opposite classroom than did the normal children;

5. the normal children in an integrated situation directed more looking, smiling, vocalizing, and touching at and were closer to their own classmates; and

6. the handicapped children in the integrated situation spent the same amount of time looking, smiling at, vocalizing to, and being close to their own classmates and the normal children and touched only their own classmates more often.

Thus, it would appear that more prosocial, child-directed and less teacher-directed, teacher-initiated behavior occurred for the handicapped children when they were playing with the normal preschool children. In addition, although the normal children continued to relate more frequently to their own classmates, the handicapped children watched and made as many social overtures to the normal peers as to their own classmates. The direction of effects suggested that the normal preschool children continued playing as if undisturbed by the addition of less developed children, whereas the handicapped children had to make a greater effort to involve themselves in the ongoing stream of activity.

Mainstreaming (Handicapped Outnumbered) Versus Matching (Equal Numbers)

In this study, a normal mainstreaming situation (mainstreaming a few handicapped children into a normal class where they were outnumbered by normal children) was compared with a situation of equal numbers handicapped and normal children (matching). In the matched numbers class, the handicapped children showed more smiling, gross motor play, parallel play, and constructive play (see Fig. 1.3). However, they also showed less fantasy play and less verbal interaction. The handicapped children interacted with other handicapped children more often in the matched numbers situation, and interacted more frequently with normal children in the mainstreamed or outnumbered situation. More attention was paid to the teacher in the matched numbers situation.

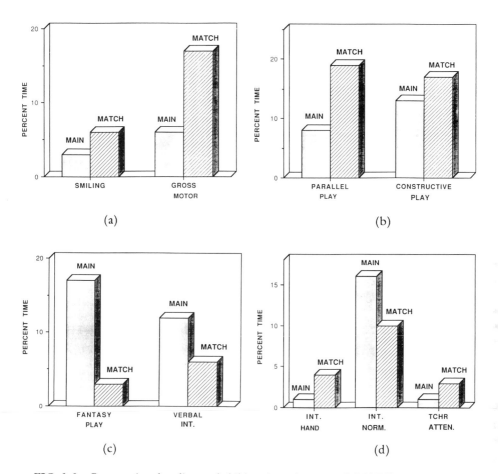

FIG. 1.3. Percent time handicapped children in mainstreamed (MAIN) group and group of equal numbers of handicapped children (MATCH) showed (a) smiling, gross motor activity, (b) parallel and constructive play, (c) fantasy play and verbal interaction, and (d) interaction with other handicapped children, interaction with normal children, and seeking attention from teacher.

Grouping With Developmentally Younger/Older Children

Hypotheses could be made that handicapped children would be advantaged by being grouped with same developmental age children. In that situation they could engage in more parallel play in which their skills were more evenly matched and they would be less frustrated. In contrast, the argument could be made that being mixed with older children would provide more modeling experiences as well as the nurturing activities of the older children.

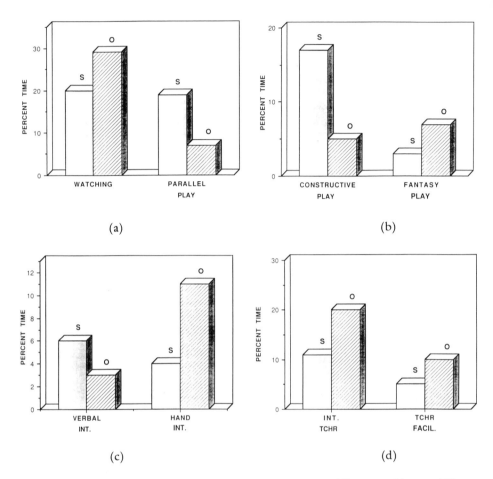

FIG. 1.4. Percent time handicapped children in same-age (S) versus older-age (O) group engaged in (a) watching and parallel play, (b) constructive and fantasy play, (c) verbal interaction and interaction with other handicapped children, and (d) interaction with teacher and teacher facilitation.

In this study we compared the same children (using the children as their own controls) in same developmental age groups and in older developmental age groups (see Fig. 1.4). Data suggested that some behaviors occurred more in one situation and some occurred more in the other. The handicapped children spent more time watching their peers in the older child situation. They spent more time in parallel and constructive play in the same age situation, but spent more time in fantasy play in the older age situation. The children spent more time in verbal interaction in the same age situation, but more interactions occurred with the handicapped in the older age situation. With respect to teacher interactions, the children interacted with the teachers more in the older age situation, and the teacher facilitated the play of the children more often in the older age situation.

Classroom Versus Playground Setting Effects

Again, using the handicapped children as their own controls, the children were observed in a classroom and playground setting. Again, their behaviors were differentially affected by the environmental variable (see Fig. 1.5). The

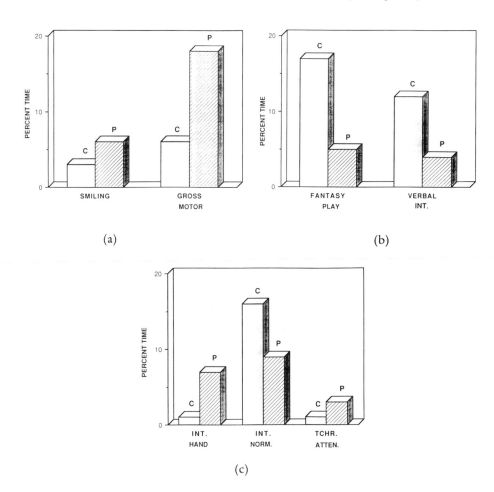

FIG. 1.5. Percent time handicapped children in classroom (C) versus on playground (P) showed (a) smiling and gross motor behavior, (b) fantasy play and verbal interaction, and (c) interaction with other handicapped children, interaction with normal children, and seeking attention from teacher.

children smiled more and engaged in more gross motor behavior on the playground versus the classroom. However, in the classroom they engaged in more fantasy play and they verbally interacted more frequently. The fact that they engaged in more fantasy play and verbal interaction in the classroom probably also explains why there were more interactions with normal children in the classroom versus the playground. In contrast, there were more interactions with the handicapped children on the playground versus the classroom. Teachers' attention was also directed at the children more often on the playground than in the classroom.

Handicapped Children With and Without Close Friends

In a study on normal preschool children who had close friends (i.e., played with one child 66% of the time) versus those who did not, the normal preschool children who had close friends were more verbal and facially expressive, more likely to take turns directing and submitting during play interactions, more likely to engage in fantasy play, and less likely to merely watch the activities of their peers (Roopnarine & Field, 1983; see Table 1.3). Thus, children who had close friends were generally "more engaging"

TABLE 1.3
Play Behaviors of Handicapped Children With and Without Friends

Behavior	With Friends	Without Friends	p Level
Wandering	10.2	14.8	.05
Watching—children	4.6	8.2	.01
—teachers	3.1	6.4	.05
Approaching—children	5.3	2.1	.001
—teachers	2.1	2.8	N.S.
Leading activity	2.3	.5	.005
Leaving activity	4.1	1.7	.001
Giving toys	.6	.3	N.S.
Taking toys	1.8	.5	.05
Touching child	2.6	1.6	N.S.
Hugging child	1.6	.1	.05
Aggressing against child	1.1	.8	N.S.
Imitation	3.0	2.0	N.S.
Fantasy play	1.6	1.1	N.S.
Vocalizing	4.3	1.6	.005
Laughing	2.7	.4	.005
Fussing	.7	.3	.005
Eye contact	8.4	7.4	N.S.
Happy face	3.9	.9	.001
Sad face	.1	.1	N.S.
Mad face	.5	.1	.05

in their social encounters and children who did not have close friends were more "watchful." Based on this study with normal preschool children, we expected to observe more expressive behavior among handicapped children who had close friends. The handicapped children were mainstreamed with normal children of equivalent developmental age inasmuch as our previous mainstreaming study had suggested that play behaviors may be facilitated in that situation (Field, Roseman, et al., 1982). Thirty-two children (16 handicapped preschoolers) who attended an all-day nursery participated in this study. The developmental age of the children averaged 20 months. The handicapping conditions included minimal CP, Down syndrome, and developmental delays.

Based on the sociogram data, only 7 of the 16 handicapped children had close friends (play with a particular peer at least 66% of the time). The remaining 9 children had no particular friend (based on their playing less than 33% of the time with a particular peer). Of the 7 children who had a friend, 1 handicapped child's friend was a normal peer, 1 handicapped child had both a handicapped and a normal friend, and 5 children had handicapped classmates as friends. The children with friends did not differ from those without friends on height, chronological age or developmental age, or type of condition. The only way they differed was on the Buck Affect Scale measuring extraversion–introversion. Children who had friends were rated by their teachers as being more extraverted.

Based on classroom observations, children who had close friends were more assertive in initiating, leading, and terminating play interactions than the children without close friends. Greater assertiveness was also suggested by more frequent hugging other children or taking toys. They were also more verbal, showed more affective displays, both positive and negative. The children who did not have friends spent more time wandering around and watching the other children.

Parallels between this study and the study on normal preschoolers are impressive. In both studies, four dimensions emerged for those children who had close friends: assertiveness, vocal activity, affective expressivity, and extraversion. These raise questions as to whether these children were simply more extraverted or whether they had developed a larger repertoire of social skills. The generally lower frequency of expressive behaviors among the handicapped children suggest a lower level of social skills in general. As Gottlieb and Leyser (1981) suggested, developmental lags in speech and language are noted in these children, and fewer affective behaviors and less assertiveness might be expected due to fear of failure. A high expectancy of failure seems to lower the level of performance below that which might be expected based on intellectual capabilities alone.

These factors may have contributed to the very small number (two of seven) of handicapped–nonhandicapped friendship pairs. Children may select equal-status friends. Although these children were approximately equivalent on developmental age, handicapped children are typically considered "lower status" among integrated groups of handicapped and normal children (Gottlieb & Leyser, 1981). In both pairs of handicapped–nonhandicapped friends, the most socially active handicapped children paired themselves with the most socially active normal children, as if the higher status children of both "hierarchies" were attracted to each other. Although Gottlieb and Leyser (1981) had suggested that the high-status child might serve as a model for behaviors to be imitated by the low-status child, and that the high-status children alter their attitudes toward low-status children after interacting with them, if the low-status children are pairing themselves with low-status children and the high-status children with high-status children, the effects of modeling and imitation may be attenuated.

One possible way to intervene is to arbitrarily pair children and reinforce that pairing to achieve the desired effect. For example, in a study entitled "A Medieval Kingdom: Leader-Follower Styles of Preschool Play" (Segal, Peck, Vega-Lahr, & Field, 1987) disruptive aggressive children were paired with nonaggressive children. The two social styles at risk for developing aggressive strategies are children who are like vassals or serfs. *Vassals*, as described by Adcock and Segal (1983), are children with relatively good social skills and moderately low social status, who seek out a strong leader as a steady playmate. These children are likely to resort to aggressive acts when their attempts to stay close to their leader are frustrated. If they are paired with a socially competent Lord who accepts them as a steady playmate, the need to maintain their position by forcibly excluding rivals is reduced. *Serfs*, on the other hand, seemingly become aggressive as a way of protesting their low position in the social hierarchy. When other children reject their attempts to be included, a vicious cycle can begin in which rejection and aggression both escalate. Pairing a serf with a Bishop-type child provides for harmonious dyadic relationships. Bishops who tend to enjoy intimate, conversational, and nonaggressive play provide the serf with nonthreatening companionship. In this study, Child A and B vassals were paired with successful Lords and Child C (an unsuccessful serf) was paired with a successful Bishop. As can be seen in Fig. 1.6, Child A and B became less aggressive after 12 weeks of this pairing. Child C first showed an increase in aggressive acts due to a bad pairing, but when paired with another Bishop showed a steady decline in aggressive behavior. These data combined pose real questions about the most optimal intervention strategy. More research is needed to determine whether modeling and imitation, social reinforcement by teachers, peer pairing or teacher coaching techniques, or combinations of the above are the most optimal.

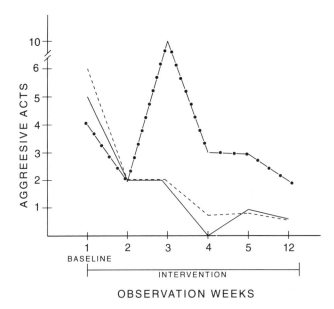

FIG. 1.6.   Mean number of aggressive acts (based on average of two observations per week) by child A(–), B(– – –) and C (– • –) during baseline observation (Week 1) and intervention period (Weeks 2–12).

PHYSIOLOGICAL INFLUENCES ON EXPRESSIVITY

Right Frontal EEG Activation in Infants

Previous research has suggested that the pattern of resting brain electrical activity recorded from anterior scalp locations may be a marker for the disposition to express negative affect and inhibition. Right frontal asymmetry has been noted in infants and young children selected for behaviors reflecting fearfulness or anxiety. Fox and colleagues reported that infants selected at 4 months of age for qualities said to predict inhibition exhibited right frontal asymmetry at 9 months of age (Calkins, Fox, & Marshall, in press). In addition, infants exhibiting stable right frontal asymmetry between 9 and 24 months of age were more likely to display fearfulness and inhibition in a series of laboratory situations (Fox, Calkins, & Bell, 1994). And, 4-year-old children who displayed reticence and social withdrawal in a peer session were more likely to display right frontal asymmetry (Fox, Rubin, et al., 1994). Finman, Davidson, Colton, Strauss, and Kagan (1989) also reported that 3-year-old children selected for behavioral inhibition were likely to exhibit right frontal asymmetry. Thus, data from normal infant and child populations suggest that right frontal asymmetry may be a marker for the temperamental disposition toward fear and shyness.

Infants of depressed mothers also show right frontal asymmetry (Field, Fox, Pickens, Nawrocki, & Soutullo, 1995). In our study on EEG asymmetry in very young infants (3- to 6-month-olds) of depressed mothers (Field et al., 1995), a greater number of depressed mothers and their infants displayed right frontal EEG asymmetry. These infants are also noted to show frequent negative affect as well as gaze aversion and lower activity levels (Cohn, Campbell, Matias, & Hopkins, 1990; Field, 1984). This "depressed" behavior appears to generalize to their interactions with adult strangers who are not depressed (Field et al., 1988). Their negative affect and mood state may reflect an endogenous trait or it may result from frequent exposure to a depressed mother. Dawson and colleagues (Dawson, Klinger, Panagitotides, Hill, & Spieker, 1992) found similar results for older infants (11- and 15-month-old infants) of mothers who had depressive symptoms. These data suggest that the depressed affect exhibited by infants of depressed mothers is associated with a pattern of brain electrical activity similar to that found in inhibited infants and children and in some depressed adults.

Vagal Tone and Its Relationship to Expressivity

Vagal tone (VT) is defined as the amount of inhibitory influence on the heart by the parasympathetic nervous system (Porges, 1985). Emotional reactivity in infants has been correlated with vagal activity (Field & Walden, 1982; Fox, 1989; Fox & Gelles, 1984; Pickens & Field, 1995; Porges, 1991; Stifter, Fox, & Porges, 1989). For example, newborns who exhibited greater HR variability were more expressive (Field & Walden, 1982), and 3-month-old infants with greater HR variability displayed longer duration interest expressions (Fox & Gelles, 1984). These data suggest that infants with higher VT are generally more reactive and more emotionally expressive.

Infants of depressed versus nondepressed mothers exhibit less "positive" and more "flat" affect as early as 3 months (Cohn, Campbell, Matias, & Hopkins, 1990; Field, 1984; Pickens & Field, 1993) and they show lower VT (Field et al., 1988). These findings, plus their higher HR and cortisol levels (Field et al., 1988), suggest that they might be more stressed during their early interactions with their mothers. In a recent study, we explored group differences and developmental changes in VT in 3- and 6-month-old infants of depressed and nondepressed mothers (Field, Pickens, Fox, Nawrocki, & Gonzalez, 1995). Lower VT was noted in infants of depressed versus nondepressed mothers at 6 months and the developmental increase in VT that occurred between 3 and 6 months for infants of nondepressed mothers did not occur for infants of depressed mothers. Correlation analyses suggested that lower VT at 6 months was related to fewer vocalizations. Vocalization is a form of emotional expressivity that is partially controlled by the vagus, and more frequent vocalizations in higher VT infants are consistent with other studies (Fox, 1989; Fox & Gelles, 1984; Porges, 1991).

Decoupling of VT and Emotional Expressions

Decoupling of VT and emotional expressions may be another manifestation of emotional dysregulation in infants. In this study, 3-month-old infants were videotaped during 3-minute face-to-face play interactions (Pickens & Field, 1995), their facial expressions were coded using the AFFEX facial expression coding system and their EKG was recorded during the interactions to assess the relationship between cardiac measures and facial expressivity. Infants of "depressed" mothers showed significantly more sad and anger expressions and fewer interest expressions than infants of nondepressed mothers. Vagal tone was correlated with joy and interest expressions and with self-comfort behaviors in the nondepressed group, but not in the depressed group, suggesting another relationship between expressivity and physiological functions.

NEUROCHEMICAL INFLUENCES ON EXPRESSIVITY

Neurochemical imbalances might also contribute to expressivity differences particularly in children with emotional and attentional handicapping conditions. Data from our labs suggest, for example, that infants of depressed mothers have noradrenergic, serotonergic, and dopaminergic dysfunction from the neonatal period that, however, normalized when they were given early intervention (Field et al., in press). Similar data have been noted for our sample of cocaine-exposed infants (Field et al., 1995). Examples of imbalances in these systems have been elaborated by Gray (1982, 1987), Quay (1988), and Rogeness, Javors, and Pliszka (1992). Gray (1982, 1987) elaborated a behavioral facilitation system (BFS) and a behavioral inhibitory system (BIS). Quay further elaborated Gray's work by hypothesizing how these systems may relate to child psychiatric disorders.

The BFS is a behavioral system that mobilizes behavior for active engagement with the environment. Examples of BFS behaviors include extraversion and aggressive behavior. The components of the BFS are thought to be integrated in the mesolimbic dopaminergic system (Gray, 1982) and to be activated primarily by rewarding stimuli. The BIS acts as an inhibitor of behavior, and its regulation appears to be centered in the septohippocampal system that appears to be noradrenergic with additional regulation from serotonergic projections from the median raphe. The BIS responds to nonreward, punishment and uncertainty. Affectively, frustration may be associated with nonreward, and fear and/or anxiety with punishment and uncertainty.

The balance of the BFS (dopaminergic system) and BIS (noradrenergic/serotonergic system) or the imbalance would reflect itself in affective behavior. For example, norepinephrine (Plaznik & Kostowski, 1983) and serotonin (Coccaro, 1989) have been shown to inhibit and dopamine to facilitate irritability and aggressivity (see Table 1.4). Serotonergic mechanisms inhibit irritable, aggressive behavior more than the noradrenergic system. The norepinephrine–dopamine (NE–DA) interactions described by Antelman and Caggiula (1977) suggested that when both NE and DA are depressed equally, one would not see the changes in behavior that occur when either one or the other is depressed. Thus, it seems to be the balance between these regulatory systems that determines normal expressivity. Expressivity may decline with decreasing age, for example, because of the decline in the dopaminergic and serotonergic systems and the relative unchange of the noradrenergic system that seems to provide increasing restraint of expressivity.

An example of imbalance comes from a study by Kraemer, Ebert, Lake, and McKinney (1989), who noted lower levels of norepinephrine in mother-deprived infants than mother-reared infants (monkey infants), which may have contributed to their heightened aggressivity. In contrast, as already mentioned, the elevated norepinephrine levels in the infants of depressed mothers may have contributed to their depressed affect. Other characteristics such as extraversion and introversion may be partially explained by the interactions of these systems.

The psychiatric disorders most commonly studied in childhood include autism, attention deficit hyperactivity disorder (ADHD), conduct disorder (CD), major depressive disorder, and Tourette's disorder. As has been suggested by Rogeness et al. (1992), all of these disorders, except for autism, could be seen as disorders secondary to dysregulation or imbalance of the three neurotransmitter systems. Rogeness reviewed data suggesting that major depression, anxiety disorder, and behavioral inhibition may be associated with high norepinephrine (NE) and serotonin (5HT) and normal to low dopamine (DA) function (see Table 1.5). For example, Kagan, Reznick, and Snidman (1987) found that children with behavioral inhibition had increased urinary NE and increased HR (the latter related to the former). Rogeness (1990) noted increased NE function in major depression and separation anxiety disorder in comparison to subjects with CD. In ADHD, a number of laboratories have found decreased norepinephrine.

Conduct disorder is associated with decreases in NE and decreases in 5HT or 5HIAA (serotonin). Although dopaminergic function has been hypothesized to be relatively high compared with NE function or 5HT

TABLE 1.4

Behaviors Associated With High and Low Levels of Dopamina (DA), Norepinephrine (NE), and Serotonin (5HT) (adapted from Rogeness et al., 1992)

	High	*Low*
Dopamine	Increased motor activity, aggressive, extroverted, reward driven	Decreased motor activity, nonaggressive, low interest in others, poor motivation
Norepinephrine	Good concentration and selective attention, conditions easily, internalizes values, easily becomes anxious, overly inhibited, introverted	Inattentive, conditions poorly, internalizes poorly, low anxiety, under inhibited
Serotonin	Good impulse control, low aggression	Poor impulse control, high aggression, increased motor activity

TABLE 1.5

Behavior Disorders Associated With High and Low Dopamine (DA), Norepinephrine (NE), and Serotonin (5HT) Combinations (adapted from Rogeness et al., 1992)

	High DA	Low DA
Low NE, low 5HT	Aggressive CD, ADD with hyperactivity, irritable, no anxiety or depression	Generally "normal," low motivation, schizoid, possible attentional problems
High NE, low 5HT	Aggressive, anxious/depressed CD, mild hyperactivity, adequate concentration	Overly inhibited and anxious, tendency to withdraw
Low NE, high 5HT	Nonaggressive CD, mild ADD with mild hyperactivity	ADD without hyperactivity, inhibited
High NE, high 5HT	Normal, extroverted and anxious, high energy, obsessive compulsive traits	Anxious, inhibited, depressed

ADD = attention deficit disorder, CD = conduct disorder

function in CD children, there are no current neurochemical data that show increased dopaminergic function in CD children.

For Tourette's disorder, the most consistent findings are an increase in dopaminergic function and a decrease in serotonergic function. According to Rogeness (1990), because serotonergic function appears to have an inhibitory and modulating role on dopaminergic function, increased serotonergic activity might be able to compensate for some of the dysregulation in the dopaminergic system.

These neurochemical dysfunctions in some of the childhood psychiatric disturbances highlight the importance of the serotonin and norepinephrine septohippocampal system and the dopamine basal ganglia system being in tune for normal expressivity to occur. Cloninger (1987) and Gray (1982, 1987) suggested, based on animal studies, that genetic or constitutional differences in the activity of these neurotransmitter systems clearly affect the way that humans express emotion.

SUMMARY

I began this chapter with a discussion of the important considerations underlying expressivity in handicapped children, starting with studies from our newborn and twin samples showing the predisposition for externalizer–internalizer type personalities or high expressivity–low expressivity. I then reviewed data from classroom studies of handicapped children (developmentally delayed, Down syndrome, CP and auditory–visual handicaps) suggesting that the severity of their handicapping condition significantly affected their temperament ratings, and that those ratings related more to the handicapping conditions than to developmental age but that they could be modified by, for example, dyadic interactions with teachers or mothers. I then reviewed a number of illustrations of modifying the environment and altering the expressivity of handicapped children by, for example, mainstreaming equal numbers of handicapped children with nonhandicapped children, by mixing them with developmentally younger versus older children, by having them play in the classroom versus the playground, and by showing differences between handicapped children who had a close friend versus those who did not.

For a discussion of the physiological and neurochemical imbalances that affects expressivity, I turned to studies on infants with right frontal EEG activation and those with low VT and decoupling of VT and behavior. These infants appear to have an affective–physiological–biochemical dysregulation that places them at risk for developmental delays (Field, 1995). Illustrations were given of neurotransmitter dysfunction in infants of depressed mothers and infants of cocaine-exposed mothers, and neurotransmitter dysfunction was discussed in the context of behavioral activation and behavioral inhibition functions involving the interaction of the noradrenergic, serotonergic and dopaminergic systems. Imbalances in these three systems could be seen in common childhood psychiatric disorders including depression, ADHD, CD, and Tourette's syndrome. Depression was associated with increased NE and serotonin and lower levels of DA, ADHD with lower levels of NE, CD with lower levels of NE and 5HT, and Tourette's syndrome with increased dopaminergic activity and decreased serotonergic function. Although the questions remain as to how all these influences including genetic, physical, environmental, physiological, and neurochemical interact, it is clear that for physically, emotionally, and behaviorally handicapped children these are important considerations, and insofar as possible they should be incorporated as measures in multivariate approaches to the problem and to designing interventions for the children.

ACKNOWLEDGMENTS

We would like to thank the children, teachers, and parents who participated in these studies and the researchers who helped with data collection and analyses. This research was supported by an NIMH Research Scientist Award (#MH00331), an NIMH Research Grant (#MH46586) to Tiffany Field, and funding from Johnson and Johnson.

REFERENCES

Adcock, D., & Segal, M. (1983). *Making friends.* Englewood Cliffs, NJ: Prentice-Hall.

Antelman, S.M., & Caggiula, A.R. (1977). Norepinephrine–dopamine interactions and behavior. *Science, 195,* 646–653.

Bryan, T.M. (1974). Peer popularity of learning disabled children. *Journal of Learning Disabilities, 7,* 621–625.

Buck, R.W. (1975). Nonverbal communication of affect in children. *Journal of Personality and Social Psychology, 31,* 644–653.

Calkins, S.D., Fox N.A., & Marshall, T.R. (in press). Behavioral and physiological antecedents of inhibition in infancy. *Child Development.*

Cicchetti, D., & Sroufe, L.A. (1978). An organizational view of affect: Illustration from the study of Down's syndrome infants. In M. Lewis & L.A. Rosenblum (Eds.), *The development of affect* (Vol. 1, pp. 309–350). New York: Plenum Press.

Cloninger, C.R. (1987). Neurologic adaptive mechanisms in alcoholism. *Science, 236,* 410–416.

Coccaro, E.F. (1989). Central serotonin and impulsive aggression. *British Journal of Psychiatry, 155,* 52–62.

Cohn, J.F., Campbell, S.B., Matias, R., & Hopkins, J. (1990). Face-to-face interactions of postpartum depressed and nondepressed mother-infant pairs at two
months. *Developmental Psychology, 26*, 15–23.

Dawson, G., Klinger, L.G., Panagitotides, H., Hill, D., & Spieker, S. (1992).
Frontal lobe activity and affective behavior of infants of mothers with depressive
symptoms. *Child Development, 63*, 725–737.

Eysenck, J.J. (1967). *The biological basis of personality.* Springfield, IL: Thomas.

Field, T. (1984). Early interactions between infants and their postpartum depressed
mothers. *Infant Behavior and Development, 7*, 517–522.

Field, T. (1995). Infants of depressed mothers. In M. Bornstein (Ed.), *Handbook of
parenting: Vol. 4. Applied and practical parenting* (pp. 85–99). Mahwah, NJ:
Lawrence Erlbaum Associates.

Field, T., Fox, N., Pickens, J., Nawrocki, T. & Soutullo, D. (1995). Right frontal
EEG activation in 3- to 6-month-old infants of "depressed" mothers. *Developmental Psychology, 31*, 358–363.

Field, T., Healy, B., Goldstein, S., Perry, S., Bendell, D., Schanberg, S., Zimmer-
man, E. A., & Kuhn, C. (1988). Infants of depressed mothers show "depressed"
behavior even with non-depressed adults. *Child Development, 59*, 1569–1579.

Field, T., Roseman, S., DeStefano, L., & Koewler, J., III. (1982). The play of
handicapped preschool children with handicapped and non-handicapped peers in
integrated and non-integrated situations. *Topics in Early Childhood Special
Education, 2*(3), 28–38.

Field, T., & Walden, T. (1982). Production and perception of facial expressions in
infancy and early childhood. In H. Reese & L. Lipsitt (Eds.), *Advances in child
development* (Vol. 16, pp. 169–211). New York: Academic Press

Field, T., Woodson, R., Greenberg, R., & Cohen, D. (1982). Discrimination and
imitation of facial expressions by neonates. *Science, 218*(8), 179–181.

Finman, R., Davidson, R.J., Colton, M.B., Strauss, A.M., & Kagan, J. (1989).
Psychophysiological correlates of inhibition to the unfamiliar in children.
Psychophysiology, 26, S24.

Fox, N.A. (1989). The psychophysiological correlates of emotional reactivity during
the first year of life. *Developmental Psychology, 25*, 364–372.

Fox, N.A., Calkins, S.D., & Bell, M.A. (1994). Neural plasticity and development
in the first year of life: Evidence from cognitive and socio-emotional domains of
research. *Development and Psychopathology.*

Fox, N.A., & Gelles, M. (1984). Face to face interaction in term and preterm
infants. *Infant Mental Health Journal, 5*, 192–205.

Fox, N.A., Rubin, K.H., Calkins, S.D., Marshall, T.R., Coplan, R.J., Porges, S.W.,
& Long, J. (1994). Frontal activation asymmetry and social competence at four
years of age: Left frontal hyper and hypo activation as correlates of social behavior in preschool children. *Child Development.*

Garcia-Coll, C., Kagan, J., & Reznick, J.S. (1984). Behavioral inhibition in young
children. *Child Development, 55*, 1005–1019.

Gottlieb, J., & Leyser, Y. (1981). Friendship between mentally retarded and nonretarded children. In S.R. Asher & J.M. Gottman (Eds.), *The development of
children's friendships* (pp. 150–181). Cambridge: Cambridge University Press.

Gray, J.A. (1982). *The neuropsychology of anxiety: An inquiry into the functions of the
septo-hippocampal system.* Oxford: Oxford University Press.

Gray, J.A. (1987). *The psychology of fear and stress.* Cambridge: Cambridge University Press.

Greenberg, R., & Field, T. (1982). Temperament ratings of handicapped infants during classroom, mother, and teacher interactions. *Journal of Pediatric Psychology, 7,* 387–405.

Iano, R.P., Ayers, D., Heller, H.B., McGettingen, J.P., & Walker, V.S. (1974). Sociometric status of retarded children in an integrative program. *Exceptional Children, 40,* 267–271.

Jones, H.E. (1950). The study of patterns of emotional expression. In M. Reymert (Ed.), *Feelings and emotions* (pp. 161–168). New York: McGraw-Hill.

Jones, H.E. (1960). The longitudinal method in the study of personality. In I. Iscoe & H.W. Stevenson (Eds.), *Personality development in children* (pp. 3–27). Chicago: University of Chicago Press.

Kagan, J., Reznick, J.S., & Snidman, N. (1987). The physiology and psychology of behavioral inhibition in young children. *Child Development, 58,* 1459–1473.

Kraemer, G.W., Ebert, M.H., Lake, C.R., & McKinney, W.T. (1989). Cerebrospinal fluid changes associated with pharmacological alteration of the despair response to social separation in rhesus monkeys. *Psychiatry Research, 11,* 303–315.

Lewis, M., Brooks, J., & Haviland, J. (1978). Hearts and faces: A study in the measurement of emotion. In M. Lewis & L. Rosenblum (Eds.), *The development of affect the genesis of behavior* (pp. 77–123) New York: Plenum Press.

Pickens, J.N., & Field, T. (1993). Facial expressivity in infants of "depressed" mothers. *Developmental Psychology, 29,* 986–988

Pickens, J.N., & Field, T. (1995). Facial expressions and vagal tone in infants of depressed and nondepressed mothers. *Early Development and Parenting, 4,* 83–89

Plaznik, A., & Kostowski, W. (1983). The interrelationship between brain noradrenergic and dopaminergic neuronal systems in regulating animal behavior: Possible clinical implications. *Psychopharmacology Bulletin, 19,* 5–11.

Porges, S.W. (1985). *Method and apparatus for evaluating rhythmic oscillations in aperiodic physiological response systems.* United States Patent Number: 4,510,944. April 16, 1985.

Porges, S.W. (1991). Vagal tone: A mediator of affect. In J.A. Garber & K.A. Dodge (Eds.), *The development of affect regulation and dysregulation* (pp. 111–128). New York: Cambridge University Press.

Quay, H.C. (1988). Attention deficit disorder and the behavioral inhibition system: The relevance of the neuropsychological theory of Jeffrey A. Gray. In L.M. Bloomingdale & J. Sergeant (Eds.), *Attention deficit disorder: Criteria, cognition, intervention* (pp. 117–125). Oxford: Pergammon Press.

Rogeness, G.A. (1990). *Norepinephrine and aggressive behavior.* Paper presented at the annual meeting of the American Academy of Child and Adolescent Psychiatry, Chicago.

Rogeness, G.A., Javors, M.A., & Pliszka, S.R. (1992). Neurochemistry and child and adolescent psychiatry. *Journal of the American Academy of Child Adolescent Psychiatry, 31,* 765–781.

Roopnarine, J., & Field, T. (1983). Peer-directed behaviors of infants and toddlers during nursery school play. *Infant Behavior and Development, 6,* 133–138.

Segal, M., Peck, J., Vega-Lahr, N., & Field, T. (1987). A medieval kingdom: Leader–follower styles of preschool play. *Journal of Applied Developmental Psychology, 8*, 79–95.

Stifter, C.A., Fox, N.A., & Porges, S.W. (1989). Facial expressivity and vagal tone in 5- and 10-month-old infants. *Infant Behavior and Development, 12*, 127–137.

– 2 –

Reading and Responding to Social Signals

Tedra Walden
Linda Knieps
Vanderbilt University

SOCIAL INTERACTION AND EMOTIONAL DEVELOPMENT

Although some aspects of emotional development are thought to be general across cultures and specific rearing experiences and thus are sometimes said to be "innate" (e.g., recognition and categorization of facial expressions; Ekman, 1992; Izard, 1992), few would argue that even these aspects of emotional functioning develop without input from the social environment. It is now recognized that the child's early interactions with the social and physical environment contribute importantly to his or her emotional functioning and emotional development (Walden & Garber, 1994). The adult–infant dyad is a mutually regulated system in which the infant and adult can assume reciprocal roles of initiator and responder. The balance of roles shifts over time, with the adult becoming less dominant as the child becomes more competent in initiating and sustaining interactions (Bronfenbrenner, 1979).

In the past, it was common to regard emotions simply as internal, private feelings. Today's view of emotion has changed dramatically, with emotions now being described by some as "processes of establishing, maintaining, or disrupting the relations between the person and the internal or external environment, when such relations are significant to the individual" (Campos, Campos, & Barrett, 1989, p. 395). Thus, emotion is seen as including the individual's understanding of the significance of an event, feelings that monitor events and one's potential for coping with them, and actual coping with the environment. Emotion regulation is seen as part of the event. Emotion is not considered to be solely intrapersonal, rather it is an interpersonal, interactive event that occurs in a context that influences its course.

EARLY SOCIOEMOTIONAL INTERACTIONS: INFANT SIGNALS AND PARENTAL RESPONSIVITY

We have been interested in one form of socioemotional regulation that occurs in caregiver–child interactions, social referencing. Social referencing is said to occur when one individual uses another's interpretation of a situation as information in constructing his or her own interpretation of a situation (Campos, 1983; Feinman, 1982).

Social referencing is an example of the interpersonal communicative context in which emotion occurs. This process of communication occurs between two or more participants who both focus on an outside stimulus or event. Referential communication such as this requires that both participants make the referent and the nature of the message clear to the partner. Thus, competent communication (both verbal and nonverbal) between individuals requires the participants to accurately send and interpret communicative social signals. The clarity of those signals and the partner's responsivity to them are important determinants of competent communicative interactions such as social referencing.

In order for parents to be responsive, the infant's signal must first be perceived and interpreted correctly, and an appropriate response selected and enacted (Lamb & Easterbrooks, 1981). Therefore, characteristics of infants' signals can impact on parental responsivity (Goldberg, 1977). Muted or ambiguous signals may be particularly difficult for parents to perceive, interpret, and respond to accurately. It has been shown that readability of infant signals is positively related to maternal responsiveness (Umbel & LaVoie, 1988).

Young infants are equipped with some behaviors that elicit parental attention and responses. Some of these behaviors are present at birth (e.g., crying), whereas others develop early in life (e.g., smiling, eye contact; Goldberg, 1977). In even the earliest parent–infant interactions, affective expressions serve as powerful communicative signals. Gianino and Tronick (1988) suggested that affect plays a crucial role in regulating parent–infant interaction. They also contended that misreading of each other's signals can interfere with reciprocity in social interaction.

Misread signals may be particularly problematic for interactions with infants and children who have developmental delays, as the affective expressions of such children may be more difficult to discern. Children with Down syndrome, for example, have been characterized as having muted or hard-to-read emotional expressions (Emde, Katz, & Thorpe, 1978). Other research indicates that these affective signals may be less predictable in infants with Down syndrome. For example Kasari, Mundy, Yirmiya, and Sigman (1990) found that infants with Down syndrome were much more labile in their affect, that is, they switched from one affective state to another more frequently than did infants without Down syndrome. The mutedness and unpredictability of infant signals may hinder smooth, responsive interactions between infants with Down syndrome and their parents.

Eye contact is another communicative signal available to young infants. However, infants with Down syndrome have also been characterized as having difficulty using this signal effectively. Jones (1980) found that infants with Down syndrome were much less likely to make referential eye contact with their parents than were nonhandicapped infants. Infants with and without Down syndrome were equally likely to make eye contact that was described as serving a personal or game purpose. Referential eye contact, however, is often the basis for communication about a third event (outside the dyad). Thus, parents of children with Down syndrome (and perhaps other developmental delays) are faced with a difficult task in interacting with their infants, as important communicative signals may be more difficult to discern in the course of interaction.

Research has shown that parents of infants and children with developmental delays do have a difficult time responding to their children's signals. Parents of children with developmental delays (particularly Down syndrome) have been described as more directive in their interactions with their children (e.g., Jones, 1980; Marshall, Hegrenes, & Goldstein, 1973). These parents have been shown to be more directive in terms of the types of communications with their children as well as in the timing or contingency between child and parent behavior. For example, Cardoso-Martins and Mervis (1985) found that the type of language differed in parents of children with and without Down syndrome; parents of children with Down syndrome used more imperatives and fewer child-appropriate labels. Others have described parents' directive behavior in terms of "responding" more during times when the infant or child is passive (i.e., offers fewer communicative signals). In this sense, parents' behavior is not contingent on their infants' behavior. Parents of children with delays tend to offer more interactional bids, even though their children are more passive in interactions. Buckhalt, Rutherford, and Goldberg (1978) found that, in an unstructured situation, parents of infants with Down syndrome interacted with their infants as much as did parents of nonhandicapped infants, even though the handicapped infants were less interactive. Buckhalt et al. also found that parents of children with Down syndrome vocalized more during a teaching interaction and appeared to be "trying harder" than did parents of non-handicapped children.

Thus, dyads with an infant with a developmental disability may have particular difficulty in communicative interactions. These infants are less likely (than infants without disabilities) to send strong, clear social signals (such as affective expressions and looking). Furthermore, parents of infants with developmental disabilities do not act as responsively to their childrens' signals.

In addition, infants with disabilities may have trouble reading the signals of their parents. Persons with mental retardation (MR) have been shown to have difficulty in decoding the emotional expressions of others. Maurer and Newbrough (1987a) found that adults with MR were less able to label photographs of basic facial expressions than were adults without MR. Generating a verbal label for facial expressions may be a relatively more difficult task than simply recognizing emotions; therefore, McAlpine, Kendall, and Singh (1991) conducted a study of the ability of adults and children with MR to recognize facial expressions when given the name (e.g., show me the person who is happy). This study also found that persons with MR were less able to recognize facial expressions of basic emotions than were adults and children without MR.

The apparent difficulty parents have in responding to their children's signals and the difficulty infants may have in reading their parents' signals may have important implications for children's development. Parental responsivity to infant signals is related to later social and emotional development. Bell and Ainsworth (1972) reported that the promptness with which mothers responded to their infants' signals predicted later reduced infant crying and superior development of alternative communicative signals (e.g., vocalizations). Responsivity may also be related to cognitive development. Lewis and Goldberg (1969) found a relation between maternal responsiveness and infants' rate of habituation to a repeated stimulus, a measure of cognitive development (Bornstein & Singer, 1986; Fagan & Sigman, 1983). Thus, parental responsivity can have important consequences in many areas of infant development.

For infants with developmental delays, responsivity to signals may be particularly important. Brinker and Lewis (1982) suggested that infants with developmental delays may have a difficult time in perceiving contingencies between their own behavior and responses to that behavior. Thus, for infants and children with delays, parents may need to be particularly responsive in order for the children to perceive the relation between their communicative signals and their parents' responses to them.

This difficulty in encoding and decoding social signals may have important consequences for socioemotional interactions such as social referencing. Social referencing is one important way in which infants and young children learn appropriate responses to novel events. As children with developmental delays have been said to exhibit more "inappropriate" behaviors, this process may be especially important in their social and emotional development. Social referencing may be one important way that "appropriate" behavior is acquired or one way "appropriate" emotional reactions to events are developed. This is because social referencing is used in forming an interpretation to events that occur.

In addition, for children who have some reaction to those events before social referencing, the match between others' reactions and one's own reaction serves as feedback about whether one is observing, interpreting, and reacting to events in similar ways as other persons. For children whose reactions differ from the reactions of other persons, social referencing can aid in calibrating those reactions in a more consensual direction. Children who do not reference those persons may never notice occasions when their responses differ from others' responses, and there will be no pressure to resolve the difference. In this way, the occurrence of social referencing serves as a socializing influence that may be absent or weak for children with developmental delays.

SOCIAL REFERENCING AND SOCIAL INTERACTION IN TYPICALLY DEVELOPING CHILDREN AND CHILDREN WITH DEVELOPMENTAL DELAYS

Social referencing is typically assessed by presenting an infant or child with ambiguous stimuli or events, and asking a parent (or other adult) to express one or more positive or negative emotional reactions to the stimuli. Several aspects of childrens' behavior may be taken as evidence that social referencing has occurred. Information-seeking, such as referential looking or asking questions, is one important aspect of behavior in social referencing situations. Another important outcome is the child's affective response; when affect regulation occurs, the child's affect reflects the affective tone of the parents' message. If the child's instrumental behavior toward the stimulus is in line with the parent's communication about that stimulus (e.g., the child approaches a stimulus associated with a positive parental message), then behavior regulation is said to have occurred.

Typically developing infants as young as 1 year of age have been shown to engage in social referencing in a variety of situations. Infants regulate their behavior according to their parents' reactions to novel events. Infants are more likely to cross a modified visual cliff when their parents express joy than when their parents express fear (Sorce, Emde, Campos, & Klinnert, 1985). Infants interact more with a stranger when their parents interact positively with the stranger (Feinman & Lewis, 1983). Infants are more likely to approach novel toys when the parent displays a positive emotional response to the toy than when the parent reacts negatively (Walden & Ogan, 1988). The affect expressed by the infant is also influenced by parents' emotional responses to the stimuli (Walden & Baxter, 1989).

Some of our research has examined social referencing in dyads with children with developmental delays. The presence of group differences in signal clarity and responsivity to social signals may have important implications for the development of social referencing. Thus, our research with delayed children was designed to be particularly sensitive to these aspects of infant signals and parental responses. In addition to measuring the typical outcome behaviors associated with social referencing (i.e., information-seeking, behavior, and affect regulation), we have included measures associated with the process of reading and responding to social signals; such as muteness and predictability of infants' affective and looking signals, and parental responsivity to infant signals.

Walden, Knieps, and Baxter (1991) reported no evidence of social referencing among delayed children as a group. In a procedure designed to elicit social referencing of a parent following an unusual and arousing event, delayed children were compared with normally developing children who were matched on mental age. The delayed children looked frequently at their parents during the social referencing procedure, but they did not regulate their behavior based on their parents' emotional messages, as was true of the normally developing children at the same developmental level. Neither did the delayed children show affective expressions that were in line with their parents' communications, as was true of normally developing children.

During the time we were collecting data in that study, we had noticed that parents of delayed children had more trouble following our instructions to give messages if and only if the child looked toward them. Data supported our observations—parents of delayed children were less contingent in providing messages in response to their children's looks. Furthermore, we found that lack of contingency went in one direction—parents of delayed children did not miss any more looks than parents of normally developing children, but they gave more messages that were not in response to children's looks (false alarms; Walden et al., 1991).

This finding fit with a description in the literature of parents of delayed children being more "directive" than parents of nondelayed children. We thought of directiveness as a description more than an explanation. We wondered why parents of delayed children did this and generated the following hypotheses about possible explanations.

One hypothesis was that parents' false alarms might help the delayed children regulate their behavior. That is, the children needed more input and direction to understand the situation and what was required of them. Maybe parents of delayed children, because of their extensive history with those children, predicted that additional input would help their children to perform appropriately and regulate their behavior based on parental messages. Thus, those parents "jumped the gun" and provided many unsolicited messages. Parents may have even realized that they were behaving noncontingently but might have done so anyway in the belief that their children's appropriate responses would be supported. However, the data indicated there was no more behavior regulation in children who received many false alarms (Walden et al., 1991). Thus, the false alarm messages did not lead to better behavior regulation for children who received them.

Another hypothesis that we have entertained is that perhaps past experience promotes development of a response bias to respond to minimal signals, perhaps more subtle or less clearly communicative signals than might be responded to for normally developing children. There was some support for this in the literature. For example, Buckhalt and colleagues (1978) found that parents of infants with Down syndrome interacted with their infants as much as did parents of infants without Down syndrome, even though the infants with Down syndrome were less interactive. Yoder and Feagans (1988) found that mothers of severely handicapped infants identified many social cues during interaction that went unnoticed by other observers. Thus, because of their experience with delayed children, parents learned to identify or to respond to more subtle, perhaps difficult-to-detect signals produced by these children. This hypothesis was consistent with data in the Walden et al. (1991) study, in which parents of delayed children produced more false alarms than parents of nondelayed children. In addition, we would expect fewer missed looks (given equally frequent child signals) if such a response bias was operating; however, the data indicated that missed looks were equally frequent for the two groups.

Yet another hypothesis that might explain the lower parental contingency for delayed children is that the children's signals are harder to decipher. There is some support in the literature for this hypothesis. For example, Emde et al. (1978) characterized social signals of infants with Down syndrome as being muted and hard to read. Maurer and Newbrough (1987b) reported that delayed children's facial expressions of four emotions (happy, sad, angry, and neutral) were less well recognized than those of nondelayed children. Signals that are less readable may make it difficult for parents to detect, interpret, and correctly respond to their children's behavior. We reasoned that unclear signals should lead to high levels of both missed looks and false alarm signals. However, in the Walden et al. (1991) study, misses were not elevated, even though false alarms were greater for delayed children.

Another study (Knieps, Walden, & Baxter, 1994), focused on affective signals of children who were normally developing and developmentally delayed. We selected children with Down syndrome because these children have been said to have aberrant affect (muted or more often neutral; when affect is expressed it is less intense and more variable). We coded affect in 10-second intervals in which the positivity–negativity of the affect expressed during each interval was rated. Keep in mind that, unlike the previous study, these affective signals were rated by highly trained (and highly reliable) coders who based their codes on videotaped records that could be reviewed and/or viewed in slow motion in order to rate them. The positivity–negativity ratings were used to construct measures of affect intensity, affect lability, and frequency of non-neutral affect. There were no differences in coder reliability for normally developing and delayed children. There was no evidence for any of the three hypothesized differences in affect expression; that is, there were no group differences in intensity, lability, or neutrality. However, similar to the findings of lack of behavior regulation among delayed children in our earlier study (Walden et al., 1991), delayed children in the social referencing procedure showed no evidence of affect regulation, as was observed for normally developing children at the same developmental level (matched on mental age). In fact, the affect expressed by infants with Down syndrome contrasted with that of the parental messages. That is, when parents appeared to be afraid, their Down syndrome children were more positive. When parents were positive, their Down syndrome children were more negative.

Therefore, in one study (Walden et al., 1991), mothers who were interacting with their own children were less contingent in responding to looks, whereas no differences in identifying affective signals of delayed and nondelayed children were found for highly trained coders in another study. We wanted to know more about this effect and its possible contribution to social interaction and emotional development in delayed and nondelayed children.

A study was designed to investigate three hypotheses about social signals produced by delayed, as compared to nondelayed, children. These hypotheses were: (a) the clarity of the signals produced by delayed and nondelayed children differs, (b) a response bias exists among parents of delayed children that involved responding to lower level or more subtle signals, and (c) experience with a particular child influences one's accuracy in identifying signals. Specifically, experience with typically developing children facilitates recognition of and responding to their social signals, whereas experience with delayed children may facilitate identifying signals produced by delayed children. Parents of both delayed and typically developing children should outperform individuals with no experience with children. Such findings were expected based on the report of Maurer and Newbrough (1987a, 1987b) that experience with mentally retarded persons improved discrimination of their emotional expressions.

The study designed was a signal detection-type method that sampled signals of delayed and typically developing children. Several participant groups were included to investigate the effects of experience with children and with children who have intellectual delays in particular. We focused on one signal, children's looks at their parents (Walden, in press).

DETECTION OF INFANT SOCIAL SIGNALS

The discriminability of social signals that were produced by normally developing and developmentally delayed toddlers was compared. The focus was on a specific social signal, social looking. This is a common and important social signal that develops very early in the life of a child. People rely heavily on looking to regulate a number of aspects of social interaction, such as turn-taking. One simple response was selected for people to make to these signals—deciding whether a child had looked toward the parent or had not looked.

Discriminability might differ for persons who have had experience interacting with intellectually delayed individuals, so three groups of judges participated. One groups of judges had extensive experience with delayed children because they were parents of a preschool child who had been diagnosed with developmental delays. Thus, these individuals had highly relevant and recent experience with young delayed children. A second group of judges had experience with normally developing children because they were parents of preschool children with no diagnosed delays. Thus, these individuals had recent experience with children but not specifically delayed children. The third group of judges had minimal experience with children in any capacity. Thus, their judgments of social behavior should be based on general experience with others, most of this with predominantly older persons. The three groups of judges differed only in their experience with children. Differences in performance among the three groups of judges would indicate that experience with particular groups of individuals influences the perception of social behavior. All the judges observed behaviors of both typically developing and delayed children; thus, specific types of experience that facilitate judgments of particular types of persons might be identified.

Each judge in the study viewed many short videotaped episodes of mothers and children interacting. After viewing each segment of interaction, the judges indicated whether the child had looked at the parent and rated their confidence in that judgment. From these responses, each judge's accuracy of detection of looks was calculated (scored as agreement with highly trained coders who repeatedly viewed videotapes in real time and in slow motion), the latency to respond to the videotape segments, and confidence in each judgment.

Results indicated that judges had more difficulty accurately detecting the social looks of children with developmental delays than typically developing children. When judges were incorrect in their judgments about the occurrence of looks, they missed more looks of delayed children. That is, the inaccuracy was due to judges missing more of the looks that did occur for children with delays. It was simply harder to figure out whether a delayed child had looked or not, and judges responded by raising their criterion for judging the looks. This result suggests that the signals produced by delayed children are less clear and that judges respond to this lack of clarity with a response bias.

In addition to being less accurate in judging the occurrence of signals produced by delayed rather than normally developing children, judges were less confident in the correctness of their responses to the signals of delayed children. Furthermore, judges reacted more slowly to the signals of delayed children, with a longer latency between the child's signal and the judge's response than was typical of responses to normally developing children. Thus, the judges were less accurate, slower to respond, and less confident in their responses to the social behavior of delayed children.

There were no effects of experience with children or experience with delayed children on the judgments of looks in this study. Even judges with recent and highly relevant experience were no different than judges with minimal experience in terms of their accuracy, latency, and confidence in making the judgments.

In the study just described, judges found signals of delayed children diffi-cult to discriminate and they responded to this difficulty with a response bias; they raised their criterion and in doing so, missed more signals. In the earlier study reported by Walden et al. (1991), parents were also less accu-rate in discriminating those same signals; however, they responded with a different response bias. Parents lowered their criterion for judging looks and, in doing so, responded more often in the absence of signals. Thus, the response biases of the impartial judges and the parents operated in different directions.

Response biases are thought to result from motivational factors. Motiva-tional influences probably differed in the two experimental studies. In the social referencing study of parents and their own children, parents may have been motivated to help their children behave as expected, that is, to engage in social referencing and regulate their behavior accordingly. Thus, parents produced many communications, some of them unsignalled, perhaps reflecting their desire for their children to look competent and well-socialized. In the signal detection study, judges were unacquainted with the children they judged and the judges' behavior in no way could influence the responses of the children on the videotapes they judged. Thus, motivational influences may have predominantly involved judges' desire to appear competent themselves by making superior judgments. The elevated criterion for responding "yes, a look occurred" may have resulted from motivation to be accurate judges.

These results suggest that the signals produced by children with intellectual delays are less clear and therefore more difficult to detect and judge than the signals of normally developing toddlers matched for mental age. Signals of delayed children were difficult to detect in both studies (Walden, in press; Walden et al., 1991). However, adults' responses to this signal difficulty varied as a function of the different contexts in which their responses were observed. The low signal clarity and the accompanying inaccuracy, slow response time, and lack of confidence it produced could lead to interactional difficulties for these children. This, in turn, may be one contribution to aberrant social behaviors observed in young intellectually delayed children. That is, the difficult-to-detect-and-understand signals produced by delayed children may make it more likely that their parents respond inappropriately and the long response time may make it less likely that they will be understood by the delayed children even when the response is appropriate. In this way, the socialization of appropriate behavior, emotional or otherwise, may be impeded.

IMPLICATIONS FOR EMOTIONAL DEVELOPMENT

Parents and others who interact with delayed children may have more trouble reading and responding to their social and emotional signals. These social partners are harder to interact with, too—they respond less contingently and more slowly, they are less accurate in identifying social signals, and they have lower confidence in their ability to read their partner's behavior. This situation may be particularly debilitating for a child who is struggling to master the vicissitudes of social interaction.

Goldberg (1977) discussed the influence of individual child characteristics such as readability, responsivity, and predictability on parent feelings of efficacy. She hypothesized that children whose signals are less readable, less responsive, and less predictable will be more difficult for parents to respond to contingently and appropriately. Parenting behaviors may therefore be less effective. These ineffective behaviors may challenge the developing feelings of parental efficacy that are an essential part of parent–child relationships.

The interactional difficulties described above also have implications for the development of social emotional behaviors of many types. Processes of development such as social referencing and communication of emotion may be disrupted because of the greater difficulty in reading and responding to social behavior. Outcomes of development, such as attachment security, may be at risk. Development of inappropriate social behavior or behavior that is poorly matched to situational contexts may be more likely.

It is likely that caregivers who develop relationships with young developmentally delayed children acquire strategies that facilitate social interaction and compensate for the interactional limitations of the young delayed child. These strategies may be general response tendencies that facilitate, prolong, or improve interaction (much as parents of younger typically developing infants devise ways of compensating for their children's limitations) or they may be very particular strategies that develop out of specific experiences with a child who tends to respond in a certain manner. One such strategy might be to attempt to influence the child's behavior before there is an apparent action or reaction to a situation that arises. These "false alarms" might facilitate interaction and coping in some circumstances, or at least caregivers may believe (or hope) they do. Thus, for a child whose behavior is difficult to decipher, a bias to respond or intervene might improve more outcomes than a bias to withhold responding. That is, it is important to recognize the possible facilitating effects of some response biases. The development of caregiving behaviors and response tendencies must be followed in a longitudinal fashion for the nature of these response patterns to be fully understood.

The process of emotional communication involves at least two partners and the contributions of one partner serve as the interactional context for the behavior of the other. Thus, the behavior of both partners in their naturally occurring sequences must be considered in understanding social interactions. Knowledge of the processes discussed in this chapter is limited to a few behaviors, often studied in a noninteractive manner. Our discussion of these processes should be regarded as hypotheses for future research rather than as conclusions.

ACKNOWLEDGMENT

The research described in this chapter was supported by grant #BNS 9109634 from the National Science Foundation to the first author.

REFERENCES

Bell, S. M., & Ainsworth, M. D. S. (1972). Infant crying and maternal responsiveness. *Child Development, 43,* 1171–1190.

Bornstein, M. H., & Sigman, M. D. (1986). Continuity in mental development from infancy. *Child Development, 57,* 251–274.

Brinker, R. P., & Lewis, M. (1982). Discovering the competent handicapped infant: A process approach to assessment and intervention. *Topics in Early Childhood Special Education, 2*(2), 1–16.

Brofenbrenner, U. (1979). *The ecology of human development: Experiments by nature and design.* Cambridge, MA: Harvard University Press.

Buckhalt, J. A., Rutherford, R. B., & Goldberg, K. E. (1978). Verbal and nonverbal interaction of mothers with their Down syndrome and non-retarded infants. *American Journal of Mental Deficiency, 82,* 337–343.

Campos, J. J. (1983). The importance of affective communication in social referencing: A commentary on Feinman. *Merrill-Palmer Quarterly, 29,* 83–87.

Campos, J. J., Campos, R. G., & Barrett, K. C. (1989). Emergent themes in the study of emotional development and emotion regulation. *Developmental Psychology, 25,* 394–402.

Cardoso-Martins, C., & Mervis, C. B. (1985). Maternal speech to prelinguistic children with Down syndrome. *American Journal of Mental Deficiency, 89,* 451–458.

Ekman, P. (1992). Are there basic emotions? *Psychological Review, 99,* 550–553.

Emde, R. N., Katz, E. L., & Thorpe, J. K. (1978) Emotional expression in infancy: II. Early deviations in Down syndrome. In H. Lewis & L. A. Rosenblum (Eds.), *The development of affect* (pp. 351–360). New York: Plenum.

Fagan, J., & Singer, L. (1983). Infant recognition memory as a measure of intelligence. In L. Lipsitt (Ed.), *Advances in infancy research* Vol. 2, (pp. 31–78). New York: Academic Press.

Feinman, S. (1982). Social referencing in infancy. *Merrill-Palmer Quarterly, 28,* 445–470.

Feinman, S., & Lewis, M. (1983). Social referencing at ten months: A second-order effect on infants' responses to strangers. *Child Development, 54,* 878–887.

Gianino, A., & Tronick, E. (1988). The mutual regulation model: The infant's self and interactive regulation coping and defense. In T. Field, P. M. McCabe, & N. Schneidernam (Eds.), *Stress and coping* (pp. 351–360). Hillsdale, NJ: Lawrence Elrbaum Associates.

Goldberg, S. (1977). Social competence in infancy: A model of parent-infant interaction. *Merrill-Palmer Quarterly, 23,* 163–177.

Izard, C. E. (1992). Basic emotions, relations among emotions, and emotion-cognition relations. *Psychological Review, 99,* 561–565.

Jones, O. (1980). Prelinguistic communication skills in Down syndrome and normal infants. In T. Field, S. Goldberg, D. Stern, & A. Sostek (Eds.), *High risk infants and children: Adult and peer interactions* (pp. 205–255). New York: Academic Press.

Kasari, C., Mundy, P., Yirmiya, N., & Sigman, M. (1990). Affect and attention in children with Down syndrome. *American Journal of Mental Retardation, 95,* 55–67.

Knieps, L. J., Walden, T., & Baxter, A. (1994). Affective expressions of toddlers with and without Down syndrome in a social referencing context. *American Journal of Mental Retardation, 99,* 301–312.

Lamb, M. E., & Easterbrooks, M. A. (1981). Individual differences in parental sensitivity: Origins, components, and consequences. In M. E. Lamb & L. R. Sherrod (Eds.), *Infant social cognition: Empirical and theoretical considerations* (pp. 127–153). Hillsdale, NJ: Lawrence Erlbaum Associates.

Lewis, M., & Goldberg, S. (1969). Perceptual-cognitive development in infancy: A generalized expectancy model as a function of the mother–infant interaction. *Merrill-Palmer Quarterly, 15,* 81–100.

Marshall, N. R., Hegrenes, J. R., & Goldstein, S. (1973). Verbal interactions: Mothers and their retarded children vs. mothers and their nonretarded children. *American Journal of Mental Deficiency, 77,* 415–419.

Maurer, H., & Newbrough, J. R. (1987a). Facial expressions of mentally retarded and nonretarded children: I. Recognition by mentally retarded and nonretarded adults. *American Journal of Mental Deficiency, 91,* 505–510.

Maurer, H., & Newbrough, J. R. (1987b). Facial expressions of mentally retarded and nonretarded children: I. Recognition by nonretarded adults with varying experience with mental retardation. *American Journal of Mental Retardation, 91,* 511–515.

McAlpine, C., Kendall, K. A., & Singh, N. N. (1991). Recognition of facial expressions of emotion by persons with mental retardation. *American Journal of Mental Retardation, 96,* 29–36.

Sorce, J. F., Emde, R. N., Campos, J., & Klinnert, M. D. (1985). Maternal emotional signaling: Its effect on the visual cliff behavior of 1-year-olds. *Developmental Psychology, 21,* 195–200.

Umbel, V. M., & LaVoie, L. (1988). *The IMCE: An attempt at the measurement of the mutual contingency experience.* Poster presented at the International Conference on Infant Studies, Washington, DC.

Walden, T. (in press). *Social responsivity: Judging signals of young children with and without developmental delays.* Child Development.

Walden, T., & Baxter, A. (1989). The effect of context and age on social referencing. *Child Development, 60,* 1511–1518.

Walden, T., & Garber, J. (1994). Emotional development. In M. Rutter, D. Hay, & S. Baron-Cohen (Eds.), *Development through life: A handbook for clinicians* (pp. 403–455). Oxford, England: Blackwell.

Walden, T., Knieps, L. J., & Baxter, A. (1991). Contingent provision of social referential information by parents of children with and without developmental delays. *American Journal of Mental Retardation, 96,* 177–187.

Walden, T., & Ogan, T. (1988). The development of social referencing. *Child Development, 59,* 1230–1240.

Yoder, P. J., & Feagans, L. (1988). Mothers' attributions of communication to prelinguistic behavior of developmentally delayed and mentally retarded infants. *American Journal on Mental Retardation, 93,* 36–43.

The Role of Situation and Child Status on Emotional Interaction

Michael Lewis
Margaret W. Sullivan
University of Medicine and Dentistry of New Jersey

Differences in socialization practices related to emotional expression and their states can be explored, at least in the early months of life, by focusing on the interactions between mothers and infants in families with normal infants and with infants who have disabilities. The focus of this chapter on emotional interchanges is based on the premise that the integration of emotional expressions, states, and experiences arise, in part, out of the interaction of the child with his or her caregivers (Lewis, 1981; Lewis & Michalson, 1983). The socialization practices of families may be studied in a variety of ways, one being the study of the interaction between mothers and their infants in regard to emotional expression. This is because we believe that meaning or emotional experiences of infants and children are developed through understanding their, as well as others, behavior in context. Infants and adults construct meaning through the observation of behavior in context (Lewis & Michalson, 1982a, 1982b). This observation takes place through affective exchanges in the daily interactions between child and caregivers. Emotional expressions are observed by both receiver and sender through contextual variables. The responses of the other and their anticipated response are based on previous experience and the actual intent of the sender's and the receiver's perception of that intent in interaction. In addition, both may use the clues made salient by the situation.

There is a growing body of research that has focused on the interaction of mothers, fathers, and other adults, as well as other children, as they interact with infants. Investigations of mother–child interaction across culture (Lusk & Lewis, 1972), gender (Lewis, 1972; Malatesta & Haviland, 1982), and social class (Freedle & Lewis, 1972; Lewis & Freedle, 1977) reveal different patterns as a function of all these variables. Although it is still too early to develop a systematic theory in regard to how interactive exchanges ultimately result in differences in emotional expression and experiences, it is clear that more information is needed, especially in regard to affective exchanges as a function of the status of the child.

Some status variables that have been explored are social class and gender, and here we see the beginnings of how affective exchanges may lead to the differences observed in adults. For example, Lewis and associates have shown that gender differences exist in terms of affective exchanges between mothers and infants as a function of gender (Goldberg & Lewis, 1969; Lewis, 1972). Female children's distress is responded to more frequently than males past 3 months of age and these differences may represent early affective expression differences among males and females. The observation that females are more apt than males to cry when distressed may have its roots in the fact that mothers are more responsive to female cries than to male cries in early infancy (Goldberg & Lewis, 1969).

Social class differences have also been observed and appear to reflect differences in communication style. Lewis and Freedle (1973) demonstrated that poor children are responded to less frequently, although maternal behavior occurs at about the same level as middle-class mothers'. The contingent nature of middle-class mothers' responses as opposed to that of poor mothers suggests that the interactive nature of affective exchanges may be different between the social classes. Lewis and Michalson (1983) also showed that mothers of 1-year-old children are more likely to interpret the distress of their infants differently as a function of social class; poor mothers are more likely to characterize the distress of their infants in terms of anger than in terms of sadness. These differences may have important implications in terms of social class differences in aggressive behavior seen in school-age children.

In this particular study, as well as others (see Brooks-Gunn & Lewis, 1982; Lewis & Michalson, 1982a, 1982b), differences in affective exchanges between mothers and their infants with disabilities are studied. The study of infants with disabilities may be particularly important because one may contrast systematic differences in interactive exchanges between normal dyads and dyads having a child with disabilities in order to study the impact of these differences on the socialization of emotional expression. The study of normal infants as well as infants with disabilities may differ through a variety of possible mechanisms: (a) children's expression of emotion may differ—that is, the facial, postural, and vocal behavior of the disabled may not be available, may be delayed, or may be different; (b) the parents interpretation of the baby's behavior may be affected—that is, their expectations may be affected and they may interpret the child's behavior as it relates to their knowledge about dysfunction in general and the disability of their particular child; (c) the socialization rules may be different for parents who have infants with disabilities versus infants who are normal; and (d) parental feelings about having a child with disabilities may affect their emotional interactions with them. In addition, differences in emotional development among different groups of children with disabilities should be of interest, because the socialization of emotions as a function of group difference may shed light on how such differences may lead to differences in affective and emotional development.

That different patterns of emotional exchange may exist for the child with disabilities and the mother is suggested by several lines of research. This research indicates that not only may the expression of a child with disabilities be different or delayed, but that the mother's interpretation of that response and her subsequent behavior may be different. Parents experience a tumultuous sequence of emotional reactions following the birth of a child with handicaps: depression, rejection, anger, and, finally, acceptance of the child (see Lewis, 1992/1995). Parents may need to mourn the death of the ideal child that they had expected and deal with their shame before accepting their child's disability. The birth of a child with disabilities or a high-risk child is a stressful event, one that may lead the mother to inadequate coping styles, difficulties in relationships, or severing ties in the social support network, all of which may result in negative emotional exchanges and experiences (Brooks-Gunn & Lewis, 1982; Lewis, Brooks-Gunn, & Fox, 1981).

Maternal feelings about the child, especially maternal feelings about a child with disabilities, are likely to be translated into particular maternal interactions. Research suggests, for example, that mothers of blind babies often feel less attached to them, presumably because of the lack of eye-to-eye contact and mutual gaze patterns (Fraiberg, 1975). Mothers of sick neonates exhibit less overall interaction than mothers of healthy neonates, possibly because of the fear of losing or harming the child rather than due to any intrinsic feature of the illness (Fox & Lewis, 1982). Moreover, infants that are disabled or at high risk are often different from infants who are normal in some skills, which may intensify affective interactions. Mothers of premature infants for whom smiling is delayed, interact less than mothers with full-term children (Field, 1980). This also may be true for infants who are disabled, especially because there is evidence to indicate that the birth of a child with physical or mental disability results in depression and shame in the parents. Harmonious interactions may be disrupted by negative affect on the part of the infant, as well as by the parent. In brief, data has already indicated that different patterns of exchanges exist between mothers and their children as a function of their status and as a function of the particular disability that they show.

CONTEXT DIFFERENCES

As we seek to understand how affective interactions between the child and parent affect subsequent development, we need to consider a very important issue, one that, unfortunately, has received relatively little attention; that of studying behavior in context. The meaning of any exchange, affective or informational in nature, is dependent on the context in which those behaviors occur. Developmental theory, focusing on the ontogenetic flow of behavior and behavioral interaction, has been somewhat unresponsive to the need to take into account situational considerations, that is, studying the behavior in context. In part, this has been due to the fact that the thrust of genetic epistemology theory has focused on the emergence of similar structures under different contexts. In fact, the major determinant of behavior, although immersed in interaction between the organism and its environment, has been the genetic enfolding of invariant sequences of behavior. This lack of concern about situational or contextual variables, as affecting both structure and such processes as equilibrium–disequilibrium, has been a major theoretical obstacle in approaching the study of context.

This disinterest in the context in which behavior occurs characterizes U.S. psychology in general (see Lewis & Freedle, 1973, 1977; Parke & O'Leary, 1976 for some exceptions). We have been unresponsive to the study of the nature of the stimulus and have concerned ourselves mostly with the questions of categorizing, observing, and assigning meaning to organisms' responses. By ignoring the stimulus or holding it constant, it has been thought that the careful study of responses would lead to the ability to understand and predict the organism's perceptions, motivations, cognitions, and actions within its environment. Thus, in the study of mother–child interactions, for example, the chief paradigm that has been used is a 2-minute observation of the mother and child in an *en face* position, where mother is instructed to play with her child. The nature of the situation is not varied because it is believed that the behavior seen in this situation is likely to characterize the mother–child interaction in all possible situations and contexts. On the face of it, this seems like an absurd assumption, and, in fact, research has indicated large variability in mother–child interaction as a function of context (see Lewis, 1978, for a review of this work).

If we are interested in situational differences, we need to develop a taxonomy of situations, although such a task is not easy and is full of complications (see, e.g., Mischel, 1973; Murray, 1938; Pervin, 1968).

Barker (1965) held to the view that the situation could be defined in objectively measurable characteristics such as room size or function. Alternatively, one could define the situation in terms of the subject's perception of it (Endler & Magnusson, 1974). The underlying assumption is that any situation must be specific in terms of the particular organism experiencing it. Such a position, however, would make study of contexts extremely difficult in infancy because all that one could do would be to consider context from the maternal, not infant, point of view. Other ways to define situations are room location, daily activities, such as washing and going to bed; and so on, or adaptive functions like teaching, play, or feeding. Skills involved, affects elicited, or people involved in the situation are other dimensions that can be considered. The only way to solve this definitional problem is to characterize the situation in relation to the particular question or issue being studied. The taxonomy, or methods derived, will not fit all cases, and thereby represent only a limited solution. Nevertheless, until more empirical attempts are made, the problem will remain at its abstract and unusable level.

There are several alternatives in how to define the concept of situation in the study of the mother–infant interaction. In the study of communication, we can characterize the setting with respect to early vocalizations of young infants. In the Lewis and Freedle (1977) study of the mother–infant communication system, it was initially assumed that the situation might be defined by the space in which the infant and mother were located. For adults, physical space usually carries with it a high degree of contextual meaning; thus, the kitchen is associated with food, eating, drinking, and certain somatic sensations, whereas the bedroom, as a space, is associated with sleeping, quiet play, and so on. With this in mind, the observation of the infant–mother communication system as a function of physical space was attempted. Surprisingly, it was found that the physical space or location by function of the very young infant was not yet differentiated by his or her caregiver. The child was not typically fed in the kitchen, played with in the livingroom or family room, washed in the bathroom, and put to sleep in the bedroom. Each of the activities, most usually associated with a room in the house, was performed by and large in any room. Physical space, such as a room, could not be used as a clear indicator of context. Interestingly enough, further observation of infants' activities in their home does reveal that by 12 months the physical space as well as the function of differentiation have been associated. This change of the first year of life speaks to the important changes in the contextual relationship of space for the infant.

Another approach—where in the room the child was situated—was considered. Eight specific categories seem to account for almost all the observed time; they were infant seat, playpen, mother's lap, crib or bed, couch or sofa, floor, changing table or bath tub, and jumper or swing. We were interested in studying prelinguistic forms of communication in order to relate them to subsequent formal linguistic activity (language) and we hope to be able to demonstrate the occurrence, at least by 3 months, of the nonrandom vocalization patterns as a function of situational context. Situational context was important because of the hypothesized possibility that meaning may initially rely on the perceptual location and recognition of features, or relational differences in the external world. Meaning is generated because the organism probably perceives such differences by noticing a significant shift in the behavioral patterns that occur in different situations. It seemed, therefore, that an exploration of the origins of semantics could be found in the communication network of the very young infant by studying situational differences.

Table 3.1, taken from Freedle and Lewis (1977), presents these eight situations. Observe that they can vary along at least five continua, such as new sensory stimulation, distance between the dyads, function—only social and other have been listed, although more would be possible—movement, and eye contact and visibility. Clearly, the situation categories and the list of features could be expanded. Thus, even the restrictions to location space does not produce a problem-free solution to the situational taxonomy issue.

Table 3.2 presents the amount of time spent in these various locations. The situational analysis revealed a distribution of time across these situations, such that the mother's lap was the most frequent situation in the 2-hour observation, followed by the crib/bed and infant seat. Relatively little time was spent on the floor or the jumper at 3 months of age. When these data were segmented by gender and socioeconomic status (SES), interesting situation-by-subject characteristics emerge. For example, for 54% of the observed time for the poor (SES V), the infant was in the mother's arms, whereas this was true for only 32% of the time for the middle-class subjects (SES I). Interestingly, no SES V mothers ever put an infant on the floor, whereas SES I babies were on the floor 3% of the observational time. Thus, situational observations differed markedly between individuals and groups, a finding reported by others.

Particularly important in the situational analysis is whether situation dimensions are useful in understanding behavior or individual differences in interactions. For example, in the study of mother–infant vocalization, it was found that the probability of a conversation (i.e., both mother and infant vocalizing to each other), continuing from one 10-second period to the next, was .49 if the infant was on its mother's lap, .63 if it was in the infant seat, and only .21 when the infant was in the crib or bed (Freedle & Lewis, 1977). Thus, vocal interaction is lowest when the infant is in the crib or bed and highest when the infant is in his or her mother's lap or infant seat. Because the assumed function of placing an infant in the crib or bed is to allow the infant to rest, the probability that the mother will engage in the simultaneous vocalizations in this particular situation will be low. On the

| Situation | New Sensory Stimulation? | Distance Between Members of Dyad | | | Function | | Free Movement for Infant? | Eye Contact and Gesture Freely Viewable? |
		Large	Medium	Small	Social?	Other?		
Tub/table	Yes (water, powder)			+	No	Clean	Not much	Yes
Jump/swing	Yes (proprioceptive feedback)		+		No	Mother busy	Semifree	Not necessarily
Couch	Maybe (texture)			+	Semisocial	Mother rest?	Semifree	Semiviewable
Floor	Yes (rug, no rug, smells, wide muscular movement)	+			No	?	Yes	Not necessarily
Mother's lap	Maybe			+	Yes		Not much	Maybe
Crib/bed	Intended lack of new stimulation	+			No	Rest infant	Not intended	No
Infant seat	Maybe		+		No	Mother busy	Not much	Not necessarily
Playpen	Maybe (toy, textures, . . .)	+			No	Mother busy	Semifree	Not necessarily

Suggested Critical Features for Vocalization

TABLE 3.2
Mean Number of 10-Second Intervals Spent in Each Situation

	Infant Seat	Play-pen	Mother's Lap	Crib/ Bed	Couch/ Sofa	Floor	Table/ Tub	Jumper	Other
Total	100.9	29.2	288.4	118.2	46.2	28.0	62.5	26.7	19.9
Male	80.2	33.0	329.5	91.6	42.0	35.1	52.9	29.7	24.0
Female	121.6	25.4	247.4	144.8	50.5	21.0	72.1	23.7	15.8
SES									
I	111.8	18.8	231.8	204.8	51.0	19.5	54.8	12.0	15.8
II	108.5	11.5	222.5	163.1	44.2	48.0	60.7	19.1	41.5
III	88.2	64.8	308.4	75.6	30.6	38.8	68.4	27.6	15.0
IV	112.8	00.0	286.8	68.4	51.6	32.4	52.8	99.6	14.4
V	90.6	36.0	387.0	67.2	57.6	00.0	69.6	9.6	00.0

other hand, when the infant is supposed to be wide awake, as when the child is in the infant seat, the mother will take the opportunity of strongly engaging the infant in conversation. Thus, a situational analysis may provide for an analysis of function through observation of differentiated behavior as a function of those situations.

A situational analysis is also invaluable in understanding individual or group differences and, likely, in understanding differences between mothers of children with disabilities and mothers of nondisabled children. It may be the case that true group differences or similarities are hidden unless situations are considered. Situations may interact with groups or individuals, such that individual or group differences may be exaggerated or reduced. Consider as an example the differences between two mothers. If Mother A was to hold her infant more often than Mother B, and if holding is related to vocalization, then differences in vocalization may be due to differences in situations between mothers, rather than the quality of mothering, per se. In order to deal with the possibility that individual differences in the dyad may be due to differences in situation, rather than in the status of the child, it is necessary to create time for each situation. From the study of individual or group differences, this procedure is necessary in order to be confident of difference per se, and for the study of the processes underlying these differences, this procedure is critical.

Figure 3.1 presents the conditional probabilities associated with state changes in conversation compared across two of the eight situations described earlier: infant seat and mother's lap (Lewis & Freedle, 1977). These two situations were chosen because they accounted for approximately 50% of observation time. Twenty poor mother dyads and 20 upper middle-class dyads were observed. Of particular interest for this discussion of group differences is the state change from one to two, which represents what was called a conversation pattern. That is, the infant vocalizes while the mother listens, followed by the infant listening while the mother vocalizes. When observation in the infant seat is compared to the mother's lap, there was relatively little interaction in the infant seat (a mean of 4%) and considerable interaction in the mother's lap (more than 25%). Note that this says nothing about the overall level of vocalization of the mother, which was as great, or greater, in the infant seat as in the lap. This analysis refers to interaction or the change from infant vocalizing to mother vocalizing. In the infant seat, the probability of exchange between speakers is less than what would be expected by chance and represents a suppression of the possible level of exchange. There were no social class differences in the amount of vocalization, just in vocal interaction. For the mother's lap situation, there were SES differences, with poor mothers showing 40% less interaction than middle-class mothers. The cause of such a difference is not pursued here (see Lewis & Freedle, 1977).

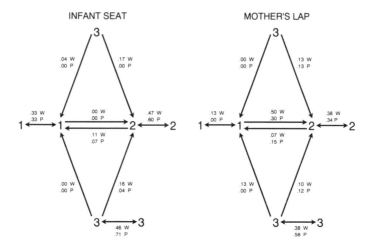

FIG. 3.1. Conversation between infant and mother as a function of situation and poverty level (from Lewis & Freedle, 1977).

This type of situational analysis is limited. More work varying the dimensions of the situation needs to be considered. A functional analysis, looking at mother–infant interaction as it relates to what parents want to do and accomplish, needs to be undertaken. Most important, such an analysis is necessary in order to understand the socialization of affect in families where there are children with dysfunctions and handicaps.

INTERACTIONS AS A FUNCTION OF MENTAL AGE AND PARTICULAR DISABILITIES

When studying children with disabilities it is important to control for mental age differences (Brooks-Gunn & Lewis, 1981). Infants with disabling conditions, such as Down syndrome or cerebral palsy (CP), may have different mental age, as well as physical handicaps. The contrasting of mental age- and chronological age-matched disability groups allows for examination of the effects of cognitive delay on the particular domain of functioning in question, be it language (Leifer & Lewis, 1983), or social behavior (Brooks-Gunn & Lewis, 1982). For example, if one were to compare one group of normal infants to a group of infants with Down syndrome, finding poorer functioning among the Down group does not isolate the source of the difference. We do not know if the poorer functioning is due to the syndrome itself, due to being atypical (i.e., any disabled group would show this same effect), or due to general cognitive delays. Information on mental age equivalence would inform us whether the effect is linked to the general cognitive functioning of the children. If a second disability group is added, comparisons between the two disability groups as well as with the normal group provides the possibility of identifying which differences are due to being disabled versus those due to having a specific condition. This methodological point has often been ignored in the literature (Lewis & Brooks-Gunn, 1982), but has special relevance to the study of mother–infant interaction where differing patterns of age and mental age differences may be observed for infant behavior and maternal behavior. Some data from the Competency Assessment Project (Brooks-Gunn & Lewis, 1982) illustrate how behaviors and interaction patterns vary as a function of mental age.

Brooks-Gunn and Lewis studied maternal and infant behaviors during a 15-minute play period using three groups of infants: a disabled group, aged 2 to 7 months (chronological age group), an older, but mental age-equivalent disabled group (mental age-equivalent group), and nondisabled children. The normal child can be compared to either the mental age or chronological age of a child with disabilities. All children with disabilities had Down syndrome. Three infant behaviors and two maternal behaviors were observed. Infant behaviors included smiles, infant vocal behavior, and fret/cries that included all negative vocalizations of the infant. Maternal behaviors were smiling and vocalizing. The frequency of each behavior expressed as a proportion of total behaviors was examined.

Figure 3.2a shows the proportion of infant smiles to all behaviors during the interaction. Infants with disabilities, whether matched for chronological or mental age equivalence, showed proportionately more smiling in response to maternal behavior during the episode than did normal infants at this age. Infant vocalizations, however, showed a different pattern than smiles, with the infants with disabilities producing proportionately less vocal behavior, regardless of chronological or mental age (see Fig. 3.2b). That both mental and chronological age-matched infants with disabilities showed the same pattern vis-à-vis the normal infants suggests that mental age is not the important factor affecting the infants with Down syndrome.

Maternal responses to these same three groups of infants' vocalizations shows that mothers of infants with disabilities, regardless of chronological or mental age, produce proportionately more vocal behavior than mothers of infants in the normal group (see Fig. 3.3). Although there was no difference between the two groups of infants with disabilities, these findings again point to the fact that mothers are responding to their infants' disability rather than to their mental age.

Data on 1-year-old children with Down syndrome support this conclusion. As shown in Fig. 3.4, mothers of normal 1-year-olds had lower levels of initiations and greater levels of response than did mental age- and chronological age-matched dyads. Again, the results for another group of

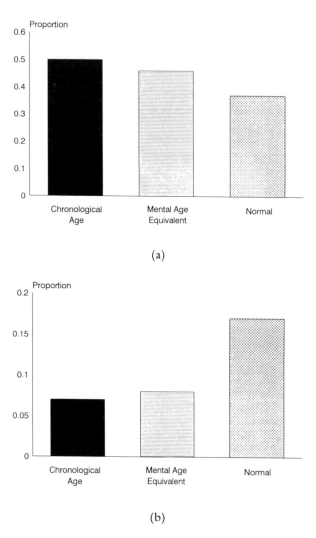

FIG. 3.2. (a) Proportion of infant smiles to all other infant behaviors (ages 2–7 months); (b) Proportion of infant vocalizations to all other infant behaviors (ages 2–7 months) (from Brooks-Gunn & Lewis, 1982).

dyads with infants having disabilities reveal that mothers are responding to the disability itself rather than the mental age. Thus, the use of chronological and mental age-matched groups with disabilities allows us to observe whether the parent–child interactions are dependent on disability status, mental age, both, or neither.

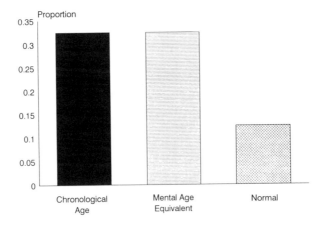

FIG. 3.3. Proportion of infant vocalizations responded to by mothers (ages 2–7 months) (from Brooks-Gunn & Lewis, 1982).

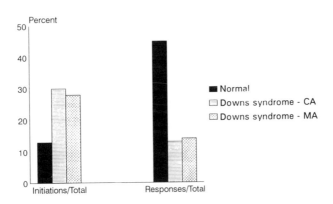

FIG. 3.4. Proportion of maternal initiations and responses as a function of all maternal behavior (age 1 year) (from Brooks-Gunn & Lewis, 1982).

SITUATION AND INFANT STATUS

In order to explore the problem of emotional interactions between mothers and infants with disabilities, the question of mental age, chronological age, and situation needed studying. Nineteen infants were divided into three groups drawn from a large database on mother–child affective exchanges.

There were seven infants who were normal and full term with no significant pre- or perinatal history of problems. They were 3 months of age and had a mental age of 3 months. The two groups of infants with disabilities included seven children with Down syndrome who were also 3 months chronological age with a 3-month mental age. They had not yet shown any developmental delay, at least as measured by the Bayley. Finally, the third group consisted five children with Down syndrome who had a mental age of 3 months but a chronological age of between 4½ and 5 months. These were the most developmentally delayed group, although matched with the other two groups on mental age. All the children were healthy at the time we observed them and there were no detectable vision or hearing problems.

The mother–infant dyads were seen for 4 minutes: 2 minutes in an *en face* situation in which the infant sat in an infant seat and the mother faced the infant within 12 to 18 inches of the infant's face; 2 minutes in a free-play situation where mothers removed the infant from the seat and played with them as they normally would do at home. Almost all mothers played with their infants on a blanket on the floor, although a few chose to keep the infants on their lap. There were no differences by group in whether the free-play situation occurred on the blanket or on the mother's lap. In the play situation, mothers maintained fairly close proximity to their children although they were not as close in face-to-face contact as they were in the *en face* situation.

The behaviors coded included a second-by-second analysis of the frequency and duration of a set of infant's behaviors, including smile, cry, look at mom, look at toy, vocalize, nonvocal sounds. Mothers' behavior included smile, laugh, vocalize, kiss, look at infant, hold, rock, touch play, touch rhythmic, touch caregiver, and give/show a toy. The reliability for the coding of these behaviors were quite good; all interobserver reliabilities had kappas at .84 or better. The results are presented for specific maternal and infant behaviors as well as for maternal contingent responsivity around affective exchanges.

Figure 3.5 shows the mean frequency of infant and maternal smile by group and by situation. As can be seen, infant smiling varied as a function of group and condition. Normal infants smiled about the same amount whether they engaged in *en face* or play behavior. Infants with Down syndrome who had the equivalent mental and chronological age smiled as much as the normal infants in the *en face* situation but less in the play situation. Finally, the group of infants with Down syndrome, who were most disabled overall, smiled significantly less than the other two groups, although there was no difference in their smiling as a function of situation. Maternal smiling, likewise, was affected by situation and group. Maternal smiling was greater in the *en face* than in the play situation for both dyads with normal infants and dyads with infants with Down syndrome who were

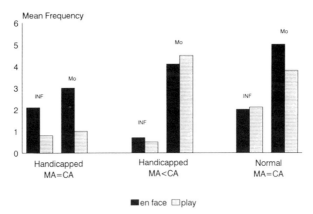

FIG. 3.5. Frequency of infant and maternal smiles as a function of situation and child's status.

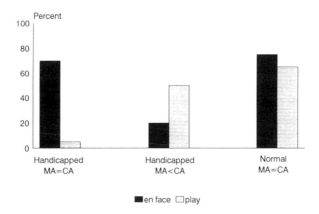

FIG. 3.6. Proportion of infant smiles responded to by mothers as a function of situation and child's status.

the same chronological age. Mothers with the most disabled infants showed no difference in their smile behavior. Overall, mothers smiled about the same amount regardless of the status of their children.

Figure 3.6 presents mothers' overall responsivity to their infants' smile. Maternal responsivity reflects the number of times the mother responded to the infant's smile with any behavior. In the group of normal infants, the proportion of times mothers were responsive to their infant's approach was 70%, with no difference as a function of situation. Mothers, who had infants who were developing normally but who had Down syndrome, responded to their infant's smiling significantly less than the normal group, although this difference was due to the fact that mothers were more likely to respond to their infants in an *en face* position than during play. The most severely disabled infants had mothers who overall responded significantly less to their infants' smile than the mothers with normal infants. Interestingly, the mothers of the most disabled infants were nearly three times as likely to respond to the infants' smile when playing with their infants than when engaging them in *en face* interactions.

The data for smiling indicates that situational differences as well as group differences affect maternal responsiveness and the mother's frequency of smiling to her infant. Mothers were more likely to be responsive to their infants' smiles in the normal than in the two disabled groups. Mothers of the most delayed infants responded proportionately less to their infants' smiles than did mothers of children with Down syndrome who were less disabled. These findings, however, interact with situational differences revealing that unless situation is taken into account, maternal–child smiling interaction cannot be fully understood.

Figure 3.7 presents the frequency of maternal kissing behavior as a function of condition and status of the child. Most important was the fact that there were significant group differences in how frequently mothers kissed their infants. Mothers with normal infants were significantly more likely to kiss their infants across all conditions than mothers with Down syndrome children. Moreover, there were interesting and significant group-by-condition interactions with mothers of normal infants and mothers of children who have Down syndrome and are seriously delayed, showing more kissing in the *en face* condition, whereas mothers with infants with less disability were more likely to kiss their children in the play situation. These findings

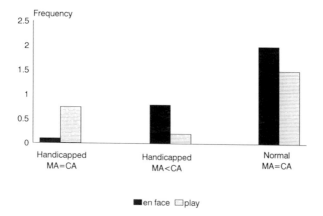

FIG. 3.7. Frequency of maternal kissing as a function of situation and child's status.

again reveal interesting differences in positive maternal behavior toward their children. They seem to indicate that children who show disabilities are receiving less positive maternal behavior. Maternal differences appear to be due to the nature of her interaction with the children.

This can be seen in maternal response to infant fret/cry behavior. All mothers were responsive to their infants' fret/cry. Thus, the question to be posed is what is the maternal latency to respond to her infant's cry? The data reveal that most of the infant's fuss/cry occurred in the play situation. The latency to respond to an infant's cry for mothers with normal children is an average of 1.25 seconds, whereas for the least disabled infants it is 1.75, and for the infants with most delay, 2.51. These differences are significant and indicate that mothers with normal infants have a significant shorter latency to respond to their children's fret/cries than mothers with disabled infants. Mothers with most delayed infants have the longest latency.

Maternal emotional responsivity seems to show that mothers with normal children are more positively responsive to their children's smiling behavior and are more quick to react to the children's cries than are mothers of disabled children. This may reflect their emotional interactive style or it may reflect mothers overall responsivity. In order to address that question, the proportion of all contingent behavior mothers show is presented in Fig. 3.8, which reveals little differences between groups or conditions. Thus, in general, mothers of infants with disabilities are as responsive to their infants as are mothers of infants with normal development. The differences reported around smiling and reaction to fret/cry appear to reflect maternal

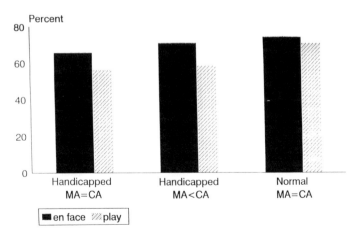

FIG. 3.8. Proportion of infant behavior responded to by mothers as a function of situation and child's status.

emotional exchanges vis-à-vis their infants who are developing normally versus those with disabilities.

MATERNAL EMOTIONAL STATE
AND MATERNAL INTERACTIONS

Goffman (1963), in a monograph entitled "Stigma," talked about the nature of self-presentation and the role of stigma in interpersonal relations. He stated that people with stigmas are thought to be not quite human: "the standard he, the person with the stigma, has incorporated from the wider society equips him to be intimately alive to what others see as his failing, inevitably causing him to agree that he does indeed fall short of what he really ought to be. Shame becomes a central possibility" (p. 4). For Goffman, stigma represents a spoiled identity, the ideal that somehow one is imperfect in regards to the standards of the society in which one lives. Although the concept of *stigma* is not easily defined, we can say that it is a mark or characteristic that distinguishes a person as being deviant, flawed, limited, spoiled, or generally undesirable. The deviant characteristics of the person are sufficient reasons for the occurrence of the stigma. Stigma relates the self to others' view and, although the feeling of being stigmatized may occur in the absence of other people, the feelings of shame associated with it come about through the anticipation of interactions with other people (Lewis, 1992/1995).

The parents of children with a stigma are themselves stigmatized and suffer the same fate as their stigmatized children. There is no question that the parents of a child who has mental retardation (MR) themselves become objects of stigma. We see the impact of stigmatization in the description of what happens to parents when they are informed that their child has MR. First, they express shock and disbelief that their child is in imperfect health. Second, they experience anger and rage. Third, sadness replaces the anger. Finally, the parents enter the coping stage. Whatever stage the parents of a child with a stigma are in, they must learn to cope with their shame and embarrassment over having such a child. The shame of having such a child can last a lifetime and can lead to many family difficulties, including a high rate of discord and divorce as each parent seeks to blame the other for the stigmatized child.

The shame of the parent has been revealed in intervention studies designed to reduce the parental stress of parents who have a child with difficulties. The most successful research projects are those that focus on parents' feelings of shame in combination with therapy for dealing with their disappointment. Frye, Greenberg, and Fewell (1989) believed that they needed to alter parents' appraisal patterns that lead to shame and embarrassment. Without dealing with this problem they could not get the parents to function appropriately. Programs treating families suffering from the stress of having stigmatized children reveal that the focus on the parents attributions and, therefore, on their shame have the best chance of altering the family dynamics and helping the children. Nixon and Singer (1993) described an intervention program to help mothers with children with MR. The program consisted of 10 hours of discussion concerning their thoughts about their children. The treatment condition focused on the cognitive distortions that contributed to self-blame and guilt and the best techniques for dealing with these distortions. The results, although modest, demonstrate that the therapy could alter the emotions of shame, guilt, and depression through altering the cognitive attributional style of parents. The authors, in discussing their findings, concluded that the treatment was effective "in reducing self-blame and guilt in parents with children who have severe disabilities. Because there were significant reductions in automatic thoughts of internal negative attributions and depression, there was evidence that cognitive distortions were effectively reconstructed" (p. 670). Therefore, there is evidence that cognitive restructuring was an important contributor to the reduction of parental self-blame and guilt.

A disability not only directly affects children's functioning but also indirectly affects children through their own shame and the shame of their parents. The impact of disabilities on children's development can only be weighed by taking into consideration both the direct and indirect affects of stigma. Parental behaviors toward their young infants and children as seen in our studies are likely to be influenced by the parental attitudes, values, and feelings they have in regard to the child with disabilities. Not only is the identity of their children spoiled, but so is their own identity as parents. These kinds of attributions, thoughts, and feelings are most likely to make themselves felt in regard to the emotional interaction between child and parent. Thus, there is good reason to suspect that the mother–child interaction is affected by maternal attributions in regard to herself and her child. These feelings of shame, sadness, and even grief are translated into the emotional interactions parents engage in with their children. Moreover, these interactions are likely to vary as a function of the situation that they are in. In the *en face* situation, mothers are more apt to engage their children directly because of the situational demands—they are very physically close and, therefore, need to interact. This may lead to high interactive behavior patterns. However, when mothers are in a more natural play situation, maternal interactions not educational in nature are revealed. This would explain why latency differences in maternal response to infant cry were revealed in the play situation, but were not apparent in the *en face* situation. In any event it is quite clear that in order to understand the emotional development of children with special needs, as well as to understand the development of emotional life of children in general, we take into account a mother's feelings about herself and the child, and to study how these feelings affect her interaction with her child.

REFERENCES

Barker, R.G. (1965). Exploration in ecological psychology. *American Psychologist,* *20,* 1–14.

Brooks-Gunn, J., & Lewis, M. (1981). Assessing the handicapped young: Issues and solutions. *Journal of the Division for Early Childhood,* 84–95.

Brooks-Gunn, J., & Lewis, M. (1982). Affective exchanges between normal and handicapped infants and their mothers. In T. Field & A. Fogel (Eds.), *Emotion and early interaction* (pp. 161–188). Hillsdale, NJ: Lawrence Erlbaum Associates.

Endler, N.S., & Magnusson, D. (1974). Interactionism, trait psychology, and situationism. *Reports from the Psychological Laboratories* (No. 418). Stockholm: University of Stockholm.

Field, T. (1980). Interactions of preterm and term infants with their lower- and middle-class teenage and adult mothers. In T. Field, S. Goldberg, D. Stern, & A. Sostek (Eds.), *High-risk infants and children: Adult and peer interactions* (pp. 113–132). New York: Academic Press.

Fox, N., & Lewis, M. (1982). Motor asymmetries in preterm infants: Effects of prematurity and illness. *Developmental Psychobiology,* *15,* 19–23.

Fraiberg, S. (1975). Intervention in infancy: A program for blind infants. In B.Z. Friedlander, G.M. Sterritt, & G.E. Kirk (Eds.), *Exceptional infant: Assessment and intervention* (Vol. 3, pp. 40–61). New York: Brunner/Mazel.

Freedle, R., & Lewis, M. (1972). Individual differences in play behavior: A mathematical analysis. In F.J. Monks, W.W. Hartup, & J. DeWit (Eds.), *Determinants of behavioral development* (pp. 461–465). New York: Academic Press.

Freedle, R., & Lewis, M. (1977). Prelinguistic conversations. In M. Lewis & L. Rosenblum (Eds.), *Interaction, conversation, and the development of language: The origins of behavior* (Vol. 5, pp. 157–185). New York: Wiley.

Frye, K.S., Greenberg, M.T., & Fewell, R.R. (1989). Stress and coping among children: A multidimensional approach. *American Journal on Mental Retardation,* *94*(3), 240–249.

Goffman, E. (1963). *Stigma.* Englewood Cliffs, NJ: Prentice-Hall.

Goldberg, S., & Lewis, M. (1969). Play behavior in the year-old infant: Early sex differences. *Child Development,* *40,* 21–31.

Leifer, J., & Lewis, M. (1983). Maternal speech to normal and handicapped children: A look at question-asking behavior. *Infant Behavior and Development,* *6,* 175–187.

Lewis, M. (1972). State as an infant-environment interaction: An analysis of mother–infant interaction as a function of sex. *Merrill-Palmer Quarterly,* *18,* 95–121.

Lewis, M. (1978). Situational analysis and the study of behavioral development. In L. Pervin & M. Lewis (Eds.), *Perspectives in interactional psychology* (pp. 49–66). New York: Plenum.

Lewis, M. (1981). Attention as a measure of cognitive integrity. In D. Radcliffe (Ed.), *Developmental disabilities in the preschool child*. New York: S.P. Medical and Scientific Books.

Lewis, M. (1995). *Shame, the exposed self*. New York: The Free Press. (Original work published 1992)

Lewis, M., & Brooks-Gunn, J. (1982). Developmental models and assessment issues. In N. Anastasiow, W. Frankenberg, & A. Fandal (Eds.), *Identifying the developmentally delayed child* (pp. 31–49). Baltimore, MD: University Park Press.

Lewis, M., Brooks-Gunn, J., & Fox, N. (1981). *Socio-affective dysfunction in high risk infants and mothers*. Unpublished manuscript, Educational Testing Service, Princeton, NJ.

Lewis, M., & Freedle, R. (1973). Mother–infant dyad: The cradle of meaning. In P. Pliner, L. Krames, & T. Alloway (Eds.), *Communication and affect: Language and thought* (pp. 127–155). New York: Academic Press.

Lewis, M., & Freedle, R. (1977). The mother and infant communication system: The effects of poverty. In H. McGurk (Ed.), *Ecological factors in human development* (pp. 205–215). Amsterdam, The Netherlands: North-Holland.

Lewis, M., & Michalson, L. (1982a). The measurement of emotional state. In C. Izard (Ed.), *Measurement of emotions in infants and children* (pp. 178–207). New York: Cambridge University Press.

Lewis, M., & Michalson, L. (1982b). Socialization of emotions. In T. Field & A. Fogel (Eds.), *Emotion and early interaction* (pp. 189–212). Hillsdale, NJ: Lawrence Erlbaum Associates.

Lewis, M., & Michalson, L. (1983). *Children's emotions and moods: Developmental theory and measurement*. New York: Plenum.

Lusk, D., & Lewis, M. (1972). Mother–infant interaction and infant development among the Wolof of Senegal. *Human Development, 15*(1), 58–69.

Malatesta, C.Z., & Haviland, J. (1982). Learning display rules: The socialization of emotional expression in infancy. *Child Development, 53*.

Mischel, W. (1973). Toward a cognitive social learning reconceptualization of personality. *Psychological Review, 80*, 252–283.

Murray, H.A. (1938). *Exploration in personality*. New York: Oxford University Press.

Nixon, C.D., & Singer, G.H.S. (1993). Group cognitive-behavioral treatment for excessive parental self-blame and guilt. *American Journal on Mental Retardation, 97*(6), 665–672.

Parke, R.D., & O'Leary, S. (1976). Father-mother-infant interaction in the newborn period: Some findings, some observations, and some unresolved issues. In K. Riegel & J. Meacham (Eds.), *The developing individual in a changing world: Vol. II. Social and environmental issues* (pp. 653–663). The Hague: Mouton.

Pervin, L.A. (1968). Performance and satisfaction as a function of individual-environment fit. *Psychological Bulletin, 69*, 56–68.

Nonverbal Communication, Joint Attention, and Early Socioemotional Development

Peter Mundy
Jennifer Willoughby
University of Miami

The display of functionally distinct nonverbal communication bids becomes increasingly apparent in the behavior of infants in the 8- to 12-month period. These bids include referential behaviors, such as protodeclarative or joint attention acts, and protoimperative or requesting acts, as well as social interaction or turn-taking behaviors (Bates, Benigni, Bretherton, Camaioni, & Volterra, 1979; Bruner & Sherwood, 1983; Sugarman, 1984).

The study of these types of nonverbal communication skills has most often been associated with research on early sociocognitive development (Bretherton, McNew, & Beeghly-Smith, 1981; Bruner, 1975; Butterworth & Jarrett, 1991; Tomasello, 1995), and the precursors of language development (Bates et al., 1979; Bruner, 1975; Golinkoff, 1983; Sugarman, 1984; Tomasello; 1988). However, research on the development of different types of nonverbal communication skills in the second year of life may also hold considerable potential for understanding socioemotional development in young children.

The most straightforward rationale for this hypothesis is based on possible links between language development and behavior disturbance. Children who evince delays or disturbance in language development are at risk for the development of emotional and behavioral disorders (Baker & Cantwell,

1987; Beitchman, Hood, & Inglis, 1990). Research also suggests that individual differences in the development of nonverbal referential and social communication skills are related to the subsequent differences in language development (Bates et al., 1979; Dunham, Dunham, & Curwin, 1993; Mundy, Kasari, Sigman, & Ruskin, 1995; Olson, Bates, & Bayles, 1984; Tomasello, 1988). Logically, then, it may be that observations of nonverbal communication skills in the second year of life can provide early information about children who, as preschoolers, develop emotional and behavioral difficulties secondary to the disturbance of linguistic communication skills.

Alternatively, it may be that nonverbal communication development in the second year reflects constitutional differences among infants, and/or environmental factors, that contribute directly to the socioemotional development of the child, rather than only indirectly through association with language development. This possibility is inherent to three related strands of theory and research.

One strand of theory and research suggests that a disturbance of nonverbal communication skills may be an important marker of difficulties in caregiver–child interactional processes that play a role in subsequent socioemotional difficulties in young children. For example, it has been argued that the display of difficult-to-read nonverbal signals, or unresponsiveness to the communicative bids of others, may potentiate child–caregiver relationship disturbance (Howlin & Rutter, 1987; Mundy, Seibert, & Hogan, 1985; Wetherby & Prizant, 1993b). Alternatively, others have suggested that a disturbance in the child–caregiver attachment system may negatively effect early nonverbal communication development (Bretherton, Bates, Benigni, Camaioni, & Volterra, 1979; Papousek, Papousek, Suoimi, & Rahn, 1991; Stern, 1985).

A second strand of theory suggests that the development of nonverbal communication skills may be indicative of developments in distinct, albeit rudimentary aspects of sociocognition (Bruner, 1975; Bretherton et al., 1981; Mundy & Hogan, 1994; Tomasello, 1995; Wellman, 1993). Research and theory also suggests that impairments or differences among children in sociocognition may play a role in emotional and behavioral regulation in social interactions (Dodge, 1986; Stern, 1985). Therefore, it may be that measures of nonverbal communication skills provide an index of individual differences in early sociocognitive development that, in turn, may be related to the emotional and behavioral regulation of young children in the social interactions.

Finally, an even more direct connection between nonverbal communication and socioemotional development has been suggested. Certain types of nonverbal communication skills, especially declarative or joint attention skills, may reflect developments in the capacity of the child to initiate shared, positive, affective states with others in reference to a third object or event (Adamson & Bakeman, 1985, 1991; Bates, Camaioni, & Volterra, 1975; Jones, Collins, & Hong, 1991; Mundy, Kasari, & Sigman, 1992; Rheingold, Hay, & West, 1976). Thus, the development of joint attention skills may mark an important aspect of the development of individual differences in the tendency to engage in what may be called *affective intersubjectivity* (Mundy et al., 1992). Hypothetically, individual differences in this characteristic may have important ramifications for emotional outcomes for young children (Stern, 1985).

Each of these related possibilities is deserving of extended consideration. Indeed, each probably warrants a chapter, or more, unto itself. However, in this chapter we focus only on the last hypothesis just enumerated. Thus, the aims of this chapter are relatively circumscribed. First, research and theory on the features that distinguish the different nonverbal communication skills that emerge in this period are discussed. Research and theory connecting these skills to sociocognitive development and language development are also highlighted. Next, the hypothesis, which states that measures of joint attention skill development reflect the tendency to initiate shared affective states vis-à-vis objects or events, is examined. As part of this discussion, two models of how individual differences in this capacity may effect emotional outcome in children are described. In one model, the potential effect of the caregiver on the development of affective sharing is described (Stern, 1985). In another model, the possibility that individual differences in affective sharing in joint attention reflect constitutional factors, as well as environmental effects that are associated with socioemotional outcome is considered.

THE DEVELOPMENT AND ASSESSMENT OF NONVERBAL COMMUNICATION SKILLS

A useful way to conceptualize the acquisition of nonverbal, gestural sociocommunication skills is in terms of a shift from dyadic to triadic, or referential communicative interactions (Bakeman & Adamson, 1984). In the first 6 to 8 months, infants and caregivers primarily engage in face-to-face, or dyadic interactions. However, after the fourth or fifth month, infants become increasingly attentive to, and interested in, manipulating objects. With this increased interest in objects, the interactions of the child and caregiver gradually expand to incorporate attention to both the social partner, and objects. This expansion continues through the second year, so that by 18 months of age, a significant portion of infant–caregiver interaction may be characterized as triadic (Bakeman & Adamson, 1984).

In seminal theory and description concerning the infant's ability to manage these triadic interactions, Bruner and colleagues distinguished between different types of sociocommunication skills that emerged in the latter part of the first year of life (Bruner, 1975; Bruner & Sherwood, 1983; Scaife & Bruner, 1975). These included the ability to engage in object-oriented offering and turn-taking routines. Another important skill domain included the infant's ability to use or respond to a visual line of regard to coordinate attention to events or objects with another person (Bruner, 1975; Scaife & Bruner, 1975). This capacity to engage in joint attention routines was not clearly manifest in most infants until the 9- to 12-month period, when infants began to consistently display the ability to follow the line of regard of others (Scaife & Bruner, 1975).

In related efforts, Bates et al. (1979) emphasized that infants' capacity to direct the line of regard of a social partner to objects appeared to bifurcate with regard to function in the 9- to 12-month period. Late in the first year of life, gestural acts were used by infants for imperative or instrumental requesting functions, such as pointing to elicit aid in obtaining an object that is out of reach. However, the functionally distinct use of gestures and eye contact for declarative purposes, such as showing an object to another person, could also be distinguished (Bates et al., 1979). Thus, by the end of the 1970s, research and theory had culminated in a taxonomy of different forms of nonverbal sociocommunication skills that emerged in the later part of the first year, and were consolidated throughout the second year of life.

Applied researchers have often called on elements of this taxonomy in their attempts to devise measures of individual differences in the development of communications skills, assuming that these measures may provide important information about development in young children (Seibert, Hogan, & Mundy, 1982; Snyder, 1978; Wetherby & Prizant, 1993b; Wetherby & Prutting, 1984). These efforts have made it possible for different researchers to use similar methods in explorations of early nonverbal communication development. Contemporary versions of these methods include the abridged version of Seibert and Hogan's Early Social-Communication Scales (ESCS; Mundy, Sigman, Kasari, & Yirmiya, 1988; Mundy, Sigman, & Kasari, 1990) and the Communication and Symbolic Behavior Scales (CSBS; Wetherby & Prizant, 1993a). These very similar instruments utilize a structured, videotaped child–tester interaction designed to elicit nonverbal communicative bids. Child–tester interactions are used to minimize the possible variability that caregivers may contribute to the display of communicative skills among young children. Both instruments yield frequency scores for the number of bids observed within three categories of nonverbal communication. Bruner and Sherwood's (1983) terminology for these categories is used in both assessment systems.

In this terminology, *social interaction skills* refer to the use of eye contact, gestures, and affective signals to elicit and maintain turn-taking with objects such as offering objects back and forth with a caregiver. *Requesting* or *behavior regulation skills* refer to the use of gestures and eye contact to direct attention and elicit aid in obtaining an object or event. An example here is giving a jar while making eye contact with an adult to elicit aid in opening the jar. Finally, *joint attention skills* are very similar to requesting skills in that they are used to direct attention. However, the function, or illocutionary force of these communicative bids appears to be to share the experience of an object or an event with someone. Thus, the function is less instrumental, but perhaps more social than with requesting. An example here might be a child who holds an interesting novel toy up to a caregiver to show the toy.

NONVERBAL COMMUNICATION AND SOCIOCOGNITION

Much of the interest in nonverbal communication skill development in the second year hinges on the judgment that the intentionality of the communicative bids of the child becomes more apparent with the emergence of triadic/referential communication bids (Bates et al., 1979; Golinkoff, 1983). The evidence for intentionality in triadic communication development is at least threefold. First, infants and toddlers increasingly combine gestures, such as reaching or pointing to objects, with eye contact suggesting that they are monitoring the degree to which the social partner may be monitoring their gestural signal. Second, infants and toddlers increasingly use conventional signals, such as pointing, suggesting that they understand something of signal value of specific types of gestures. Finally, and perhaps most important, with the emergence of triadic skills, infants and toddlers begin to display communicative repair when their initial gestural bids do not yield desired responses (Golinkoff, 1983). For example, a child may first simply extend his or her arm with a hand-open gesture toward a cookie that is out of reach, then add eye contact and a vocalization if the reaching gesture fails to elicit aid in obtaining the cookie.

With the premise of intentionality comes the important corollary assumption that the development of referential or triadic nonverbal communication skills reflect aspects of the infants' burgeoning awareness of self and other (Bruner, 1975). To be intentional with regard to communicative acts suggests that the child has some sense of self and other as capable of sending and receiving signals. Extending this notion, Bretherton et al. (1981) suggested that referential nonverbal communication skills reflect rudimentary aspects of a developing "theory of mind" in infants and toddlers. That is, triadic nonverbal communicative acts indicate that the child can appreciate that others have perceptions and intentions relative to objects or events, and that these perceptions or intentions can be affected by the child's behaviors. Subsequently, numerous researchers working on issues in normal and atypical development have explored the notion that referential nonverbal communication skills reflect an awareness that self and others can experience common covert psychological phenomenon relative to objects and events (Baron-Cohen, 1989; Bretherton et al., 1981; Hobson, 1993; Moore & Corkum, 1994; Mundy, Sigman, & Kasari, 1993; Stern, 1985; Tomasello, 1995; Wellman, 1993).

Two convergent examples of these elaborations may be found in somewhat divergent literatures. In an attempt to understand interpersonal development, Stern (1985) argued that the sociocommunication behaviors of infants between 7 and 12 months of age suggest that they have the capacity to share three aspects of mental states with others. Accordingly, infants in this period can: *share intentions* or a common goal orientation with regard to objects or events; engage in joint attention and *share a common visual/sensory perspective* on objects or events; and *share affective states* or a common emotional response to objects and events. Similarly, Wellman (1992), in describing early cognitive development, proposed that in the last quarter of the first year of life, infants understand people in terms of three aspects of behavior: *desire* or that people can seek to attain the same objects or experiences; *perception* or that people can see, hear, or feel the same object or event; and *emotion* or that people can have the same affective reactions to objects or events.

The aspects of sociocognition described by Stern and Wellman may be directly related to the three categories of nonverbal communication skills described by Bates, Bruner, and others. The ability to recognize that self and other can experience intentions, or goal orientations, may be reflected by the capacity of the child to initiate and respond to nonverbal requests. The capacity to understand that both self and other can share a common visual perspective of an event or object may be involved in both joint attention and requesting, as these both involve coordinating attention between self and another person vis-à-vis an object or event. Finally, as we discuss in more detail later, both social interaction and joint attention skills may involve affective sharing. In the former, affective sharing occurs in the face-to-face enterprise of turn-taking. In the latter, the tendency to share affective states may have a more sophisticated expression as the child initiates shared affective states in a triadic context that is referenced to an object or event (Mundy, Kasari, & Sigman, 1992).

This line of theory would suggest that different measures of nonverbal communication skills may reflect distinct aspects of sociocognitive and socioemotional development in young children. However, as a prerequisite to a consideration of this hypothesis it is first important to document that joint attention and other types of nonverbal communication skills may actually reflect distinct aspects of early psychological development. This issue has received relatively little attention in research on normal development. However, direct support for the importance of the distinctions among nonverbal communication skills made by Bruner, Bates, and others is apparent in applied research on children with developmental disorders.

NONVERBAL COMMUNICATION
AND DEVELOPMENTAL DISORDERS

Young children with distinct forms of biologically based developmental disorders display different profiles of development across nonverbal communication skills (Mundy et al., 1988; Mundy, Sigman, Ungerer, & Sherman, 1986; Wetherby & Prizant, 1984b; Wetherby, Yonclas, & Bryan, 1989). Young children with autism display a profound disturbance of joint attention skill development, a moderate disturbance of social interaction skill development, and only a mild disturbance of requesting skill development (Loveland & Landry, 1986; McEvoy, Rogers, & Pennington; 1993; Mundy et al., 1986; Mundy, Sigman, & Kasari, 1994; Wetherby & Prizant, 1984b; Wetherby et al., 1989). Alternatively, children with Down syndrome display a disturbance of nonverbal requesting skill development, a possible mild enhancement of social interaction performance, and no differences from mental age-matched controls on referential joint attention skills (Mundy et al., 1988; Mundy et al., 1995; Wetherby et al., 1989).

It is difficult to understand the contrasting pattern of nonverbal communication skill development observed across these groups simply in terms of caregiver or other environmental effects (Kasari, Sigman, Mundy, & Yirmiya, 1988; Mundy et al., 1988). On the other hand, this segregation of disturbance in nonverbal communication skills across groups with organic forms of developmental disorders suggests that different nonverbal communication skills may reflect distinct and, to some degree constitutional, aspects of early psychological development in young children. Additional evidence of the distinct nature of these skills may be found in research on language development and nonverbal communication.

NONVERBAL COMMUNICATION
AND LANGUAGE DEVELOPMENT

Several studies on normal development have reported moderate relations between measures of nonverbal communication and language development (Bates et al., 1979; Olson, Bates, & Bayles, 1984; Tomasello, 1988). However, even though distinctions among skills may have been recognized (Bates et al., 1979), these distinctions have not been emphasized in exploring the relations between nonverbal and verbal communication development. Rather, a primary focus has been on analysis of the child–caregiver interactional process that may provide a connection between nonverbal communication skills, especially joint attention, and language development (Bruner, 1975; Dunham et al., 1993; Tomasello, 1988, 1992; Tomasello & Farrar, 1986; Werner & Kaplan, 1963).

On the other hand, applied research involving children with developmental disorders has begun to explore the links between language development and children's performance on measures of different types of nonverbal communication skills. This research suggests that joint attention and social interaction skill development may have especially strong ties to language development in children with normal and atypical development (Mundy et al., 1990; Mundy et al., 1995; Paul, 1991). Indeed, in one recent study, joint attention and social interaction skills were found to predict language development across a 13-month period in a sample of 22 toddlers, even after taking variance in initial Bayley mental age or Reynell receptive and expressive language age estimates into account (Mundy et al., 1995). Requesting skills were also predictive of language development, but not after taking variance in initial developmental status into account.

Although only tentative conclusions may be drawn from this limited empirical base, these data suggest that different types of nonverbal communication skills may not be equal in their links to early language development. This observation is consistent with the hypothesis that different types of nonverbal communication skills may reflect different aspects of early psychological development. Studies on the cognitive and affective correlates of nonverbal communication skills provide further support for this hypothesis.

THE COGNITIVE CORRELATES
OF NONVERBAL COMMUNICATION SKILLS

Theory and research have long held that the emergence of gestural communication skills is linked to development in the capacity for representational thinking (Bates et al., 1979). However, theory on the dissociation between the development of joint attention skills versus requesting or social interaction skills in children with autism suggests that the former may involve more sophisticated representational processes than the latter (Baron-Cohen, 1989). In this regard, Mundy et al. (1993) reported that individual differences in symbolic play were correlated with joint attention skills, but not requesting or social interaction skills, in a sample of 15 preschool children with mental retardation (MR). Again, firm conclusions may not be drawn from one small study. Nevertheless, to the extent that symbolic play measures index representational development, these data suggest that joint attention skills may differ from requesting and social interaction skills in the degree to which they ultimately come to involve higher order, symbolic-representation processes (Werner & Kaplan, 1963).

Another interesting study also suggests that joint attention skills involve different cognitive processes than do requesting skills. McEvoy, Rogers, and Pennington (1993) reported a significant relation between joint attention and social interaction skills, as assessed on the ESCS, and a putative measure of executive functions in children with autism and comparison groups of children. A comparable relation was not observed for requesting skills. Executive functions refer to the regulatory processes that enable planned and flexible problem solving. Theoretically, executive functions are mediated by neurological processes associated with the frontal lobes. McEvoy et al. (1993) interpreted these results to suggest that deficient joint attention, and better requesting skill development in children with autism could be explained by the different degree to which joint attention and requesting skills may reflect executive-cognitive, and frontal-neurological processes.

Neurological data consistent with this conclusion have been reported in a study of intervention for young children with intractable seizure disorders (Caplan et al., 1993). In this study, Positron Emission Tomography (PET) indices of individual differences in metabolism in the frontal hemispheres of 13 children with seizure disorders predicted joint attention development in these children, but did not predict requesting or social interaction skill development. These results suggested that individual differences in the functioning of the frontal lobes, as indexed by a measure of metabolic rate, may be more strongly related to joint attention skills than other types of nonverbal communication skills.

Thus, recent research has begun to suggest that different types of nonverbal communication skills reflect different types of cognitive and neurological processes. In general, these studies suggest that measures of joint attention skills may be particularly sensitive indices of both cognitive-representational and frontal-neurological processes as applied to the domain of early sociocommunication development. It is noteworthy, however, that research has also begun to suggest that affective processes may distinguish joint attention skills from other forms of nonverbal communication skills. For the present discussion, this may be the most important aspect of the contemporary literature on nonverbal communication development.

THE AFFECTIVE CORRELATES
OF NONVERBAL COMMUNICATION SKILLS

In their initial work, Bates and her collaborators observed that joint attention acts serve not only to direct the attention of the adult to an object, but also are simultaneously used for primarily socioaffective sharing purposes. Bates et al. (1975) stated, "Long before he can understand the utilitarian value of sharing information, the child will engage in "declaring" for primarily social purposes" (p. 115). Accordingly, children's declaring or joint attention acts involve the "use of an object (through pointing, showing, giving, etc.) as a means to attain adult attention" (p. 115). Moreover, the attention-getting component, as described by Bates et al. (1975), appeared to involve the conveyance or exchange of affective signals. They suggested that the development of joint attention acts mark the emergence of attempts to "seek a more subtle kind of adult response—laughter, comment, smiles and eye contact" (p. 121) in reference to the coordinated attention to an object and event.

Other researchers have expressed similar views of joint attention development. Rheingold et al. (1976) interpreted joint attention acts as a means to share experience with others. They described this "experience-sharing" function as distinct from the function of imperative, requesting gestures. Bruner (1981) also perceived that there may be "some primitive mood marking procedure to distinguish indicating from commanding or requesting" (p. 67) among proverbial acts of communication. These observations suggest that joint attention acts may involve the attempts of young children to convey or share their affective experience of an object with others. Alternatively, affective sharing may play a lesser role in imperative requesting acts. Thus, there is a suggestion in the literature that nonverbal joint attention may involve affective sharing to a greater extent than does nonverbal requesting.

The empirical literature supports and expands on this view of joint attention behaviors. Whereas Bates et al. (1975) suggest joint attention bids may involve *seeking* an affective response from adults, research also suggests that by 10 months of age, infants may also *initiate* positive affective exchanges in a joint attention context. In play with objects, they often first express positive affect to objects, and then turn to display this affect to a social partner (Jones et al., 1991). Jones and Raag (1989) also presented data that suggests that, by 18 months, the tendency of toddlers to share positive affect vis-à-vis an object is as strong with strangers as it is with familiar caregivers. In addition, Adamson and Bakeman (1985) reported that higher proportions of all affective displays occur within joint attention episodes than in face-to-face interactions in caregiver–child interaction observations conducted with 6-, 9-, 12-, 15-, and 18-month-olds (Adamson & Bakeman, 1985, Table 2). Thus, these data suggest that joint attention episodes may be a prepotent context in mother–infant interaction for the conveyance of affect.

Although important and informative, these studies did not attempt to directly distinguish between joint attention and requesting behaviors. However, a direct comparison of the affective components of nonverbal joint attention and requesting has recently been presented in an attempt to understand the disassociation between these types of acts in the development of children with autism (Kasari, Sigman, Mundy, & Yirmiya, 1990). In this study, both the nonverbal communication skills and facial affect of children with autism and comparison children were carefully observed. The results indicated that children with normal development displayed much more positive affect in conjunction with joint attention bids, as compared to requesting bids. On the other hand, the children with autism displayed equivalent levels of affect in conjunction with both types of communicative behavior and displayed significantly less positive affect in conjunction with joint attention bids, than did the comparison children. A related study has been conducted with a sample of 32 normal infants (Mundy et al., 1992). The results indicated that these infants displayed more positive affect in conjunction with each of four types of joint attention acts relative to four types of requesting acts. The results of this study were interpreted to suggest that the assessment of joint attention bids on the ESCS reflects a tendency to initiate states of "affective intersubjectivity," or states of shared positive affect vis-à-vis objects or events (Mundy et al., 1992).

Although affective sharing, in general, appears to be associated with bids for joint attention, data suggest that infants and toddlers display considerable individual differences in affective intersubjectivity in structured measures of gestural communication development. Wetherby and Prizant (1993a) assessed 208 children who were either prelinguistic or used holophrastic speech with the CSBS. One measure on the CSBS is an index of "shared positive affect." It is not clear to what degree this CSBS measure is derived from observations of joint attention bids or other nonverbal communication bids. Nevertheless, the data suggest that considerable individual differences in the tendency to display positive affect to the tester in a structured nonverbal communication measure may be displayed by young children. Let us discuss the potential importance of these individual differences.

JOINT ATTENTION AND SOCIOEMOTIONAL DEVELOPMENT

Much more research is needed before a definitive perspective on the nature of nonverbal communication skills is at hand. However, the foregoing review provides the basis for some interesting, if tentative, conclusions. Research and theory suggest that the types of nonverbal communication skills that develop in the second year of life may reflect partially independent domains of early psychological development. Data on the correlates of nonverbal communication skills suggests that the domain assessed under the rubric of joint attention may reflect higher order representational mental processes to a greater extent than requesting and social interaction skills. Moreover, research has begun to suggest that joint attention skills reflect self-regulatory and behavior organization mechanisms associated with executive functions and frontal-neurological processes to a greater degree than requesting, and perhaps social interaction skills. Data on language development also suggests that the link between joint attention skills development and early lexical acquisition may be especially strong. Finally, and perhaps most important, joint attention skills may provide a window onto individual differences in the tendency of infants and toddlers to initiate states of positive affective sharing with others relative to objects or events.

Whereas the empirical links between joint attention and socioemotional behavior development in children as yet are few, the theoretical links are readily accessible. This is especially so when joint attention is viewed as involving affective sharing. Stern (1985) suggested that the "capacity to share affective states is the most pervasive and clinically germane feature of intersubjective relatedness" that arises in infants and toddlers (p. 138).

Intersubjectivity refers to the "similarity in thought-feeling content of two dyad members that develops as a consequence of their interaction" (Ickes, Tooke, Stinson, Baker, & Bissonette, 1988, p. 61). As noted earlier, nonverbal communication skills theoretically reflect the developing awareness in infants and toddlers that the self and other can have similar goals, perceptions, or feelings regarding objects or events. Moreover, it appears that joint attention behaviors may be especially important in the development of affective sharing (Mundy et al., 1992). For Stern, the development of this capacity, or the capacity for affective intersubjectivity or "interaffectivity" (p. 132), constitutes a critical step in the socioemotional development of the child.

In Stern's (1985) view, it is most important to consider how caregivers respond when infants and toddlers initiate a potential state of shared affect in reference to objects or events. Caregiver responsiveness was referred to as *affective attunement* or the degree to which a parent aligned his or her response appropriately to the affect expressed by his or her child. So, for example, a parent might smile and laugh along with a child's positive affect, but display concern and extend comfort in response to a child's negative affect. Parental attunement was viewed as critical to emotional development because it enabled young children to begin to understand what was, and what was not within the realm of shareable personal, emotional experience. Moreover, the effects of attunement were thought to become increasingly robust as triadic nonverbal communications emerged, and the child became more capable of processing intersubjective information on shareable experiences that were anchored to a greater variety of referents in the world.

The potentially pathogenic expression of affective attunement was called "selective attunement" (Stern, 1985, p. 207). Selective attunement occurs in all caregiver–child dyads to some degree. However, in some situations, selective attunement occurs with such frequency that there is a systematic bias toward responsiveness to one affective valence or another. For example, a parent may be responsive to positive affective expressions, but intolerant of negative expressions, or visa versa. In Stern's (1985) view, selective attunement was primary in the development of self-pathology because the child would come to emphasize "the portion of inner experience that can achieve intersubjective acceptance with the inner experience of other, at the expense of the remaining, equally legitimate portion of inner experience" (p. 210). In other words, selective attunement to affective states in infants, was thought to precipitate the early disavowal or repression of segments of the child's affective experience. Thus, a lack of integration in children's sense of self was fostered, with certain aspects of their emotional life split off or invalidated. This process, in the view of Stern and other self psychologists, is a primary contributor to the development of behavior disturbance in children, as well as adults.

According to this interactional view, the degree to which children express positive affect in the context of joint attention can largely be an effect of caregiver affective attunement or selective attunement. Accordingly, joint attention skills may well be one marker of the "mental health" of a caregiver–child dyad with too little, or too much affective expression in joint attention contexts indicative of a possible problem. For example, one could well imagine that stressed, ambivalent or inadequate caregivers might not be well attuned to the expression of positive affect in their children. Consequently, one may expect to observe a decrease in joint attention bids among children exposed to this type of caregiving.

This hypothesis is plausible and warrants empirical consideration. However, an alternative, more nativistic view of the meaning of shared affect in joint attention bids is also possible. In this model, it is assumed that joint attention, and affective sharing are influenced not only by caregiver effects, but also by inherent qualities of the child. This view emerges from applied research on nonverbal communication in children with autism (Mundy, 1995), but may have implications for research on nonverbal communication and socioemotional development in all children.

JOINT ATTENTION AND SOCIOEMOTIONAL APPROACH BEHAVIOR

Why do toddlers initiate joint attention bids? It is tempting to address this question in terms of the cognitive processes that are involved in coordinated attention and reference to objects (e.g., Butterworth & Jarrett, 1991; Tomasello, 1995). However, such an approach may be more appropriate for understanding how a child is able to initiate a joint attention bid, but not necessarily why a child initiates joint attention bids. To understand why toddlers initiate joint attention bids it may be important to consider motivational processes.

In this regard, recall Bates et al.'s (1975) observation that joint attention bids mark the emergence of attempts to "seek a more subtle kind of adult response—laughter, comment, smiles and eye contact" in episodes involving reference to an object or event (p. 121). Also recall research that suggests that joint attention bids may reflect the tendency of toddlers to share their own positive affect with others relative to objects or events (Kasari et al., 1990; Mundy et al., 1992). If these observations are valid, then individual differences in joint attention bids may reflect differences in the degree to which children are motivated by the reinforcement value of a social partners' positive regard, and/or the experience of establishing shared positive affect with others.

This motivational hypothesis of the initiation of joint attention bids leads to a corollary hypothesis. The degree to which the child is disposed to positive affective sharing in communication with others may be expected to play a role in the degree to which the child is able to establish a positive sense of relatedness with caregivers and other less familiar people. According to this hypothesis, joint attention bids may be regarded as an index of the socioemotional approach tendency of children (Mundy, 1995). This tendency may have a positive effect on the potential for bonding between children and other potential caregivers.

It may be argued that a major component of joint attention development and the disposition toward positive socioemotional approach behaviors may be explained in terms of learning processes (e.g., Moore & Corkum, 1994). Stern's model of affective attunement provides an illustration of how one might expect caregiver influences, for example, to entrain more or less joint attention and positive socioemotional approach behavior in young children. However, several lines of reasoning may also be marshalled to suggest that neurobiological variability among children also contributes to individual differences in the disposition toward joint attention bids and socioemotional approach behaviors.

First, observations of the profound disturbance in joint attention development among autistic children draws one to consider the development of joint attention and positive affective sharing from a biological perspective. Much of the current research on autism suggests that the primary causal path in the etiology of this disorder is neurobiological (see Schopler & Mesibov, 1987). Moreover, several proposals about the constituents of the biological disorder of autism suggest that mechanisms specific to socioemotional motivation processes that potentiate children's movement toward establishing states of positive affective intersubjectivity may be disturbed in children with autism (Fotheringham, 1991; Mundy, 1995; Panksepp & Sahley, 1987). Indeed, one of the lessons of research on autism for the field of normal development may be that there is a very large degree of variability in the degree to which people tend to establish states of positive affective intersubjectivity with others, and that some portion of this variance is due to neurobiological differences among people. Second, evidence that individual differences in joint attention development could be predicted from individual differences in frontal functioning among young children with histories of intractable seizure disorders (Caplan et al., 1993) provides some support for the notion that joint attention development reflects individual differences in neurobiological processes. Moreover, this finding provides a bridge to a most interesting finding in developmental psychobiological research.

Before the end of the first year of life, neurological subsystems may be organized, and lateralized to regulate social approach behaviors as opposed to social withdrawal behaviors (Fox, 1991). In particular, left frontal processes appear to play a role in behaviors that are child-initiated, involve a focus on a social object, and include the display of positive affect to the social partner (Davidson, Ekman, Saron, Senulis, & Friesen, 1990; Dawson, 1994; Fox, 1991). In the first year of life, reaching to a caregiver while smiling would be prototypical of a social approach behavior. Hypothetically, positive affective sharing in joint attention bids in the second year of life reflects an elaboration of this frontally mediated, socioemotional approach tendency (Mundy, 1995). This speculation is bolstered a bit by the finding that left, rather than right frontal functioning was most powerfully related to joint attention development in the study of children with seizure disorders (Caplan et al., 1993). This possible lateralization of neurological processes would also be consistent with the notion that some component of individual differences in positive socioemotional approach disposition, as measured by frequency of joint attention bids, is associated with differences innate in neurobiological propensities.

The foregoing hypotheses and assumptions provide the framework for a model that is, admittedly, on the speculative side of current research and theory on joint attention skill development. However, it is not so speculative as to be beyond the pall of empirical verification or refutation. There are at least two studies that provide some support for the notion that joint attention skill development may play a role in bonding between children and potential caregivers. These studies suggest that joint attention skill development is related to caregivers' positive perceptions of their children as social partners.

JOINT ATTENTION AND SOCIAL BEHAVIOR

Paul (1991) reported a study in which 30 two-year-olds with specific expressive language delays were compared with 30 children displaying a more typical pattern of expressive language development. The results indicated that parents of late talkers reported observing more evidence of disruptive and hyperactive behavior than did the parents of children with more typical language. The reports of parents of late talkers also yielded lower scores on the socialization index of the Vineland even when items associated with language development, such as saying "please," were excluded (Paul, 1991). The critical items on this measure include showing interest in children or peers, playing simple interactive games, showing desire to please the caregiver, and imitating complex tasks displayed by others. Finally, Paul also reported that the late talkers produced significantly fewer overall communicative acts with their mothers, and that this difference was primarily due to an attenuated tendency of the late talkers to initiate joint attention acts. Indeed, late talkers displayed a higher mean for regulatory (requesting) acts (6.3, SD = 5.1) than did the comparison children (4.2, SD = 3.1), but a much lower mean for joint attention acts (23.27, SD = 12.3 vs. 40.7, SD = 15.2, respectively; Paul & Shiffer, 1991).

The interpretation of these data is not straightforward. On the one hand, it may be that processes specific to delayed language development account for the links observed in this study between socialization, behavior disturbance, and joint attention behaviors in 2-year-olds. However, the uneven profile of communicative functions displayed by the late talkers leaves open an alternative. Paul (1991) suggested that this profile was indicative of a child who may engage in social interactions for instrumental purposes but who was limited in tendency to engage in communicative interaction for the more social purposes inherent to joint attention bids. Thus, a tentative hypothesis raised in this study was that an attenuation of joint attention bids reflected a reduced drive to initiate communicative bids that involve social experience sharing. This reduced drive may be linked both to language delays and behavior disturbance in some children (Paul, 1991).

A related, if serendipitous finding has recently been reported in a study of 30 preschool children with autism and comparison children, including a sample of 30 normal children (mean age approximately 20 months) on the ESCS and parent's report of symptoms on the Autism Behavior Checklist (ABC). The ABC yields measures of impairment in five areas:

1. a Relating scale that assesses the tendency to use and respond to touching, eye contact, facial affect, imitation, and to establish friendships,
2. a Language scale that measures frequency of language use and atypical vocal behavior,
3. a Social/Self Help scale that assesses temperament and adaptive behavior,
4. a Sensory scale that measures hypersensitivity and hyposensitivity to stimulation, and,

5. a Body/Object Use scale that measures stereotypes and repetitive actions.

The results indicated that nonverbal joint attention skill was correlated with parents reports on the Relating scale of the ABC for both the children with autism ($r = -.37$, $p < .05$), *and for the children with normal development* ($r = -.40$, $p < .05$). Higher scores on the ABC Relating scale indicated that parents confirmed more negative observations about the social behavior of their children such as "not responding to others affect, resisting being touched or held, not imitating others in play, and not developing friendships." Thus, in both the autistic and normal samples, children who reportedly had fewer positive social behaviors by parental report also had lower ESCS joint attention scores. These data suggest that the frequency of joint attention behaviors, as assessed in interaction with a tester, may be related to the degree that parent's perceive the display of positive social behaviors among normally developing toddlers, as well as among children displaying atypical social development. Although tentative, these results are consistent with the notion that joint attention behavior, via effects associated with caregiver perceptions of the social behavior of young children, could have an effect on caregiver–child bonding. Let us now extend this notion to consider how joint attention skill development and social approach behaviors may relate to the development of attachment.

JOINT ATTENTION AND ATTACHMENT

The social approach model leads to an interesting premise regarding a possible interaction between joint attention skill development and attachment. To recapitulate, in this model we assume that joint attention bids, at least those associated with the expression of positive affect, reflect a disposition toward socioemotional approach behavior in children. Moreover, it is assumed that socioemotional approach behaviors play a facilitating role in establishing bonds or a positive sense of relatedness between the child and others. Finally, we also assume that individual differences in joint attention development are affected by both environmental, especially caregiver effects, and by innate, neurobiological characteristics of the child. This suggests the possibility of different types of environmental and biological combinations that may affect joint attention, and more importantly socioemotional approach tendencies in children.

If one focuses on caregiver effects, the tendency is to suggest that a child's joint attention skill development may be augmented by positive caregiving and attenuated by negative caregiving. However, if it is also assumed that a child has an innate reaction range with regard to the development of joint attention skills, then a more transactional perspective may be adopted. From this perspective, one of the more interesting potential combinations is the child with a biological disposition toward higher frequencies of joint attention, or social approach bids, who is growing up in an environment that presents a risk for poor caregiving. The poor caregiver environment may have a negative effect on the socioemotional development of a child. However, one hypothesis is that a child with a higher inherent predisposition toward joint attention and socioemotional approach behavior may be less vulnerable to the negative effects of a poor caregiver environment. Although poor caregiving may decrease socioemotional approach tendencies, children with higher biological predispositions toward joint attention skills development may have a sufficiently broad reaction range to express an adaptive level of socioemotional approach behaviors with the primary caregiver, and with other potential caregivers. This, in turn, may allow the child to elicit whatever positive social interactions are possible in the poor caregiving environment. Perhaps more importantly, it may increase the likelihood that the child will establish bonds with others that mitigate the negative effects of the primary caregiver interactions. Thus, the display of good joint attention skills by a toddler with a tester may be one significant indicator of the degree to which a child may be more or less vulnerable to negative caregiving effects.

This hypothesis leads to a testable prediction. To the degree that the assessment of attachment via the strange situation reflects something of quality of caregiving, we may expect ratings of toddler's behavior in the strange situation, and ratings of toddler's joint attention bids to testers to yield partially independent predictors of early socioemotional behavioral development. In particular, we might expect data from attachment measures and joint attention measures to interact in their prediction of behavioral outcome with positive attachment indices mitigating the possible negative effects of poor joint attention development, and positive joint attention development mitigating the negative effects associated with indices of disturbed attachment. Furthermore, the toddler with both poor attachment and joint attention indices may be at higher risk than other children for the development of behavior disturbance.

Of course these predictions presuppose that attachment and the tendency to display joint attention bids follow at least partially independent paths in early development. In this regard, it should be noted that the EEG correlates of infants' responses to separation situations and social approach situations appear to be different (Fox, 1991). Furthermore, research on autism suggests that although these children display profound joint attention disturbance, the behavior they display in the strange situation is not disturbed relative to control children with MR (Sigman & Mundy, 1989). Similarly, individual differences in joint attention behavior do not appear to be correlated with attachment ratings of children with autism, although nonverbal requesting does appear to correlate with attachment in these children (Capps, Sigman, & Mundy, 1994). Thus, although scant research may currently be brought to bear on this important issue, the data that exist are not inconsistent with the hypothesis that joint attention and attachment measures may provide independent but complimentary indices of risk for socioemotional disturbance in preschool children. We are currently examining this hypothesis in a longitudinal study of infants and toddlers who are at risk for the development of behavior disturbance.

SUMMARY

In this chapter we have attempted to argue that the study and assessment of nonverbal communication skills development, especially in the second year of life, may be of considerable value for research on early socioemotional development. Several systems of assessment of nonverbal communication skills have been developed. However, all too often these assessments are considered only in conjunction with research on language development, or perhaps sociocognitive development. Nevertheless, both new and old research and theory suggest that nonverbal communication development, especially joint attention development, may reflect processes that are critical to adaptive and maladaptive socioemotional development in preschool children. To illustrate this point, we briefly described how Stern's (1985) theory on early intersubjectivity and affective attunement between caregivers and toddlers may be related to the development of nonverbal communications skills. We have also described a sociomotivational model of joint attention development and extrapolated from this model the hypothesis that joint attention and attachment measures may be complimentary, but independent predictors of behavior development in preschool children. At the outset, however, we noted that the circumscribed views presented here did not do justice to the numerous possible connections between early nonverbal communication and subsequent socioemotional development in children. We hope this chapter serves to encourage others to begin to examine this potentially important linkage in early development.

ACKNOWLEDGMENT

The preparation of this chapter was supported by NIDCD Grant # 00484.

REFERENCES

Adamson, L., & Bakeman, R. (1985). Affect and attention: Infants observed with mothers and peers. *Child Development, 56,* 582–593.

Adamson, L., & Bakeman, R. (1991). The development of shared attention during infancy. In R. Vasta (Ed.), *Annals of child development* (Vol. 8, pp. 1–41). London, UK: Kingsley.

Bakeman, R., & Adamson, L. (1984). Coordinating attention to people and objects in mother–infant and peer–infant interactions. *Child Development, 55*, 1278–1289.

Baker, L., & Cantwell, D. (1987). A prospective psychiatric follow-up of children with speech/language disorders. *Journal of the American Academy of Child and Adolescent Psychiatry, 26*, 546–553.

Baron-Cohen, S. (1989). Joint-attention deficits in autism: Towards a cognitive analysis. *Development and Psychopathology, 3*, 185–190.

Bates, E., Benigni, L., Bretherton, I., Camaioni, L., & Volterra, V. (1979). *The emergence of symbols: Cognition and communication in infancy.* New York: Academic Press.

Bates, E., Camaioni, L., & Volterra, V. (1975). The acquisition of performative prior to speech. *Merrill-Palmer Quarterly, 21*, 205–224.

Beitchman, J., Hood, J., & Inglis, A. (1990). Psychiatric risk in children with speech and language disorders. *Journal of Abnormal Child Psychology, 18*, 283–296.

Bretherton, I., Bates, E., Benigni, L., Camaioni, L., & Volterra, V. (1979). Relationship between cognition, communication and quality of attachment. In E. Bates, L. Benigni, I. Bretherten, L. Camaioni, & V. Volterra (Eds.), *The emergence of symbols: Cognition and communication infancy* (pp. 223–269). New York: Academic Press.

Bretherton, I., McNew, S., & Beeghly-Smith, M. (1981). Early person knowledge as expressed in verbal and gestural communication: When do infants acquire a theory of mind? In M. Lamb & L. Sherrod (Eds.), *Infant social cognition* (pp. 333–373). Hillsdale, NJ: Lawrence Erlbaum Associates.

Bruner, J. (1975). From communication to language: A psychological perspective. *Cognition, 3*, 255–287.

Bruner, J. (1981). Learning how to do things with words. In J. Bruner & A. Garton (Eds.), *Human growth and development* (pp. 62–84). London, UK: Oxford University Press.

Bruner, J., & Sherwood, V. (1983). Thought, language and interaction in infancy. In J. Call, E. Galenson, & R. Tyson (Eds.), *Frontiers of infant psychiatry* (pp. 38–55). New York: Basic Books.

Butterworth, G., & Jarrett, N. (1991). What minds have in common is space: Spatial mechanisms serving joint visual attention in infancy. *British Journal of Developmental Psychology, 9*, 55–72.

Caplan, R., Chugani, H., Messa, C., Guthrie, D., Sigman, M., Traversay, J., & Mundy, P. (1993). Hemispherectomy for early onset intractable seizures: Presurgical cerebral glucose metabolism and postsurgical nonverbal communication patterns. *Developmental Medicine and Child Neurology, 35*, 582–592.

Capps, L., Sigman, M., & Mundy, P. (1994). Attachment security in children with autism. *Development and Psychopathology, 6*, 249–261.

Davidson, R., Ekman, P., Saron, C., Senulis, J., & Friesen, W. (1990). Approach–withdrawal and cerebral asymmetry: Emotion expression and brain physiology. *Journal of Personality and Social Psychology, 58*, 330–341.

Dawson, G. (1994). Development of emotional expression and emotion regulation in infancy: Contribution of the frontal lobe. In G. Dawson & K. Fischer (Eds.), *Human behavior and the developing brain* (pp. 518–536). New York: Guilford Press.

Dodge, K. (1986). A social information processing model of social competence in children. In M. Perlmutter (Ed.), *Minnesota symposium on child psychology, Vol. 18: Cognitive perspectives as children's social and behavior development* (pp. 72–125). Hillsdale, NJ: Lawrence Erlbaum Associates.

Dunham, P., Dunham, F., & Curwin, A. (1993). Joint-attentional states and lexical acquisition at 18 months. *Developmental Psychology, 29*, 827–831.

Fotheringham, J. (1991). Autism: Its primary psychological and neurological deficit. *Canadian Journal of Psychiatry, 36*, 686–692.

Fox, N. (1991). It's not left, it's right: Electroencephalograph asymmetry and the development of emotion. *American Psychologist, 46*, 863–872.

Golinkoff, R. (1983). The preverbal negotiation of failed messages: Insights into the transition period. In R. Golinkoff (Ed.), *The transition from prelinguistic to linguistic communication* (pp. 57–78). Hillsdale, NJ: Lawrence Erlbaum Associates.

Hobson, P. (1993). *Autism and the development of mind.* Hillsdale, NJ: Lawrence Erlbaum Associates.

Howlin, P., & Rutter, M. (1987). The consequences of language delay for other aspects of development. In W. Yule & M. Rutter (Eds.), *Language development and language disorders* (pp. 187–213). Philadelphia: Lippincott.

Ickes, W., Tooke, W., Stinson, L., Baker, V., & Bissonette, V. (1988). Social cognition: Intersubjectivity in same sex dyads. *Journal of Nonverbal Behavior, 12*, 58–84.

Jones, S., Collins, K., & Hong, H. (1991). An audience effect on smile production in 10-month-old infants. *Psychological Science, 2*, 45–49.

Jones, S., & Raag, R. (1989). Smile production in older infants: The importance of a social recipient for the facial signal. *Child Development, 60*, 811–818.

Kasari, C., Sigman, M., Mundy, P., & Yirmiya, N. (1988). Caregiver interactions with autistic children. *Journal of Abnormal Child Psychology, 16*, 45–56.

Kasari, C., Sigman, M., Mundy, P. & Yirmiya, N. (1990). Affective sharing in the context of joint attention interactions of normal, autistic and mentally retarded children. *Journal of Autism and Developmental Disorders, 20*, 87–100.

Loveland, K., & Landry, S. (1986). Joint attention and language in autism and developmental language delay. *Journal of Autism and Developmental Disorders, 16*, 335–349.

McEvoy, R., Rogers, S., & Pennington, R. (1993). Executive function and social communication deficits in young, autistic children. *Journal of Child Psychology and Psychiatry, 34*, 563–578.

Moore, C., & Corkum, V. (1994). Social understanding at the end of the first year of life. *Developmental Review, 14*, 349–372.

Mundy, P. (1995). Joint attention and social emotional approach behavior in children with autism. *Development and Psychopathology, 7*, 63–82.

Mundy, P., & Hogan, A. (1994). Joint attention, intersubjectivity and autistic psychopathology. In D. Cicchetti & S. Toth (Eds.), *Rochester symposium on developmental psychopathology: Disorder and dysfunction of the self* (pp. 1–31). Rochester, NY: University of Rochester Press.

Mundy, P., Kasari, C., & Sigman, M. (1992). Nonverbal communication, affective sharing, and intersubjectivity. *Infant Behavior and Development, 15,* 377–381.

Mundy, P., Kasari, C., Sigman, M., & Ruskin, E. (1995). Nonverbal communication and early language acquisition in children with Down syndrome or normal development. *Journal of Speech and Hearing Research, 38,* 157–167.

Mundy, P., Seibert, J., & Hogan, A. (1985). Communication skills in mentally retarded children. In M. Sigman (Ed.), *Children with emotional disorders and developmental disabilities.* Orlando, FL: Grune & Stratton.

Mundy, P., Sigman, M., & Kasari, C. (1990). A longitudinal study of joint attention and language development in autistic children. *Journal of Autism and Developmental Disorders, 20,* 115–123.

Mundy, P., Sigman, M., & Kasari, C. (1993). The theory of mind and joint attention deficits in autism. In S. Baron-Cohen, H. Tager-Flusberg, & D. Cohen (Eds.), *Understanding other minds: Perspective from autism* (pp. 181–203). Oxford, UK: Oxford University Press.

Mundy, P., Sigman, M., & Kasari, C. (1994). Joint attention, developmental level, and symptom presentation in young children with autism. *Development and Psychopathology, 6,* 389–401.

Mundy, P., Sigman, M., Kasari, C., & Yirmiya, N. (1988). Nonverbal communication skills in Down Syndrome children. *Child Development, 59,* 235–249.

Mundy, P., Sigman, M., Ungerer J.A., & Sherman, T. (1986). Defining the social deficits in autism: The contribution of non-verbal communication measures. *Journal of Child Psychology and Psychiatry, 27,* 657–669.

Olson, S., Bates, J., & Bayles, K. (1984). Mother–infant interaction and the development of individual differences in children s cognitive competence. *Developmental Psychology, 20,* 166–179.

Papousek, H., Papousek, M., Suomi, S., & Rahn, C. (1991). Preverbal communication and attachment: Comparative views. In J. Gewirtz & W. Kurtines (Eds.), *Intersections with attachment* (pp. 97–122). Hillsdale, NJ: Lawrence Erlbaum Associates.

Panksepp, J., & Sahley, T. (1987). Possible brain opiod involvement in disrupted social intent and language development of autism. In E. Schopler & G. Mesibov (Eds.), *Neurobiological issues in autism* (pp. 357–372). New York: Plenum Press.

Paul, R. (1991). Profiles of toddlers with slow expressive language development. *Topics in Language Disorder, 11,* 1–13.

Paul, R., & Shiffer, M. (1991). Communicative initiations in normal and late-talking toddlers. *Applied Psycholinguistics, 12,* 419–431.

Rheingold, H., Hay, D., & West, M. (1976). Sharing in the second year of life. *Child Development, 83,* 898–913.

Scaife, M., & Bruner, J. (1975). The capacity for joint visual attention in the infant. *Nature, 253,* 265–266.

Schopler, E., & Mesibov, G. (1987). *Neurobiological issues in autism.* New York: Plenum Press.

Seibert, J.M., Hogan, A.E., & Mundy, P.C. (1982). Assessing interactional competencies: The Early Social-Communication Scales. *Infant Mental Health Journal, 3,* 244–245.

Sigman, M., & Mundy, P. (1989). Social attachments in autistic children. *Journal of the American Academy of Child and Adolescent Psychiatry, 28,* 74–81.

Snyder, L. (1978). Communicative and cognitive abilities in the sensorimotor period. *Merrill-Palmer Quarterly, 24,* 161–180.

Stern, D. (1985). *The interpersonal world of the infant.* New York: Basic Books.

Sugarman, S. (1984). The development of proverbial communication. In R. L. Schiefelbusch & J. Pickar (Eds.), *The acquisition of communicative competence* (pp. 23–67). Baltimore, MD: University Park Press.

Tomasello, M. (1988). The role of joint attention in early language development. *Language Sciences, 11,* 69–88.

Tomasello, M. (1995). Joint attention as social cognition. In C. Moore & P. Dunham (Eds.), *Joint attention: Its origins and role in development* (pp. 103–130). Hillsdale, NJ: Lawrence Erlbaum Associates.

Tomasello, M., & Farrar, J. (1986). Joint attention and early language. *Child Development, 57,* 1454–1463.

Wellman, H. (1993). Early understanding of the mind: The normal case. In S. Baron-Cohen, H. Tager-Flusberg, & D. Cohen (Eds.), *Understanding other minds: Perspectives from autism* (pp. 40–58). Oxford, UK: Oxford University Press.

Werner, H., & Kaplan, S. (1963). *Symbol formation.* New York: Wiley.

Wetherby, A.M., & Prizant, B. (1993a). *Communication and Symbolic Behavior Scales.* Chicago: Riverside.

Wetherby, A.M., & Prizant, B. (1993b). Profiling communication and symbolic abilities in young children. *Journal of Childhood Communication Disorders, 15,* 23–32.

Wetherby, A.M., & Prutting, C.A. (1984). Profiles of communicative and cognitive-social abilities in autistic children. *Journal of Speech and Hearing Research, 27,* 367–377.

Wetherby, A.M., Yonclas, D., & Bryan, A. (1989). Communicative profiles of handicapped preschool children: Implications for early identification. *Journal of Speech and Hearing Disorders, 54,* 148–158.

Emotions in Cocaine-Exposed Infants

Margaret Bendersky
*University of Medicine and Dentistry
of New Jersey*

Steven M. Alessandri
Medical College of Pennsylvania

Michael Lewis
*University of Medicine and Dentistry
of New Jersey*

EMOTIONAL FUNCTIONING IN COCAINE-EXPOSED INFANTS

Emotions are studied as the infant's primary means of communicating with the outside world. Emotional expressions are seen as influencing and reflecting the quality of the infant's interaction with his or her social environment. Recent theory and research on infant emotion has demonstrated that infant emotional reactivity is an important feature of the infant's temperament and that the display of affect is an important mediator of interpersonal relationships in the first year of life (Cicchetti, Ganiban, & Barnett, 1991; Lewis & Michalson, 1983; Malatesta, Culver, Tesman, & Shepard, 1989). In regard to the study of infant emotions, this implies examining endogenous infant traits, their emotional expression, and their interaction with socialization experiences to produce particular patterns of emotional behavior.

Studies that attempt to explore dispositions or temperamental styles have noted that an infant's emotionality, activity level, and attention are likely to be stable over time and reflected in similar responses across different emotional elicitors (Goldsmith, 1993; Goldsmith & Campos, 1986; Rothbart, 1986). This approach assumes a biological component to individual differences in emotional behavior. Research on infant emotion also has focused on the expression of emotion with particular emphasis on the primary and secondary emotions and their developmental course (Izard, 1993; Lewis, 1993a, 1993b). Infants display a varied repertoire of emotional expressions very early in life and these expressions serve as signals of communication with their caregivers. The infant's facial expressions, vocalizations, direction of gaze, and capacity for affective involvement serve to initiate, maintain, and terminate interactions with others (Lewis & Michalson, 1983). Thus, infant expression and regulation of emotions play a key role in the formation of early social relationships. It is fair to say that temperament, emotion expression, and social behavior are elements of an emotional system that interact dynamically (Goldsmith, 1993; Rothbart, 1989; Thompson, 1990).

This chapter is divided into three sections. First, we briefly discuss the psychophysiological properties of cocaine, with special emphasis on its effect on the emotion system. Second, we describe the research on emotion, temperament, and socioemotional development in cocaine-exposed infants and the interrelations across these domains. Last, we present evidence from our longitudinal study on the effects of prenatal cocaine exposure that implicates cocaine as playing an important role in the development of early emotional behavior.

COCAINE AND THE EMOTION SYSTEM

Cocaine is a short-acting (15–30 minute) central nervous system (CNS) stimulant that causes peripheral vasoconstriction, tachycardia, and a rapid increase in blood pressure. It also blocks the reuptake of dopamine, which results in loss of appetite, overactivity, euphoria, sexual excitement, and extroverted behavior. Moreover, cocaine decreases serotonin, which increases sleeplessness. Cocaine generally results in an initial arousal followed by depression and anxiety. The depression probably reflects acute neurotransmitter depletion caused by the cocaine use. Cocaine is absorbed readily into the bloodstream and reaches the brain quickly by the intranasal route (snorting), the inhalation route (free basing or smoking crack), or the intravenous route (shooting up).

The placenta does not protect the fetus from cocaine exposure. Cocaine readily crosses from maternal to fetal circulation where it may remain for up to 2 weeks because immature liver and kidneys metabolize the cocaine more slowly. Thus, cocaine has a longer half-life in the fetus than in the adult.

Cocaine's potential impact on development is thought to be due to both direct effects on developing neurotransmitter systems and indirect effects via decreased blood flow and nutrients to the fetal brain. Cocaine's action in blocking the reuptake of the monoaminergic neurotransmitters including norepinephrine, serotonin, and dopamine appears to interfere with neuronal differentiation and brain structure formation (Cregler & Mark, 1986; Mayes & Bornstein, 1995; Ritchie & Greene, 1985). Recent evidence suggests that the monoaminergic neurotransmitters in the fetal CNS are critical to cell proliferation, neural outgrowth, and synaptogenesis (Lauder, 1988; Mattson, 1988). In addition, they regulate the timing of neurogenesis (Lauder, 1991). Thus, brain structure in areas consisting of predominantly monoamingeric neurons can be impaired by prenatal cocaine exposure. The extent of the disruption of the normal processes of growth and differentiation is likely due to such factors as time and amount of exposure. The functional systems involved include those thought to control arousal and attention modulation, the regulation of anxiety and other emotional states, the regulation of reactivity, the level of arousal induced by novel stimulation, and the reinforcing properties of stimuli (Mayes & Bornstein, 1995). These functions are components of emotional reactivity and expression.

Indirect effects of cocaine are likely to have less specific developmental consequences. Cocaine alters fetal oxygenation by reducing uterine blood flow and impairing oxygen transfer to the fetus (Moore, Sorg, Miller, Key, & Resnick, 1986; Ritchie & Greene, 1985; J. Woods, Plessinger, & Clark, 1987). Nutritional deprivation may result from the anorexic effect of chronic cocaine use (Scherling, 1994). Increased maternal stress, sexually transmitted diseases, lack of prenatal care, and other psychosocial risk factors are associated with cocaine use during pregnancy (Bendersky, Alessandri, Gilbert, & Lewis, in press; N. Woods, Behnke, Eyler, Conlon, & Wobie, 1995). These mechanisms may result in more general cognitive deficits as well as growth retardation (Hadeed & Siegel, 1989; Mayes, Granger, Frank, Bornstein, & Schottenfeld, 1993).

Studies have documented neurobehavioral effects of in utero cocaine exposure in neonates. These findings include hyperirritability, high respiratory and heart rates, poor feeding patterns, startles, frequent crying and poor consolability, and irregular sleeping patterns (Schutter & Brinker, 1992). Findings using the Brazelton Neonatal Behavioral Assessment Scale (NBAS) have been inconsistent. Cocaine-exposed neonates have been reported to show diminished orientation, motor, and state regulatory behaviors (Chasnoff, Lewis, Griffith, & Willey, 1989) and deficits in habituation (Eisen et al., 1990; Mayes et al., 1993), although not all studies using the NBAS have found differences. Lester and colleagues (1991) found both excitable and depressed cry characteristics in the newborn associated with cocaine exposure. Excitable cry characteristics (e.g., long duration, high fundamentals, and variable frequency) were hypothesized to be related directly to cocaine exposure and may reflect withdrawal, whereas depressed cry characteristics (e.g., few utterances, low amplitude) were thought to be due to the indirect effects of cocaine secondary to low birthweight.

Studies of effects beyond the neonatal period have primarily focused on general developmental functioning utilizing the Bayley Scales of Infant Development (Bayley, 1969) and IQ tests. The most recent and method-ologically sound studies have reported few differences on these measures between cocaine-exposed infants and various comparison groups (Arendt, Singer, & Minnes, 1993; Billman, Nemeth, Heimler, & Sasidharan, 1991; Chasnoff, Griffith, Freier, & Murray, 1992; Scherling, 1994; Zuckerman & Frank, 1992). Reports of differences in more specific developmental functions are starting to appear. Deficits in attention and state or arousal regulation in tasks such as habituation, recognition memory, and reaction to novelty, have been described (Hawley & Disney, 1992; Mayes & Bornstein, 1995). In our research, we focused on the examination of the emotion system in cocaine-exposed infants with special attention directed to temperament and emotional expressions (Alessandri, Sullivan, Bendersky, & Lewis, 1995; Alessandri, Sullivan, Imaizumi, & Lewis, 1993).

TEMPERAMENT, EMOTION EXPRESSION, AND SOCIAL BEHAVIOR IN COCAINE-EXPOSED INFANTS

Much attention has been given to the definition and measurement of temperament in infancy with numerous reviews of the construct and its assessment appearing in recent years (Bates, 1987; Bornstein, Gaughran, & Homel, 1985; Goldsmith & Campos, 1982, 1986). Although no single definition of temperament has gained universal acceptance, most researchers would agree that temperament includes individual behavioral differences in attention, emotional expressivity, motor activity, soothability, and self-regulation (Campos, Barrett, Lamb, Goldsmith, & Stenberg, 1983; Derryberry & Rothbart, 1984; Goldsmith et al., 1987; Lewis, 1989; Thomas & Chess, 1989). Individual differences are presumed to have genetic and psychobiological bases, although the environment is seen as a factor that molds temperament styles (Buss & Plomin, 1984; Rothbart & Derryberry, 1981; Thomas & Chess, 1980).

Research comparing the variability of temperamental characteristics among "at-risk" and normal infants is important for identifying individual differences that may be of consequence to the caregiver–infant relationship. An infant's tendency to be easily frustrated, difficult to soothe, and have a high activity level, as well as failure in regulating distress, will have an impact on interactions with caregivers (Brazelton, Koslowski, & Main, 1979; Malatesta & Haviland, 1982).

Cocaine exposure may affect behavioral domains linked to underlying temperamental differences. Is there, for example, a cluster of temperamental characteristics that typifies the cocaine-exposed infant? We have recently collected data that addresses this question (Alessandri et al., 1995). We selected the Rothbart (1978) Infant Behavior Questionnaire (IBQ) as the measure of temperament because it measures individual differences in reactivity and self-regulation such as activity and emotionality, and because a primary goal in its construction was to investigate both developmental continuity and change in infant behavior as observed by the caregiver in the home (Rothbart, 1981). The results of our work indicated that cocaine-using mothers rated their infants on the IBQ lower in activity level, lower in smiling and laughter, and lower in distress to limitations compared to nonusing mothers who were equated in all respects except for cocaine use. In addition, cocaine-using mothers rated their infants as lower in both positive reactivity and lower in negative reactivity. It appears that the mothers of cocaine-exposed infants perceive their infants' emotional behavior as flat with regard to both positive and negative affective responsivity. As is discussed later, this will have important social implications for parent–child interactions.

It is clear that discrete emotion expressions can be seen in very young infants. Emotional expressions are seen by some as the manifestation of internal states (Ekman & Friesen, 1975), although the relation between expressions and emotional states is still unclear (Lewis, 1992; Lewis & Michalson, 1983). Formal coding systems have been developed for measuring emotional behavior and identifying emotional expressions. The most comprehensive are Ekman and Friesen's (1978) anatomically based Facial Action Coding System (FACS) and two coding systems by Izard: Maximally Discriminative Facial Movement Coding System (MAX; Izard, 1979) and (AFFEX; Izard, Dougherty, & Hembree, 1983). These coding systems have provided researchers with important tools for the objective description of facial behavior and its relation to emotion.

Although emotional expressions may be connected to internal emotional states, context plays an important role in determining the meaning of a particular emotional expression (see Lewis & Sullivan, chapter 3, this volume). For example, when an infant shows a fearful facial expression toward an adult wearing a scary mask, we are more likely to interpret the infant's expression as an indication that the infant is in a state of fear than if the same facial expression were shown toward its caregiver (Lewis & Michalson, 1983). Thus, the context in which the facial expression is observed lends a degree of validation to the connection between facial expressions and internal states.

For this reason, we have studied facial expressions in a contingency or instrumental learning context (Alessandri, Sullivan, & Lewis, 1990; Lewis,

Alessandri, & Sullivan, 1990; Sullivan, Lewis, & Alessandri, 1991). We observed infant facial responses as they learned a simple association between pulling a string in order to turn on a picture and music. In the course of learning this association, we observed infants showing interest, surprise, and joy, particularly at the point of discovery that arm pulling produces the outcome. In addition, infants showed angry faces when the contingency between arm pulling and outcome no longer existed. Thus, the ability to master even simple contingencies is an emotionally arousing and motivating experience for very young infants.

We recently extended this methodology to study emotional behavior in cocaine-exposed infants (Alessandri et al., 1993). The capacity to modify one's behavior in response to stimuli is a critical skill related to the infant's developing cognitive and emotional abilities. If apathy and underarousal are characteristics of the effects of in utero cocaine exposure (Lester et al., 1991), such effects may be observed in the emotional behavior of infants in the contingency procedure. We found that infants exposed to cocaine showed less overall arousal and expressed less interest and joy during learning even though there was no difference in learning between the groups. This is an important finding because it has been shown that increased expressions of joy often occur when a problem is mastered (Lewis et al., 1990; Lewis & Goldberg, 1969; Sullivan & Lewis, 1989; Watson, 1972). Moreover, cocaine-exposed infants expressed less anger when frustrated and showed lack of interest in reinstating the contingency. Anger is typical of infants when they experience loss of control over the contingency and it disappears once the association is reinstated and the infant's expectancy regarding control is reaffirmed (Lewis et al., 1990). Cocaine-exposed infants are unable to persevere in the face of obstacles. Rather than being able to behave in order to reinstate a positive stimulus and to overcome their frustration, cocaine-exposed infants are unable to organize their response. This lack of instrumental behavior persisted even in the face of restoration of control of the stimulus. Such deficiencies in arousal and emotional responsivity in cocaine-exposed infants are consistent with the mechanisms of the effects of cocaine on the developing CNS (Mayes & Bornstein, 1995). It appears that in utero cocaine exposure may place the infant at risk for deficiencies in emotional responsivity that persist over the first months of life. This lack of emotional responsiveness may be a precursor of a global motivational deficit that may result in failure to develop feelings of competency and efficacy (Lewis & Goldberg, 1969).

A lower level of emotional responsivity in cocaine-exposed infants should have important implications for social development. Cocaine-exposed infants may be compromised in their emotional capacity for participation in both the subtle give-and-take of interaction and the communication about their states and needs through smiles, frowns, cries, and eye contact. If cocaine-exposed infants exhibit a lower activity level and lower affective responsivity, caregivers would have difficulty modulating their stimulation to match their infants' arousal and stimulation needs.

This may be especially problematic because the parents of cocaine-exposed infants themselves often suffer from events that can compromise their ability to meet the needs of their infants. Factors such as poverty, a history of child abuse, family instability and violence, and a history of psychiatric illness can compromise caregivers' abilities to be sensitive to their exposed infants' needs. Because of the highly addictive nature of cocaine, drug-abusing mothers are at risk for dysfunctional parenting and failure in meeting the special needs of their infants that may significantly contribute to developmental morbidity. Some studies have found that mothers engage their infants less if they are difficult or irritable (Crockenberg & Acredolo, 1983; Linn & Horowitz, 1983), and there have been reports of associations between early interactional disturbances and later, school-age behavioral and emotional problems including short attention span, hyperactivity, and disturbed social interactions (Bakeman & Brown, 1980; Field, 1984).

Thus, children who experience prenatal exposure to cocaine are even more at risk when they do not experience the consistent parenting children need to thrive, and, therefore, may be at greater risk for poorer developmental outcomes at later ages. Although resiliency and change are always possible for the child, resiliency cannot be taken for granted. Rodning, Beckwith, and Howard (1991) examined quality of attachment in children prenatally exposed to PCP and cocaine and found that the majority of drug-exposed infants were insecurely attached to their caregivers and that this did not differ in three caregiving environments in which the infants were being raised (i.e., mother care, kinship care, or foster care).

Thus, emotional behavior, even early in infancy, has enormous repercussions for the social and cognitive growth of children. Given the theoretical and empirical cause for concern about the development of prenatally cocaine-exposed infants, further information about this area of functioning is critical to our understanding the consequences of this significant societal problem.

ELICITING EXPRESSIONS IN COCAINE-EXPOSED INFANTS

In our longitudinal study of prenatal cocaine exposure the examination of emotional behavior in exposed and nonexposed infants is being conducted in a number of different contexts. We discuss findings of several procedures explored in a sample of infants and parents from Trenton, New Jersey and Northwest Philadelphia. Both sites are relatively impoverished, predominantly African-American urban centers. Prenatal substance use was established in several ways. The meconium of subjects born at participating hospitals was screened by radioimmunoassay for metabolites of cocaine, cannabinoids, opiates, phencyclidine, and barbiturates. Positive screens were confirmed by gas chromatography/mass spectrometry. Meconium begins to form in the fetal gastrointestinal tract at about the 16th week of gestation. This is a sensitive and reliable method of detecting substance exposure from approximately the second trimester through the end of pregnancy (Ostrea, 1995). In addition, all women were interviewed in depth about prenatal substance use. Interviews were conducted between the 38th week of pregnancy and 1 month postdelivery. Women were guided by trained interviewers through questions about the frequency and amount of use of a variety of medications, recreational and illegal substances of abuse during each trimester and the month prior to pregnancy. Prenatal maternal and neonatal urine screens if available, were considered as well. In addition to exposure to cocaine, we were able to determine whether the fetus was exposed to other toxic substances known to place it at risk, in particular, marijuana, cigarettes, and alcohol. As marijuana, cigarettes, and alcohol have been shown to affect development themselves (e.g., Fried & Watkinson, 1990; Fried, Watkinson, Dillon, & Dulberg, 1987; Streissguth, Bookstein, Sampson, & Barr, 1993) they become confounding variables when we attempt to understand the unique impact of prenatal cocaine exposure.

In order to look at the effects of exposure to cocaine and other substances on emotional reactivity, a matched sample procedure was used. Nineteen cocaine-exposed infants were matched to 19 control infants, keeping exposure to all other substances constant. This enabled us to examine the specific impact of the cocaine exposure. To compare emotional expressivity between these two groups of infants, we observed infants and mothers in three situations: an *en face* play interaction with their mothers, a tickle, and an arm restraint situation. The first looked at emotions during play, the second and third examined emotion during physical interaction.

Caregiver–Infant *En Face* Procedure

In this procedure, the mother's attention to her infant during a face-to-face play interaction was experimentally manipulated. Subjects were placed in an infant seat on a small table at the mother's eye level. The mothers were seated facing their infants and engaged them in interaction, including touching. This play period lasted 2 minutes after which mothers stopped interacting and dropped their heads. This turn-away period lasted 45 seconds. Mothers resumed interacting as before for 1 minute. Infants' faces were videotaped throughout using the MAX system. Enjoyment, anger, sadness, and fear were coded. Facial expressions were coded every second

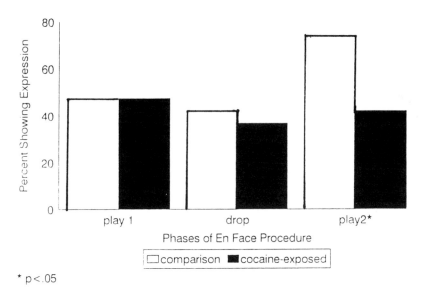

* p < .05

FIG. 5.1. Enjoyment during *en face* procedure.

for the last 15 seconds of the first 2-minute, interaction period (Play 1), the 45 seconds during which the mothers withdrew their attention (drop), and the first 45 seconds following resumption of the interaction (Play 2). The last 15 seconds of the first interaction period were deemed representative of the undisturbed *en face* interaction behavior.

Enjoyment. As can be seen in Fig. 5.1, the proportion of subjects who showed enjoyment during the first play period was exactly the same for cocaine and control subjects. About half of these 4-month-olds smiled as their mothers smiled, spoke to, and touched them. When the mothers lowered their heads (drop), the number of infants showing enjoyment decreased slightly in both groups. There was no difference between the cocaine-exposed and control infants. When mothers resumed the playful interactions, subjects who had been exposed to cocaine did not increase their expressions of joy, whereas the subjects in the nonexposed group did. The difference between the two groups during the Play 2 phase was significant.

Negative Affect. The three negative expressions were combined into a single negative affect score (see Fig. 5.2). In general, the pattern of negative expressions was the mirror image of that for enjoyment. About 16% of the

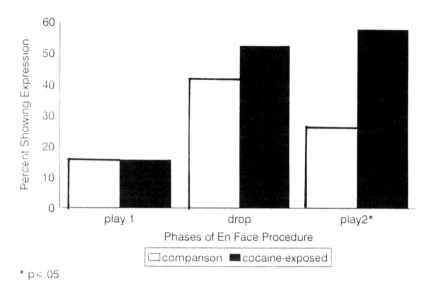

FIG. 5.2. Negative expressions during *en face* procedure.

subjects in each group expressed negative affect during the initial play period. The number of subjects showing negative expressions increased significantly when the mothers withdrew their attention. When mothers resumed their play (Play 2), cocaine-exposed infants continued to express negative affect, whereas the noncocaine-exposed infants decreased their negative affect, returning to their base levels. Although there were no negative affect differences between groups for the play and drop conditions, there was a significant group difference in the second play phase.

These findings suggest that exposed infants may have a problem in modulating their emotions. These infants seem to show the appropriate emotional reactions to their mothers during play, and they get upset when their mothers abruptly withdraw their attention; however, once upset, a significant proportion of the cocaine-exposed infants are not able to calm down and reengage in a pleasant interaction. Thus, differences between the cocaine-exposed and control infants were not in the amount of emotion expressed at 4 months but the modulation of emotion, especially negative emotion, when it occurred.

While the first affect-eliciting situation was designed to observe emotional expression during play, the second and third situations were designed to observe emotional expression during physical interaction: The tickle situation was intended to elicit enjoyment, and the arm restraint to elicit negative affect.

Tickle and Arm Restraint

In these procedures, the experimenter, rather than the mother was used to elicit emotional expression. In the tickle situation, the experimenter faced the infant who was seated in an infant seat. The experimenter smiled and talked pleasantly for 6 seconds and then gently tickled the infant's sides and abdomen for 9 seconds. We considered this interaction to have a predominantly positive affective valence, especially for 4-month-olds who would not necessarily experience stranger anxiety. In the arm restraint situation, the experimenter, still seated opposite the infant, firmly held the infant's arms down for 30 seconds. The experimenter maintained a neutral facial expression throughout the procedure. We considered this situation to have a predominantly negative affective valence.

As in the play situation, the infants were videotaped and a second-by-second coding of joy, anger, sadness, and fear, was done using the MAX system. For these two procedures, data were available for 30 cocaine-exposed and 30 matched infants.

Enjoyment. Figure 5.3 indicates that there were no differences between the two groups in the amount of enjoyment expressed. More than 60% of the infants in both groups smiled and expressed pleasure in the tickle interaction, whereas less than 20% of both groups showed enjoyment during arm restraint. The significant difference in enjoyment between the two situations

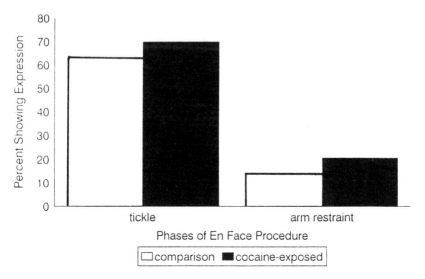

FIG. 5.3. Enjoyment during eliciting expressions procedure.

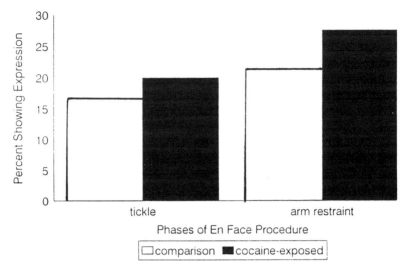

FIG. 5.4. Negative expressions during eliciting expressions procedure.

confirms our belief that enjoyment is more likely to be elicited during tickling than arm restraint.

Negative Affect. Although the tickling situation elicited enjoyment, there were some subjects who also showed negative expressions. Between 15% and 20% of the infants expressed negative affect (see Fig. 5.4). There were no group differences in negative expression to tickle. During arm restraint, the proportion of subjects who showed negative emotion was higher than during the tickle, but again there were no group differences. Thus, in both situations, prenatal cocaine exposure did not appear to affect either positive or negative emotional reaction.

COCAINE EXPOSURE AND EMOTIONAL EXPRESSION

In our earlier work, 4-month-old infants exposed to cocaine, showed that they could learn a task as well as nonexposed infants, but that their emotional expressions during learning and during extinction were different (Alessandri et al., 1993). Finding similar learning ability in cocaine-exposed and unexposed infants is consistent with other studies that have reported no differences in global cognitive functioning, but differences in underlying abilities, such as attending to novel tasks and perseverance (Azuma & Chasnoff, 1993; Chasnoff et al., 1992; Hawley & Disney, 1992). Similarly, Mayes and Bornstein (1995) reported that among infants who complete an habituation procedure, there is no difference between cocaine-exposed and unexposed infants in number of trials to meet the criterion of habituation or in recovery to a novel stimulus. However, a greater number of cocaine-exposed infants do not complete the procedure because of difficulty beginning or irritability early in the procedure. Thus, there is converging evidence that cognitive skills per se, may not be affected by prenatal cocaine exposure so much as the attentional, motivational, and regulatory capacities necessary to maximize performance.

In the present studies, emotional reactivity was studied in three different situations. The use of these different situations allowed us to examine whether the emotional expression of cocaine-exposed infants was different than that of infants not exposed to cocaine across a range of events. No differences in emotional expressivity were found across the first mother play period, the tickle, and the arm restraint situations, leading us to believe that at least for some situations, there was little emotional difference between groups. However, one finding does stand out and it is consistent with our earlier work. Cocaine-exposed infants, when disrupted, appear to be less able to reorganize themselves once the disruption is over. In this case, once the mothers dropped their gaze and ceased interacting, the cocaine-exposed infants were distressed and unable to recover when their mothers looked up and resumed their interactions. This finding is consistent with the results from the Alessandri et al. (1993) study. In that study, cocaine-exposed infants were able to learn the task as well as the nonexposed infants, but once disrupted, in this case frustrated by the failure of their learned response to produce the outcome, they were unable to recover from the frustration, became upset, and could not resume their instrumental behavior once control of the outcome was returned to them.

Such consistent findings suggest that cocaine may affect the ability of infants to recover once frustrated or upset. In contrast, noncocaine-exposed infants seem not to have difficulty with this. These findings fit remarkably well with the hypothesized effects of disruptions on the functioning of the dopamine-rich nigrostriatal system and the posterior attentional system, which has heavy noradrenergic innervation (Mayes & Bornstein, 1995; Posner & Peterson, 1990). Theoretical and empirical evidence suggests that cocaine exposure specifically affects these developing brain regions. The nigrostriatal system is involved in arousal and attentional modulation and the regulation of emotional states. The posterior attentional system gates the processing of novel stimuli and the ability to move on to another situation.

Of course, we cannot rule out the possibility of other explanations for these differences in emotional reactivity. For example, there are well-documented differences in mothers who use cocaine and those who do not. Our own work with this sample has found that during pregnancy, women who used cocaine had less stable, more isolated experiences, with less support and resources than the pregnant women who did not use cocaine (Bendersky et al., in press). These findings agree with those reported by others (e.g., Eyler, Behnke, Conlon, Woods, & Frentzen, 1994; MacGregor, Keith, Bachicha, & Chasnoff, 1989; MacGregor et al., 1987; Richardson & Day, 1991). Such differences might affect the woman's ability to interact optimally with her young infant. In fact, research has confirmed that cocaine users may have parenting difficulties. Higher rates of child abuse and neglect have been found in homes with cocaine-abusing adults (Black & Mayer, 1980; Wasserman & Leventhal, 1993). In addition, several small, but suggestive studies of direct mother–infant interaction, have found mothers who used cocaine during pregnancy to be less responsive and more passive during play episodes at 2 weeks and 8 to 11 months postdelivery (Burns, Chethik, Burns, & Clark, 1991; Gottwald & Thurman, 1994). It is possible that cocaine-exposed infants, even as young as 4 months of age, have a poorer capacity to regulate reactions because caregivers normally help infants develop this skill. Women who used cocaine during pregnancy, and have possibly continued using, may be particularly poor at structuring and directing attention during interactions with their infants (Mayes & Bornstein, 1995), which might be necessary to facilitate the development of emotional regulation and modulation.

Whatever the basis for such behavioral changes, an early difficulty in modulating emotional reactions is likely to have profound consequences on developing social relationships. As we suggested earlier, an impairment of emotional control in the child in a high-risk social environment may lead to considerable psychosocial problems in the longterm.

Both in this study, as well as the earlier work, there were differences in emotional reactions across the situations. The *en face* procedure is a highly arousing, primarily social situation. The infants are engaged in pleasant and, hopefully, familiar play interactions with their mothers. Because they have had similar experiences before, the infants expect a certain pattern of the interaction. Suddenly, and unexpectedly, their mothers withdraw their attention but do not leave the area, a highly unusual event. This results in distress and frustration at the failure of their usual repertory of social behaviors to reengage their mothers. Similarly, in the contingency procedure, the infants learn that they control the onset of a pleasant stimulus. As in a play interaction with the caregiver, the infants have built an expectancy about the situation. Suddenly, they lose control over the stimulus. This violation of their expectation of control results in frustration and distress.

The tickle procedure is also a familiar social situation. The infants, unafraid of the nice, albeit unfamiliar, adult who is interacting with them, respond with apparent pleasure. No expectancies are violated and the infants all react appropriately. The arm restraint procedure is different from the others. It is not familiar to the infants and they have no expectation about it. Most infants fail to show distress despite the fact that an adult is not permitting them to move their arms as they would like. The explanation for this finding may be that the infants are too young to be frustrated in such a situation. Stenberg, Campos, and Emde (1983) observed that anger to arm restraint did not emerge until 4 to 6 months of age. It has been hypothesized that anger is not felt until an infant has the cognitive capacity to understand that some instrumental activity might accomplish a goal (Darwin, 1872/1965; Lewis, 1991). Such an understanding of means–ends relationships does not generally emerge until at least 4 months of age (Piaget, 1952). We see it during the contingency procedure because the infants can learn that their actions accomplish a goal. Infants who fail to learn the contingency do not show frustration when the contingency is no longer in effect. Thus, we suspect that our subjects did not have the capacity to be frustrated by their inability to move their arms for 30 seconds, reducing the amount of negative affect expressed.

Sound, prospective investigations of the impact of prenatal cocaine exposure on emotional functioning of the children are only in the early stages. The evidence to date, suggesting particular difficulties in the ability to recover emotional control following perturbations, indicates that this may be a critical area of examination. The capacity to recover one's equilibrium and move on to new situations is fundamental to the development of satisfying and nurturant social relationships, as well as to the capacity to adapt and to learn from objects, situations, and the people in one's environment. Further research must confirm and refine our understanding of the phenomenon and its etiology and approaches to modifying detrimental consequences.

ACKNOWLEDGMENT

Preparation of this chapter was supported by grant #DA07109 to Michael Lewis from the National Institute on Drug Abuse.

REFERENCES

Alessandri, S.M., Sullivan, M.W., Bendersky, M., & Lewis, M. (1995). Temperament in cocaine-exposed infants. In M. Lewis & M. Bendersky (Eds.), *Mothers, babies, and cocaine: The role of toxins in development* (pp. 273–285). Hillsdale, NJ: Lawrence Erlbaum Associates.

Alessandri, S.M., Sullivan, M.W., Imaizumi, S., & Lewis, M. (1993). Learning and emotional responsivity in cocaine-exposed infants. *Developmental Psychology, 29,* 989–997.

Alessandri, S.M., Sullivan, M.W., & Lewis, M. (1990). Violation expectancy and frustration in early infancy. *Developmental Psychology, 26*, 738–744.

Arendt, R., Singer, L., & Minnes, S. (1993). Development of cocaine exposed infants. *Society for Research in Child Development Abstracts*.

Azuma, S.D., & Chasnoff, I.J. (1993). Outcome of children prenatally exposed to cocaine and other drugs: A path analysis of three-year data. *Pediatrics, 92*, 396–402.

Bakeman, R., & Brown, J.V. (1980). Early interaction: Consequences for social and mental development at three years. *Child Development, 51*, 437–447.

Bates, J.E. (1987). Temperament in infancy. In J.D. Osofsky (Ed.), *Handbook of infant development* (2nd ed., pp. 1101–1149). New York: Wiley.

Bayley, N. (1969). *Bayley Scales of Infant Development: Birth to two years*. New York: Psychological Corporation.

Bendersky, M., Alessandri, S., Gilbert, P., & Lewis, M. (in press). Characteristics of pregnant substance abusers in two cities in the Northeast. *The American Journal of Drug and Alcohol Abuse*.

Billman, D., Nemeth, P., Heimler, R., & Sasidharan, P. (1991). Prenatal cocaine exposure: Advanced Bayley Psychomotor Scores. *Clinical Research, 39*, 697A.

Black, R., & Mayer, J. (1980). Parents with special problems: Alcoholism and opiate addiction. *Child Abuse and Neglect, 4*, 45–54.

Bornstein, M.H., Gaughran, J., & Homel, P. (1985). Infant temperament: Theory, tradition, critique, and new assessments. In C.E. Izard & P.B. Read (Eds.), *Measurement of emotions in infants and children* (Vol. 2, pp. 172–199). New York: Cambridge University Press.

Brazelton, T.B., Koslowski, B., & Main, M. (1979). The origins of reciprocity: The early mother/infant interaction. In M. Lewis & L.A. Rosenblum (Eds.), *The effect of the caregiver on the infant* (pp. 49–77). New York: Wiley.

Burns, K., Chethik, L., Burns, W.J., & Clark, R. (1991). Dyadic disturbances in cocaine-abusing mothers and their infants. *Journal of Clinical Psychology, 47*, 316–319.

Buss, A.H., & Plomin, R. (1984). *Temperament: Early developing personality traits*. Hillsdale, NJ: Lawrence Erlbaum Associates.

Campos, J.J., Barrett, K.C., Lamb, M.E., Goldsmith, H.H., & Stenberg, C. (1983). Socioemotional development. In M.M. Haith & J.J. Campos (Eds.), *Handbook of child psychology: Vol. 2. Infancy and developmental psychobiology* (pp. 783–915). New York: Wiley.

Chasnoff, I.J., Griffith, D.R., Freier, C., & Murray, J. (1992). Cocaine/polydrug use in pregnancy: Two-year follow-up. *Pediatrics, 89*, 284–289.

Chasnoff, I.J., Lewis, D.E., Griffith, D.R., & Willey, S. (1989). Cocaine and pregnancy: Clinical and toxicological implications for the neonate. *Clinical Chemistry, 35*, 1276–1278.

Cicchetti, D., Ganiban, J., & Barnett, D. (1991). Contributions from the study of high-risk populations to understanding the development of emotion regulation. In J. Garber & K. Dodge (Eds.), *The development of emotion regulation and dysregulation* (pp. 15–49). New York: Cambridge University Press.

Cregler, L.L., & Mark, H. (1986). Special report: Medical complications of cocaine. *New England Journal of Medicine, 315*, 1495–1500.

Crockenberg, S., & Acredolo, C. (1983). Infant temperament ratings: A function of infants, mother, or both. *Infant Behavior and Development, 6*, 61–72.

Darwin, C. (1965). *The expression of emotion in animals and man.* Chicago: University of Chicago Press. (Original work published 1872)

Derryberry, D., & Rothbart, M.K. (1984). Emotion, attention, and temperament. In C.E. Izard, J. Kagan, & R. Zajonc (Eds.), *Emotion, cognition, and behavior* (pp. 132–167). New York: Cambridge University Press.

Eisen, L.N., Field, T.M., Bandstra, E.S., Roberts, J.P., Morrow, C., Larson, S.K., & Steele, B.M. (1990). Perinatal cocaine effects on neonatal stress behavior and performance on the Brazelton Scale. *Pediatrics, 88,* 477–480.

Ekman, P., & Friesen, W. (1975). *Unmasking the face: A guide to reorganizing emotions from facial clues.* Englewood Cliffs, NJ: Prentice-Hall.

Ekman, P., & Friesen, W.V. (1978). *The Facial Action Coding System: A technique for the measurement of facial movement.* Palo Alto, CA: Consulting Psychologists.

Eyler, F.D., Behnke, M., Conlon, M., Woods, N.S., & Frentzen, B. (1994). Prenatal cocaine use: A comparison of neonates matched on maternal risk factors. *Neurotoxicology and Teratology, 16,* 81–87.

Field, T.M. (1984). Early interactions between infants and their postpartum depressed mothers. *Infant Behavior and Development, 7,* 527–532.

Fried, P.A., & Watkinson, B. (1990). 36- and 48-month neurobehavioral follow-up of children prenatally exposed to marijuana, cigarettes, and alcohol. *Developmental and Behavioral Pediatrics, 11,* 49–58.

Fried, P.A., Watkinson, B., Dillon, R.F., & Dulberg, C.S. (1987). Neonatal neurological status in a low-risk population after prenatal exposure to cigarettes, marijuana, and alcohol. *Developmental and Behavioral Pediatrics, 8,* 318–326.

Goldsmith, H.H. (1993). Temperament: Variability in developing emotion systems. In M. Lewis & J.M. Haviland (Eds.), *Handbook of emotions* (pp. 353–364). New York: Guilford.

Goldsmith, H.H., Buss, A.M., Plomin, R., Rothbart, M.K., Thomas, A., Chess, S., Hinde, R.A., & McCall, R.B. (1987). Roundtable: What is temperament? Four approaches. *Child Development, 58,* 505–529.

Goldsmith, H.H., & Campos, J.J. (1982). Toward a theory of infant temperament. In R.N. Emde & R.J. Harmon (Eds.), *The development of attachment and affiliative systems* (pp. 161–193). New York: Plenum.

Goldsmith, H.H., & Campos, J.J. (1986). Fundamental issues in the study of early temperament: The Denver Twin Study. In M.E. Lamb & A. Brown (Eds.), *Advances in developmental psychology* (pp. 231–283). Hillsdale, NJ: Lawrence Erlbaum Associates.

Gottwald, S.R., & Thurman, S.K. (1994). The effects of prenatal cocaine exposure on mother-infant interaction and infant arousal in the newborn period. *Topics in Early Childhood Special Education, 14,* 217–231.

Hadeed, A.J., & Siegel, S.R. (1989). Maternal cocaine use during pregnancy: Effect on the newborn infant. *Pediatrics, 84,* 205–210.

Hawley, T.L., & Disney, E.R. (1992). Crack's children: The consequences of maternal cocaine abuse. *Social Policy Report of the Society for Research in Child Development, 6,* 1–22.

Izard, C.E. (1979). *The Maximally Discriminative Facial Movement Coding System (MAX).* Newark: Instructional Resources Center, University of Delaware.

Izard, C.E. (1993). Organizational and motivational functions of discrete emotions. In M. Lewis & J.M. Haviland (Eds.), *Handbook of emotions* (pp. 631–641). New York: Guilford.

Izard, C.E., Dougherty, L., & Hembree, E. (1983). *A system for identifying affect expressions by holistic judgements (AFFEX)*. Newark: Instructional Resources Center, University of Delaware.

Lauder, J.M. (1988). Neurotransmitters as morphogens. *Progressive Brain Research, 73*, 365–387.

Lauder, J.M. (1991). Neuroteratology of cocaine: Relationship to developing monamine systems. *National Institute of Drug Abuse Research Monographs, 114*, 233–247.

Lester, B.M., Corwin, M.J., Sepkoski, C., Seifer, R., Peucker, M., McLaughlin, S., & Golub, H. (1991). Neurobehavioral syndromes in cocaine-exposed newborn infants. *Child Development, 62*, 694–705.

Lewis, M. (1989). Culture and biology: The role of temperament. In P. Zelazo & R. Barr (Eds.), *Challenges to developmental paradigms* (pp. 203–226). Hillsdale, NJ: Lawrence Erlbaum Associates.

Lewis, M. (1991). Ways of knowing: Objective self-awareness or consciousness. *Developmental Review, 11*, 231–243.

Lewis, M. (1992). *Shame, the exposed self.* New York: The Free Press.

Lewis, M. (1993a). The emergence of human emotions. In M. Lewis & J. Haviland (Eds.), *Handbook of emotions* (pp. 223–235). New York: Guilford.

Lewis, M. (1993b). Self-conscious emotions: Embarrassment, pride, shame, and guilt. In M. Lewis & J. Haviland (Eds.), *Handbook of emotions* (pp. 563–573). New York: Guilford.

Lewis, M., Alessandri, S.M., & Sullivan, M.W. (1990). Violation of expectancy, loss of control and anger in young infants. *Developmental Psychology, 26*, 745–751.

Lewis, M., & Goldberg, S. (1969). Perceptual-cognitive development in infancy: A generalized expectancy model as a function of the mother-infant interaction. *Merrill-Palmer Quarterly, 15*(1), 81–100.

Lewis, M., & Michalson, L. (1983). *Children's emotions and moods: Developmental theory and measurement.* New York: Plenum.

Linn, P., & Horowitz, F. (1983). The relationship between infant individual differences and mother/infant interaction during the neonatal period. *Infant Behavior and Development, 6*, 415–427.

MacGregor, S., Keith, L.G., Bachicha, J.A., & Chasnoff, I.J. (1989). Cocaine abuse during pregnancy: Correlation between prenatal care and perinatal outcome. *Obstetrics and Gynecology, 74*, 882–885.

MacGregor, S.N., Keith, L.G., Chasnoff, I.J., Rosner, M.A., Chisum, R.N., Shaw, P., & Minoque, J. (1987). Cocaine use during pregnancy: Adverse perinatal outcome. *American Journal of Obstetrics and Gynecology, 157*, 686–690.

Malatesta, C.A., Culver, C., Tesman, J., & Shepard, B. (1989). The development of emotion expression during the first two years of life. *Monographs of the Society for Research in Child Development, 50* (1-2, Serial No, 219).

Malatesta, C.A., & Haviland, J.M. (1982). Learning display rules: The socialization of emotion expression in infancy. *Child Development, 53*, 991–1008.

Mattson, M.P. (1988). Neurotransmitters in the regulation of neuronal cytoarchitecture. *Brain Research Reviews, 13*, 179–212.

Mayes, L.C., & Bornstein, M.H. (1995). Developmental dilemmas for cocaine abusing parents and their children. In M. Lewis & M. Bendersky (Eds.), *Mothers, babies, and cocaine: The role of toxins in development* (pp. 251–272). Hillsdale, NJ: Lawrence Erlbaum Associates.

Mayes, L.C., Granger, R.H., Frank, M.A., Bornstein, M., & Schottenfeld, R. (1993). Neurobehavioral profiles of infants exposed to cocaine prenatally. *Pediatrics, 91, 778–783.*

Moore, T.R., Sorg, J., Miller, L., Key, T., & Resnick, R. (1986). Hemodynamic effects of intravenous cocaine on the pregnant ewe and fetus. *American Journal of Obstetrics and Gynecology, 155,* 883–888.

Ostrea, E.M., Jr. (1995). Meconium drug analysis. In M. Lewis & M. Bendersky (Eds.), *Mothers, babies, and cocaine: The role of toxins in development* (pp. 179–202). Hillsdale, NJ: Lawrence Erlbaum Associates.

Piaget, J. (1952). *The origins of intelligence in children.* New York: International Universities Press.

Posner, M.I., & Peterson, S.E. (1990). The attention system of the human brain. *Annual Review of Neuroscience, 13,* 25–42.

Richardson, G.A., & Day, N.L. (1991). Maternal and neonatal effects of moderate cocaine use during pregnancy. *Neurotoxicology and Teratology, 13,* 455–460.

Ritchie, J.M., & Greene, N.M. (1985). Local anesthetics. In A.G. Gilman, L.S. Goodman, T.N. Ral, & F. Murad (Eds.), *The pharmacologic basis of therapeutics* (7th ed., pp. 309–310). New York: Macmillan.

Rodning, C., Beckwith, L., & Howard, J. (1991). Quality of attachment and home environments in children prenatally exposed to PCP and cocaine. *Development and Psychopathology, 3,* 351–366.

Rothbart, M.K. (1978). *Infant Behavior Questionnaire.* Unpublished manuscript, University of Oregon, Eugene, OR.

Rothbart, M.K. (1981). Measurement of temperament in infancy. *Child Development, 52,* 569–578.

Rothbart, M.K. (1986). Longitudinal observation of infant temperament. *Developmental Psychology, 22,* 350–365.

Rothbart, M.K. (1989). Temperament and development. In G.A. Kohnstamm, J.E. Bates, & M.K. Rothbart (Eds.), *Temperament in childhood* (pp. 187–248). Chichester, England: Wiley.

Rothbart, M.K., & Derryberry, D. (1981). Development of individual differences in temperament. In M.E. Lamb & A.L. Brown (Eds.), *Advances in developmental psychology* (Vol. 1, pp. 37–86). Hillsdale, NJ: Lawrence Erlbaum Associates.

Scherling, D. (1994). Prenatal cocaine exposure and childhood psychopathology. *American Journal of Orthopsychiatry, 64,* 9–19.

Schutter, L.S., & Brinker, R.P. (1992). Conjuring a new category of disability from prenatal cocaine exposure: Are the infants unique biological or caretaking casualties? *Topics in Early Childhood Special Education, 11,* 84–111.

Streissguth, A.P., Bookstein, F., Sampson, P., & Barr, H. (1993). *The enduring effects of prenatal alcohol exposure on child development: Birth through seven years, a partial least squares solution.* Ann Arbor: University of Michigan Press.

Stenberg, C.R., Campos, J.J., & Emde, R.N. (1983). The facial expression of anger in seven-month-old infants. *Child Development, 54,* 178–184.

Sullivan, M.W., & Lewis, M. (1989). Emotion and cognition in infancy: Facial expressions during contingency learning. *International Journal of Behavioral Development, 12,* 221–237.

Sullivan, M.W., Lewis, M., & Alessandri, S. (1991). Interface between emotion and cognition. In R.M. Downs, L.S. Liben, & D.S. Palermo (Eds.), *Visions of* aesthetics, the environment, and the development: The legacy of J.F. Wohlwill (pp. 241–261). Hillsdale, NJ: Lawrence Erlbaum Associates.

Thomas, A., & Chess, S. (1980). *The dynamics of psychological development*. New York: Bruner-Mazel.

Thomas, A., & Chess, S. (1989). Temperament and personality. In G.A. Kohnstamn, J.E. Bates, & M.K. Rothbart (Eds.), *Temperament in childhood* (pp. 249–263). New York: Wiley.

Thompson, R.A. (1990). Emotion and self-regulation. In R.A. Thompson (Ed.), *Nebraska Symposium of Motivation: Vol. 36. Socioemotional development* (pp. 367–467). Lincoln: University of Nebraska Press.

Wasserman, D.R., & Leventhal, J.M. (1993). Maltreatment of children born to cocaine-dependent mothers. *American Journal of Diseases of Children, 147,* 1324–1328.

Watson, T. (1972). Smiling, cooing and the game. *Merrill-Palmer Quarterly, 18,* 323–339.

Woods, J.R., Plessinger, M.A., & Clark, K.E. (1987). Effect of cocaine on uterine blood flow and fetal oxygenation. *Journal of the American Medical Association, 251,* 957–961.

Woods, N.S., Behnke, M., Eyler, F.D., Conlon, M., & Wobie, K. (1995). Cocaine use among women: Socioeconomic, obstetrical, and psychological issues. In M. Lewis & M. Bendersky (Eds.), *Mothers, babies, and cocaine: The role of toxins in development* (pp. 305–332). Hillsdale, NJ: Lawrence Erlbaum Associates.

Zuckerman, B., & Frank, D.A. (1992). Prenatal cocaine and marijuana exposure: Research and clinical implications. In I.S. Zagon & T.A. Slotkin (Eds.), *Maternal substance abuse and the developing nervous system* (pp. 125–154). Boston: Academic Press.

Expression and Understanding of Emotion in Atypical Development: Autism and Down Syndrome

---

Connie Kasari
Marion Sigman
University of California, Los Angeles

Emotional expressions serve an integral role in communication. Facial expressions communicate to others particular feeling states. These communicated feeling states, in turn, influence others to respond. For example, mothers are motivated to respond differentially to positive versus negative facial expressions of their infants (Huebner & Izard, 1988; Malatesta & Haviland, 1982). Even children modify their behavior in response to other's expressions (Izard & Malatesta, 1987). Thus, facial expressions of emotion can have a potent effect on the behavior of others.

A disruption in this emotional signaling system can have a deleterious effect on social interactions. This effect is dramatically illustrated by children whose emotional expressions are delayed or different. For example, a delay in the onset of infant smiling may cause the mother to interact less with her child (Field, 1980). Deviance in expressive behavior (e.g., expressions that do not fit the situation) can seriously hamper the caregiver's ability to "read" the child's expressions (Goldberg, 1977). Thus, both delay and deviance in expressive behavior may directly affect the interactive behavior of the social partner with possible long-term, cumulative effects.

Disruptions in the signaling system may also result in indirect influences on social interactions. The infant who does not smile within the expected frame of time can cause disappointment and depression in the caregiver (Emde & Brown, 1978). Adult feelings of efficacy are reduced when infant behaviors lack clarity, and are difficult for others to read (Goldberg, 1977). Thus, the negative perceptions and feelings that may result from disruptions in emotional signaling can also affect the social interactions of the child. Without intervention, many dyads may not be able to overcome their interactive differences.

There are two prototypical cases that reflect delays and differences in emotional expressions, autism and Down syndrome. According to Hobson (1991), children with autism lack "intersubjective personal engagement with others" (p.10) and this deficiency constitutes a fundamental feature of the disorder. Kanner (1943) originally suggested that autistic children have "inborn disturbances of affective contact" with others (p. 250). As infants, children with Down syndrome demonstrate delays in their acquisition of affect displays (Cicchetti & Sroufe, 1978). They also display qualitative differences in their facial expressions, such as "dampening" of expression (Emde, Katz, & Thorpe, 1978). However, in contrast to children with autism, children with Down syndrome are often described as emotionally connected to others and socially precocious (Baron, 1972).

These two prototypical cases are similar in that both groups of children demonstrate a disruption in their emotional signaling system. They differ, however, in whether emotions are deviant or delayed, and in the centrality of this disruption for understanding the nature of the disorder. It is likely that in autism, the emotional characteristics of the children are more deviant than merely delayed and that understanding the emotional difficulties of these children is central to our understanding of the autistic disorder. This does not seem as clearly the case in Down syndrome. Emotions are more often delayed in children with Down syndrome and although there are some qualitative differences that suggest disturbance, this disturbance is milder than in the case of autism.

Infants with Down syndrome are typically identified at birth and the genetic abnormality that gives rise to the syndrome is well known. The cause of autism is unknown. Moreover, there is controversy as to the underlying or core deficits that characterize the autistic disorder. Although a deficit in personal engagement is a diagnostic criteria of autism, an ongoing controversy concerns whether this deficit stems from a cognitive or affective base. The majority of research conducted in autism concerns older autistic children and the results of these studies seem to suggest a cognitive base. Often the children are unable to take another person's perspective, to understand their beliefs or desires as different from their own. Such an inability may result in the pattern of emotional responses that we observe in these children. On the other hand, it may be that there is a core affective deficiency, much like Kanner (1943) originally described. As Hobson

(1991) noted, the lack of basic experiences in the emotional realm may result in a pattern of cognitive and social deficits characteristic of autism. Research on emotional and cognitive abilities of autistic children has yet to clarify this relation. Still, the nature of affective deficits is likely to be central to our understanding of autism, perhaps, even helping us to understand its etiology.

In this chapter, we address several aspects of emotional development: facial expressions, responding and recognition of emotion, the development of complex emotions, and the ability to talk about emotions. Following a description of these aspects in typical development, we describe studies of children with autism and children with Down syndrome. We close our discussion with some methodological considerations and implications of the findings on atypical development to pursuing new lines of research with both typical and atypical populations.

EMOTIONS IN TYPICALLY DEVELOPING CHILDREN

From the very beginning, infants are capable of expressing emotion. At birth or shortly after, facial expressions of infants include interest, disgust, sadness, anger, and joy (Izard & Malatesta, 1987). Facial expressions of children, particularly nonverbal children, are important because expressions are seen as outward, expressive signals of internal emotional experiences. Thus, smiling in an infant is seen as a reliable and accurate index of positive emotional feelings.

Facial expressions also are important social displays that communicate information to another person. A child's smile may encourage the adult to interact with the child, whereas a frown may prompt the adult to change something in the child's environment (e.g., change position). Expressions may also prompt the labeling of emotion, thus providing important avenues of socialization for the child (Lewis & Michalson, 1983).

Children are also very attentive to the emotions of others. As young as 6 months, infants are able to differentially respond to happy and sad expressions of their mothers (Cohn, Campbell, Matias, & Hopkins, 1990; Termine & Izard, 1988). By 12 months, many children are able to regulate their own behavior in relation to emotions displayed by their mothers (Klinnert, Campos, Sorce, Emde, & Svejda, 1983). If the mother displays a fearful face, the child does not approach a novel toy, but if the mother shows joy, the child is more apt to approach the toy. Moreover, the same toys used in subsequent free-play sessions are approached or avoided depending on whether the mother previously displayed a positive or negative emotion toward the toy (Hornik, Risenhoover, & Gunnar, 1987; Walden & Ogan, 1988). By 2 to 3 years of age, children can recognize happy, sad, angry, and scared emotions from vignettes involving puppets to depict emotions (Denham & Couchoud, 1990), and they respond to distress in others with prosocial behaviors (Zahn-Waxler, Friedman, & Cummings, 1983).

Children also begin to talk about emotions. Toward the end of the second and into the third year, children begin to label emotion states. The terms are basic in the beginning—happy, mad, sad, and scared (Bretherton & Beeghly, 1982; Izard, 1971; Smiley & Huttenlocher, 1989). As their cognitive abilities advance, children begin to attribute emotions to their dolls and animals in play, to talk about past and future emotional states, and to give reasons for feeling different emotions (Bretherton & Beeghly, 1982). Talking about emotion also serves to regulate emotion in young children. Dunn, Brown, and Beardsall (1991) described how children's conversations about feeling states with their mothers are often associated with conflict resolution.

All of these abilities—displaying reliable facial expressions, responding and recognizing emotions in others, and talking about emotions—are evident in the first 2 years of life. These same abilities become differentiated and more complex as children get older (Lewis, 1993). For example, complex emotions—emotions requiring greater cognitive skill—are often not evident until the second year or later. These emotions include embarrassment, pride, empathy, and guilt. Their emergence is marked by certain cognitive antecedents, such as knowing the self as distinct from others and the ability to compare one's own performance to some external standard.

Understanding of emotions in others expands greatly between 3 and 5 years of age. At this age, children begin to appreciate the subjective nature of emotions. They recognize that another person's emotions are determined by how that person appraises the situation and that this appraisal may differ from their own appraisal (Harris, 1989). Thus, children are beginning to develop a "theory of mind" that considers the contributions of desires and beliefs.

NATURE OF EMOTIONAL DIFFICULTIES IN ATYPICAL DEVELOPMENT

Although the foregoing literature suggests a natural progression in understanding and expression of emotion among typical children, children with atypical development frequently have difficulties with emotional expression and understanding. The nature of the difficulty, however, may be quite different among different groups of children. In our aim to examine studies of children with Down syndrome or autism, two issues complicate comparability. These issues center on diagnostic and measurement issues.

The first issue concerns the timing of diagnosis. Children with autism usually are not formally diagnosed until after infancy—typically around the second or third birthday—whereas infants with Down syndrome are routinely diagnosed at birth. Due to the later timing of diagnosis, early emotional development has been nearly impossible to study in infants with autism.

Despite the lack of prospective studies on the early emotional development of children with autism, there are data suggesting that early emotional differences exist among infants later diagnosed as autistic. These data are largely gathered through parental recollections of children's early development and non-systematic gathering of data, such as home movies. Reports of parental recollections of their autistic children's development vary in terms of when certain behaviors appeared in the children's early development and how abnormal these behaviors may have been (Ornitz, Guthrie, & Farley, 1978). Parents' retrospective reports are complicated by issues of the parents' own knowledge of child development, their observational skills in detecting differences in development, and memory for those differences. Thus, it is difficult to know if certain early behaviors were indeed lacking, and thus, predictive of the later autism diagnosis.

Two interesting studies show that deficiencies in emotional signaling occur early in the development of autism. One examined the videotaped records of twins who were seen at 4 months of age (Kubicek, 1980). The aim of this study was not to examine the early development of autism, but the opportunity arose when one of the twins was later diagnosed as autistic. The early videotape recordings suggest that there were some curious differences between the fraternal twins. The one later diagnosed as autistic lacked eye contact, and displayed neutral facial expressions and rigid posturing. Thus, this twin lacked the normal affective reciprocity evident in the typically developing twin's interactions.

In a second study, home movies of first birthdays were examined of children who were diagnosed with autism and children with typical development (Osterling & Dawson, 1994). The children later diagnosed with autism differed from the typical children in that they looked less to others, rarely showed or pointed to objects or things, and failed to orient to their name. Thus, these studies show that affective differences early on may differentiate children with autism and typically developing children.

A second issue complicating the comparison of Down syndrome and autism concerns the applicability of measures requiring high language and cognitive abilities. Although some individuals with autism can achieve normal levels of intelligence (about 25%), this is rarely the case in Down syndrome. Thus, measures that require verbal responses and a high degree of cognitive ability are often appropriate for only a small percentage of children with autism and generally inappropriate for children with Down syndrome.

With these two limitations in comparability of autism and Down syndrome studies, we now turn our attention to areas of emotional development previously discussed. To the extent possible, evidence is presented on the emotional development of children with autism and children with Down syndrome.

Facial Expressions of Emotion

Emotional expressions are present at birth and are the foundation for communication between parent and child. Thus, the infant's first smiles or cries are potent elicitors of contact and caregiving. Any disruption in this signaling process, whether delayed or deviant, can have an immediate and profound effect upon those individuals who care for the child.

Autism. In Kanner's (1943) original description of 11 cases of "infantile autism," deviances in facial expressions were common. For example, he commented about Case 11 that, "Her expression was blank, and she made no communicative gestures; she had no real contact with the persons in the office" (p. 240). Subsequent clinical descriptions of children with autism have ranged from "apparent absence of emotional reaction" (American Psychiatric Association, 1987, p. 35) to "extremes of emotion in a way which is quite inappropriate for their age and the social situation" (Ricks & Wing, 1975, p. 201).

Despite the rich clinical descriptions, empirical studies of facial expressions in autism did not exist before the mid-1980s. One of the earliest studies examined facial expressions of affect as children interacted with an unfamiliar adult (Yirmiya, Kasari, Sigman, & Mundy, 1989). Using an anatomically based measure of affect, Izard's (1979) Maximally Discriminative Movement system (MAX), autistic children showed similar amounts of positive and negative emotion. There was one interesting difference, however. When blends of expressions (a combination of facial movements that indicate more than one emotion, such as joy and interest) were examined, the autistic children showed many more combinations of facial expressions, and some that did not fit any discrete emotion described by Izard's system.

Because of the great variety of blends observed in our study of facial expressions, we categorized them as positive (e.g., interest and joy), negative (e.g., fear and sadness), and incongruous (e.g., joy and sadness). This categorization resulted in the autistic children showing significantly more negative and incongruous blends. In contrast, not a single typical child showed incongruous blends.

Despite the difference in blends overall, we were struck by the few differences in facial expressions of these different groups of children. This finding was particularly surprising given the clinical literature that so powerfully described deficiencies in facial expressions of autistic children. We wondered if the presence of incongruous and negative blends in an otherwise pleasant interaction might contribute to caregivers difficulty in reading the emotional signals of their children (Kasari, Sigman, Yirmiya, & Mundy, 1992). Therefore, even though children showed negative and incongruous blends for a very small percentage of the total interaction, their presence might nevertheless be significant in the emotional signaling of the autistic children. A brief expression that appears odd and does not fit the tone of the interaction may significantly disrupt the flow of the interaction.

We also had a sense that some important element was missing. Most people know that a smile is meant to communicate a feeling if an individual looks at you while smiling. Smiling may have even greater meaning if the smile is also accompanied with a gesture or word. Yet, in examining facial expressions of children in the Yirmiya et al. (1989) study, it became apparent that the occurrence of facial expression was only one component of children's communication with others. It was not clear that the autistic children's facial expressions were socialized (i.e., coordinated with other communicative behaviors) in the same way as in nonautistic children. If they were not, this lack of coordination might help explain the clinical feeling that the child with autism lacks a sense of "intersubjective personal engagement" (Hobson, 1991, p. 10).

To study coherence of emotional communication, we examined several other behaviors in addition to facial expressions of affect. We were particularly interested in whether affect was used in a communicative fashion that was appropriate to the interaction context. Using Izard's MAX system, we again coded facial expressions of children as they interacted with an adult. This time we also coded where children were looking and whether they engaged in communicative gestures of requesting or joint attention.

Whether children engaged in communicative acts that involved requesting or joint attention interactions was important to examine for two reasons. First, previously published reports have noted deficits in joint attention gestures, but not requesting gestures, among children with autism (Loveland & Landry, 1986; Mundy, Sigman, Ungerer, & Sherman, 1986). Second, theories regarding communication development suggest that the tendency to gesture for requesting or for joint attention have different purposes. For example, the child may point to a toy to request it or point to a toy to indicate interest. The purpose of the former pointing behavior may be for behavior regulation, whereas the purpose of the latter pointing behavior is merely to indicate and share interest in some event or object vis-à-vis another person. Thus, requesting behaviors (including pointing, reaching, and giving) are primarily for behavior regulation. Joint attention behaviors (including pointing, showing, and referential eye gaze) are used for sharing and regulating attention.

We found that the coherence of affect and other communicative behaviors was different between the children with and without autism (Kasari, Sigman, Mundy, & Yirmiya, 1990). Compared to matched controls, the autistic children did not show much positive affect when engaged in joint attention interactions, even when the amount they engaged in joint attention was statistically controlled. Their performance was unlike typically developing children who show more positive affect during joint attention interactions than requesting interactions (Mundy, Kasari, & Sigman, 1992). Thus, the autistic children did not show positive affect in situations in which positive affect was expected. This difference in signaling behavior might further contribute to difficulties others have in "reading" the affective signals of children with autism.

These results suggested that autistic children were similar to other children in their display of positive affect; however, positive affect used in a communicative fashion was less coherent. Two additional papers build on these findings. Dawson, Hill, Spencer, Galpert, and Watson (1990) examined young autistic children's use of positive affect in interaction with their mothers around snack time. Similar to the previous studies, they found that the amount of positive affect was similar for autistic and normal children matched on mental age. However, positive affect *shared* with the mother was different. The autistic children were less likely to look at the mother while smiling.

In another study, Snow, Hertzog, and Shapiro (1987) examined young children's use of positive affect in interactions with a peer partner and an adult partner. Overall, compared to mentally retarded children, the autistic children used less positive affect. Importantly, they found that the autistic children were less likely to use positive affect that was directed to the partner and more likely to use positive affect during play with objects.

The foregoing studies suggest that autistic children are capable of displaying affect expressions, but that they use these expressions less often in a coordinated and communicative fashion. There may also be some unusual qualities to the expressions, such as the presence of incongruous blends.

Down Syndrome. Unlike the majority of studies on children with autism, studies of children with Down syndrome have examined facial expressions within the first year of life. Emde et al. (1978) described the dampened smiles of infants with Down syndrome. Absent from these early smiles of the infants was the brightening of the eyes and the excited waving of the arms and legs that usually accompanies the smiles of typically developing infants. Cicchetti and Sroufe (1978) also noted the lessened intensity of affective expressions of infants with Down syndrome. In addition, they documented delays in the onset of facial expressions and the far less frequent smiles of these infants.

More recent studies vary as to the overall amount of affect, particularly positive expressions, that children with Down syndrome display relative to comparison children. Landry and Chapieski (1990) found that infants with Down syndrome displayed more positive affect than a high-risk preterm sample of infants. The greater amount of positive affect in the infants with Down syndrome was due to the greater amount displayed in an independent, object-centered play interaction than an interaction centered on their mothers. This pattern was the opposite of the comparison children who displayed greater positive affect during the mother-centered interaction.

Brooks-Gunn and Lewis (1982) also examined positive affective expressions during mother–child interactions. Compared to developmentally delayed, physically impaired, and typically developing children, children with Down syndrome displayed less positive affect than the other children. Even when developmental abilities were considered, results still indicated reduced frequency of positive affect for the children with Down syndrome.

Kasari, Mundy, Yirmiya, and Sigman (1990) examined positive affect expressions of toddler and preschool-aged children with Down syndrome as they interacted with an experimenter. In contrast to the previous studies, the children with Down syndrome displayed similar amounts of affect compared to mental-age matched typical children. However, some qualitative differences in positive affect were found, namely in the greater display of slight smiles (i.e., smiles that did not involve the entire face), and more frequent shifts in facial expression.

The three studies just cited varied in their outcomes of positive affect in children with Down syndrome. The different results may be due to methodological differences in how facial expressions were coded and/or to the age of the children studied. Also, in both the Landry and Chapieski (1990) and the Kasari, Mundy et al. (1990) studies, children with Down syndrome looked to the adults more frequently than did the comparison children. Thus, when the children with Down syndrome did display positive affect, it was most often shared with another person.

In summary, the results of studies of expressive behavior in autistic and Down syndrome children suggest some similarities and differences among the groups. Several studies found that the occurrence of facial expressions was similar when comparing children with autism or children with Down syndrome to comparison children. Each group, however, also displayed etiologically specific differences in these expressions. Children with autism showed more incongruous blends and expressions that were not tied to the partner in a communicative fashion. Children with Down syndrome showed briefer expressions that were less intense and that did not involve the entire face.

The most striking difference between autism and Down syndrome, however, was the manner in which the children share affect. Sharing of affect lacks coherence in children with autism. These children rarely coordinate facial expressions with other aspects of communication, thereby giving the impression they are less connected and interested in the interaction. In contrast, children with Down syndrome typically show positive affect while looking to the person in ways expected for the interaction. Thus, their expressions may appear more coherent.

Recognizing and Responding to Emotion in Others

As the foregoing studies indicate, several unique qualities of emotional expression are found in children with autism and Down syndrome. Given the differences in facial expressions, one might wonder the extent to which these children are able to recognize emotions in others and to respond in appropriate ways. Studies on responsiveness have tended to focus on young children, whereas studies of recognition have focused on older, more verbal children.

Autism. Responsiveness to others' emotions has been examined using emotion-eliciting paradigms common to typically developing samples. In a study of young autistic children, children's responses were examined as they observed adults showing negative emotions of fear, distress, and discomfort (Sigman, Kasari, Kwon, & Yirmiya, 1992). Developmentally matched 3- to 6-year-old samples of autistic, mentally retarded, and typically developing children were studied. One paradigm was a traditional social referencing situation, where a robot entered the room and the mother and adult experimenter displayed expressions of fear. A second paradigm exposed the child to distress in the mother, when the mother pretended to cry after she hit her finger with a pounding toy. The third paradigm had the mother feign illness. She lay moaning on a sofa during a free-play episode with the child.

Each paradigm was videotaped and later coded for affective and attentional responses. Interestingly, in each of these paradigms there were few affective responses of any of the children. Most of the children remained neutral. But the normal and mentally retarded children were very attentive to the adult's expressions in all three experimental situations. In contrast, many of the autistic children appeared to ignore or not notice the adults showing these negative affects.

It is unclear what the consequences of this failure to attend to others' emotions might mean for the children's later development of emotional understanding and learning. The failure to attend to others' affects may be a specific deficit in the development of affect. Alternatively, the failure to attend to others' emotions may be early evidence of a cognitive deficit; that is, because autistic children are less aware that another person has a perspective or interest in their experience, they pay little attention to this person.

To investigate these possibilities, longitudinal studies would be helpful. Yet, few longitudinal studies exist concerning the emotional responsivity in children with autism. In a recent study, Dissanayake, Sigman, and Kasari (in press) followed young children with autism over 5 years. Children's responses to distress and anger in others were examined initially when the children were between 3 and 6 years of age. These same children were seen again twice—the first time, 1 1/2 years later, and the second time, 5 years after the initial testing. At each assessment, the child's responses were examined as they observed negative emotions in others. For example, 1 1/2 years later, their reactions to someone who pretended to hurt herself and cry were observed. Five years later, the children's reactions to an angry telephone conversation were observed. The children who were very attentive to negative emotion in others at the initial testing were more attentive to negative emotions in others 5 years later. Thus, these results point to significant stability in emotional responses over a 5-year period.

In terms of recognizing emotion, a number of studies have examined the ability of older children and adults with autism. Hobson and colleagues have reported a series of studies examining the extent to which autistic individuals are able to match facial expressions of affect with other aspects of emotion (i.e., bodily movements, sound, activity; Hobson, 1986; Hobson, Ouston, & Lee, 1989). The children with autism were less proficient at matching emotion-related items than they were at matching nonemotion-related items. However, these differences mostly disappear when children are matched for verbal abilities (Hobson et al., 1989; Ozonoff, Pennington, & Rogers, 1990).

These studies lead one to question whether children with autism are just not very attentive to a person's facial features in general. If not, this may explain some of their difficulty in recognizing emotions in others. On the other hand, recognizing facial features may be somewhat unusual in children with autism. Weeks and Hobson (1987) and Jennings (1973) both gave autistic children photographs of various individuals to sort. In the Weeks and Hobson study, the children could sort these photos on the basis of gender, age, and facial expression of emotion or the type of hat they were wearing. When compared by the children's sorting "strategy," mentally retarded and nonretarded children sorted the photos by people's facial expression, whereas the autistic subjects sorted by type of hat. These findings suggest that either autistic children do not view facial expressions of emotion as very salient or they are unable to decipher the meaning of different expressions.

Down Syndrome. The responsiveness of children with Down syndrome to emotions in others is in some ways both similar to and different from children with autism. Similar to children with autism, children with Down syndrome are not different in facial expressions of affect compared to typically developing children in a social referencing situation (Kasari, Freeman, Sigman, & Mundy, 1995; Knieps, Walden, & Baxter, 1994). But there are differences in attention or in matching affect to the situation. Kasari et al. (1995) found that, compared to typical children, children with Down syndrome less often shift attention between an ambiguous stimulus and the person displaying the emotion. Instead, the children with Down syndrome look to the adult longer and to the ambiguous stimulus for shorter amounts of time. It appeared that the children with Down syndrome were attracted to the person's face and were less able to make the connection between the stimulus and the emotional message of the adult. This pattern of attention is quite different from children with autism who tend not to pay much attention to the adult (Sigman et al., 1992).

Knieps et al. (1994) found differences in children's ability to match emotional expressions to their mothers. Unlike the typically developing infants, the children with Down syndrome tended to display positive affect when their parents showed fearful expressions. Thus, it appeared that the children actually displayed facial expressions opposite of their parents whereas the typical children more often matched their parent's expressions.

Responsiveness to distress in others also has been examined in children with Down syndrome. Similar to studies in autism, the responses of children with Down syndrome have been examined when an adult pretends to hurt her finger and cry (Kasari, Mundy, & Sigman, 1990). In this situation, children with Down syndrome and children with typical development seem differentially affected by the simulated situation. Children with Down syndrome display a greater amount of both neutral and negative affect, whereas the typical children display more interest expressions. There also are differences in looking patterns between the two groups over age. The children with Down syndrome decrease looking to the experimenter over age, whereas the typical children increase looking. In addition, the children with, Down syndrome appear to react to the adult's distress with distress themselves. In contrast, the children with typical development look to others and show interest (e.g., quizzical) expressions more often. It may be that the typical children were unsure how sincere the person was and tried to get confirmation from others about the situation.

In terms of responsiveness to others' emotions, children with Down syndrome appear to pay a great deal of attention to the person displaying the emotion. This attraction to the person may result in an inability to appraise a situation meaningfully, thus, failing to make connections between the emotion and an event (Kasari et al., 1990; Kasari et al., 1995; Knieps, Walden, & Baxter, 1994).

In terms of emotion recognition, most studies have examined emotion recognition abilities in mixed groups of mentally retarded individuals. In nearly all of these studies, the children with mental retardation are impaired in recognition of emotions whether they are compared to typical children of the same mental age (McAlpine, Kendall, & Singh, 1991) or the same chronological age (Adams & Markham, 1991; Mauer & Newbrough, 1987).

Researchers rarely separate children with Down syndrome from other children with mental retardation in studies of emotion recognition. However, Kasari, Hughes, and Freeman (1994) examined emotion recognition in 4- to 6-year-old children with Down syndrome. Two groups of typically developing children were matched to the Down syndrome children, one group matched for mental age and one for chronological age. Three different tasks were administered that examined the children's ability to recognize basic emotions of happy, sad, anger, and fear. Children were asked to verbally label faces of a puppet (expressive task) and then choose the face requested by the experimenter (receptive task). Following these two tasks, children were told simple stories using puppets to depict an emotion. For example, a story depicting happiness involved one puppet giving another puppet ice cream. Two stories for each emotion were randomly presented.

In this study, the samples of children matched for developmental abilities did not differ in their abilities to verbalize, recognize, or identify the emotions from the different tasks. All of the children were more accurate in recognizing happy and sad than anger and fear. When the errors were analyzed, however, the children with Down syndrome tended to answer with "happy." Thus, they may have had a more positive "set" response than the typically developing children.

In summary, young children with Down syndrome appear to be as responsive, if not more so, to the negative affects of others. They are also equally able to recognize and label the emotions of others as are mental age-matched typical children. In contrast, children with autism appear fairly unresponsive to the negative emotions of others, in large part because they fail to even pay rudimentary attention to the person. Children with autism also appear to have difficulty in recognizing emotions in others, although the extent of the difference may depend on the developmental matching criteria used for the comparison group.

Complex Emotions

The development of complex emotions, such as embarrassment, guilt, empathy, and pride, requires certain cognitive prerequisites. For example, pride develops once a child has a sense of self separate from others and can reflect on his or her own performance relative to some standard (Heckhausen, 1984; Stipek, 1983). Some degree of self-evaluation is involved in feelings of pride, guilt, and embarrassment, whereas personal responsibility and an audience are involved to varying degrees. For example, a sense of personal responsibility is critical to experiencing pride, but not so critical to embarrassment, whereas an audience is critical to experiencing embarrassment, but not to pride.

Autism. Because of the cognitive requirements associated with complex emotions, studies have not often been conducted with samples of atypically developing children. However, one study of empathy has been reported on a sample of high-functioning adolescents with autism (Yirmiya, Sigman, Kasari, & Mundy, 1992). In this study, adolescents with autism with IQs in the normal range, were asked how they felt after viewing videotaped segments designed to elicit empathic responses (Feshbach, 1982). Overall, the adolescents with autism were less accurate and their abilities were more highly correlated with current language and cognitive abilities than those for the comparison sample of typically developing youngsters.

Investigation of complex emotions often requires verbal skills. However, many of these emotions also are associated with behavioral responses. For example, embarrassment is often associated with blushing or coy behavior (Lewis, 1993). Behavioral responses associated with pride-like behaviors include smiling and calling attention to one's accomplishment and clapping for oneself (Stipek, Recchia, & McClintic, 1992).

Recently, pride has been examined in a sample of young autistic children. Kasari, Sigman, Baumgartner, and Stipek (1993) examined young autistic children's positive expressions, task completion, and social orientation responses in an achievement context. Children were given two developmentally appropriate puzzles to complete and were praised for completing the second, but not the first puzzle. Children with autism were just as likely as other children to smile when they completed the puzzles. However, they did not look up to others and smile or draw another's attention to the task. In response to praise for completing a puzzle, the autistic children actually showed avoidant responses. Based on the results of the study, it is impossible to say that the autistic children did not experience pride. However, the degree to which pride is socially mediated and the situations in which pride is experienced (e.g., social vs. independent) may be different for children with and without autism.

Down Syndrome. Like children with autism, children with Down syndrome demonstrate significant cognitive and language deficiencies. Unlike children with autism, however, children with Down syndrome rarely function in the normal range of cognition. This may be why studies of complex emotions are not reported for children with Down syndrome. However, Hughes and Kasari (1995) reported a study of Down syndrome children's expression of pride in children between 4 and 6 years of age. In this study, children were observed completing moderately challenging puzzles in interactions with their mothers. Positive affect expressions, social orientation, and task completion behaviors of the children were examined. Results indicated that children with Down syndrome (with average mental ages of 40 months) displayed greater social orientation and more task-related behaviors than typically developing children of equivalent mental ages. Thus, in this situation, the children with Down syndrome were more expressive of prideful behaviors than the children with typical development.

As in the previous study, it is not possible to say with confidence that children with Down syndrome are experiencing pride to a greater degree than other children. The nature of pride and the situations in which it is experienced may be different for children with autism and children with Down syndrome.

Talking About Emotion

Because children with autism and children with Down syndrome are grossly deficient in communication and language skills, talking about emotions has rarely been examined. No studies of children with Down syndrome were found. However, a few studies have been reported of high-functioning individuals with autism (individuals with normal IQ and adequate comprehension and expressive skills). Capps et al. (1992) examined the ability of high-functioning adolescents to provide examples of times they felt a specific emotion. Somewhat surprisingly, these adolescents with autism had little difficulty talking about their own experiences of basic emotions, such as happiness, sadness, anger, and fear. They were even able to describe times they felt proud or embarrassed—clearly more complicated emotions that require greater cognitive skills. Pride involves the reflection of a standard for self and embarrassment involves the presence of an audience. Even with this ability there were some notable differences. The autistic children often used examples that seemed "scripted" or expected. Whereas the typical child might give an example of anger from a specific fight with his brother, the autistic child might say "When someone hits me." Thus, the examples given by the autistic children often seemed to be learned responses, perhaps the result of cognitive compensation for deficiencies in emotional understanding.

Jaedicke, Storoschuk, and Lord (1994) found that autistic individuals were as capable of providing examples of the emotions happy, sad, afraid, worried, and angry as were language-matched children with mental retardation (MR) or typical development. However, the autistic children less often related an emotion to reaching a goal or to social interactions. As in the Capps et al. (1992) study, they seemed to give concrete examples of an event.

These studies suggest that high-functioning individuals with autism can accurately talk about emotions, giving appropriate examples of a range of emotion. The scripted nature of their examples, however, may indicate the use of cognitive compensation in their understanding of emotion. Although studies have not been conducted with Down syndrome individuals, it is important to know whether adults with Down syndrome understand and talk about complex emotions in their conversations with others. Such information can yield important insights into the emotional lives of autistic and Down syndrome individuals.

SOME METHODOLOGICAL CONSIDERATIONS

Given the foregoing discussion, the study of emotional development in atypical populations raises a number of issues. One issue is the extent to which emotions might be separable from cognitive ability. Appraisal and conceptual processes are important contributors to children's recognition and understanding of emotion. Studies of children with atypical development often find that cognitive abilities are more highly linked to emotional abilities than in the comparison samples of typically developing children. Thus, the measures used to match comparison samples becomes an important issue.

The expression and understanding of emotions is influenced by developmental abilities and experience. Depending on the behaviors under investigation, the matching criteria for comparison samples may include developmental criteria (e.g., mental age, language abilities), experiential criteria (i.e., age), or both. Different study results have been obtained depending on the matching criteria used. Hobson (1986) found that autistic adolescents were impaired on emotion recognition tasks relative to a mental age matched comparison sample of typically developing children. However, in subsequent studies when autistic children were matched with typical children on verbal mental age (rather than full-scale or performance scores), differences were not significant (Hobson et al., 1989; Ozonoff et al., 1990).

Another issue concerns the composition of comparison samples. The majority of children with autism are also mentally retarded (Rutter, 1985). In order to determine if an attribute is specific to autism and not to developmental delay, comparison samples are usually employed of children with MR. Children with Down syndrome are one of the earliest identified and most common genetic forms of MR. Thus, comparison groups are often composed of children with Down syndrome. Yet, we have argued in this chapter that children with Down syndrome have some unique aspects of their emotional responding. Thus, using children with Down syndrome as a contrast to children with autism may not be the best test of whether an attribute is associated with autism or to MR. It may be that the difference is due to Down syndrome and not autism. Studies that utilize several different samples of children may be more informative (Brooks-Gunn & Lewis, 1982).

CONCLUSIONS/FUTURE DIRECTIONS

Overall, children with autism appear to have difficulty with "affective contact." Their emotional expressions often lack coherence with other communicative behaviors. They pay less attention to others' emotional displays and they show less responsiveness to others. Even with high cognitive abilities, children with autism have difficulty with emotional understanding (Capps, Sigman, & Yirmiya, 1995). In contrast, children with Down syndrome are very attentive to others and are sometimes as responsive to others as are typically developing children at the same developmental age. Both children with autism and children with Down syndrome display facial expressions with qualities that impede readability by others.

The emotional abilities of children with Down syndrome and autism, however, are not always different from typical samples matched for developmental level. Whereas autistic children may not differ, as in the ability to talk about basic emotions, they rarely perform better on emotion tasks than the comparison samples. In contrast, children with Down syndrome may have greater emotional responsivity when compared to developmental agemates. Thus, although children with autism nearly always display weakness on emotion-related tasks, children with Down syndrome at times show strength. Studies are needed that continue to examine the factors associated with strengths and weaknesses in emotional development among these children.

Although a rich research base exists on emotional behavior in both autism and Down syndrome, there is a general lack of study on the socialization of emotion. Few studies have examined the effect of the autistic or Down syndrome child's disrupted signaling system on the behaviors or feelings of others. However, there are some indications that deleterious effects are achieved. For example, mothers of autistic children do not smile in response to their children's smiling as often as mothers of normal children (Dawson et al., 1990). Because the autistic children rarely combined smiling and looking to the caregiver simultaneously, the lack of coherence in the autistic child's signaling behavior may have resulted in less contingent smiling on the part of their mothers. Similarly, mothers of Down syndrome children smiled less in response to their children's smiles and did not increase responsive smiling over time despite increases in children's smiling (Brooks-Gunn & Lewis, 1982).

Other evidence of a mismatch in parental responding with Down syndrome children comes from a study by Walden, Knieps, and Baxter (1991). These researchers found that parents of children with developmental delays (many of whom had Down syndrome) tended to "over shoot" their children's signals for information. Thus, in a social referencing situation when the parent was to display a facial expression only after the child looked to them for information, parents of children with developmental delays were more likely to display the expressions before the child had clearly looked to the parent. Similarly, Sorce and Emde (1982) found that in comparison to parents of typically developing infants, parents of Down syndrome infants interpreted less clear expressions of emotion as meaningful, suggesting caregiving strategies for intervention.

These studies suggest that the lack of clarity in facial expression may directly influence the parent to respond in certain ways (Sorce & Emde, 1982). The disruption in the emotional signaling system may also indirectly lead to negative reactions in the parent by increasing a sense of despair with their child. Studies of infants with Down syndrome suggest that their dampened expressions cause greater depression in their parents (Emde, Katz, & Thorpe, 1978). Kasari and Sigman (in press) found that perceptions of more difficult temperaments in children with autism were associated with the caregiver's sense of greater parenting stress. Observations of interactions between child and caregiver found that these same parents tended to have less active engagement of their children in interactions.

Future studies need to examine the socialization of emotion in children with typical and atypical development. Findings from these studies may be most useful for designing appropriate interventions. With specific interventions, many parents, peers and the children themselves may be able to overcome the interactive difficulties presented by the child's atypical emotional development.

REFERENCES

Adams, K., & Markham, R. (1991). Recognition of affective facial expressions by children and adolescents with and without mental retardation. *American Journal on Mental Retardation, 96*, 21–28.

American Psychiatric Association. (1987). *Diagnostic and statistical manual of mental disorders* (3rd ed., rev.). Washington, DC: Author.

Baron, J. (1972). Temperament profile of children with Down's syndrome. *Developmental Medicine and Child Neurology, 14*, 640–643.

Bretherton, I., & Beeghly, M. (1982). Talking about internal states: The acquisition of an explicit theory of mind. *Developmental Psychology, 18*, 906–921.

Brooks-Gunn, J., & Lewis, M. (1982). Affective exchanges between normal and handicapped infants and their mothers. In T. Field & A. Fogel (Eds.), *Emotion and early interaction* (pp. 161–212). Hillsdale, NJ: Lawrence Erlbaum Associates.

Capps, L., Sigman, M., & Yirmiya, N. (1995). Self-competence and emotional understanding in high-functioning children with autism. *Development and Psychopathology, 7*, 137–150.

Capps, L., Yirmiya, N., & Sigman, M. (1992). Understanding of simple and complex emotions in non-retarded children with autism. *Journal of Child Psychology and Psychiatry, 33*, 1169–1182.

Cicchetti, D., & Sroufe, L.A. (1978). An organizational view of affect: Illustration from the study of Down syndrome infants. In M. Lewis & L.A. Rosenblum (Eds.), *The development of affect* (pp. 309–350). New York: Plenum.

Cohn, J.F., Campbell, S.B., Matias, R., & Hopkins, J. (1990). Face-to-face interactions of postpartum depressed and nondepressed mother-infant pairs at 2 months. *Developmental Psychology, 26*, 15–23.

Dawson, G., Hill, D., Spencer, A., Galpert, L., & Watson, L. (1990). Affective exchanges between young autistic children and their mothers. *Journal of Abnormal Child Psychology, 18*, 335–345.

Denham, S., & Couchoud, E.A. (1990). Young preschoolers' understanding of emotion. *Child Study Journal, 20*, 171–192.

Dissanayake, C., Sigman, M., & Kasari, C. (in press). The stability of response to other's emotions in children with autism. *Journal of Child Psychology and Psychiatry.*

Dunn, J., Brown, J., & Beardsall, L. (1991). Family talk about feeling states and children's later understanding of others' emotions. *Developmental Psychology, 27*, 448–455.

Emde, R., Katz, E.L., & Thorpe, J.K. (1978). Emotional expression in infancy: II. Early deviations in Down syndrome. In M. Lewis & L.A. Rosenblum (Eds.), *The development of affect* (pp. 351–360). New York: Plenum.

Emde, R.N., & Brown, C. (1978). Adaptation to the birth of a Down's syndrome infants grieving and maternal attachment. *Journal of the American Academy of Child Psychiatry, 17*, 299–323.

Feshbach, N.D. (1982). Sex differences in empathy and social behavior in children. In N. Eisenberg (Ed.), *The development of prosocial behavior* (pp. 315–338). New York: Academic Press.

Field, T. (1980). Interactions of preterm and term infants with their lower-and middle-class teenage and adult mothers. In T. Field, S. Goldberg, D. Stern, & A. Sostek (Eds.), *High-risk infants and children: Adult and peer interactions* (pp. 113–132). New York: Academic Press.

Goldberg, S. (1977). Social competence in infancy: A model of parent–infant interaction. *Merrill-Palmer Quarterly, 23*, 163–177.

Harris, P.L. (1989). *Children and emotion: The development of psychological understanding.* Oxford, UK: Blackwell.

Heckhausen, H. (1984). Emergent achievement behavior: Some early developments. In J. Nicholls (Ed.), *Advances in motivation and achievement: Vol. 3: The development of achievement motivation* (pp. 1–32). Greenwich, CT: JAI Press.

Hobson, R.P. (1986). The autistic child's appraisal of expressions of emotion. *Journal of Child Psychology and Psychiatry, 27,* 321–342.

Hobson, R.P. (1991). What is autism? *Psychiatric Clinics of North America, 14,* 1–17.

Hobson, R.P., Ouston, J., & Lee, A. (1989). Naming emotions in faces and voices: Abilities and disabilities in autism and mental retardation. *British Journal of Developmentl Psychology, 7,* 237–250.

Hornik, R., Risenhoover, N., & Gunnar, M. (1987). The effects of maternal positive, neutral, and negative affective communications on infant responses to new toys. *Child Development, 58,* 937–944.

Huebner, R.R., & Izard, C.E. (1988). Mothers' responses to infants' facial expressions of sadness, anger, and physical distress. *Motivation and Emotion, 12,* 185–196.

Hughes, M., & Kasari, C. (1995). *Caregiver child interactions and the expression of pride in children with Down syndrome.* Manuscript submitted for review.

Izard, C.E. (1971). *The face of emotion.* New York: Appleton-Century-Crofts.

Izard, C.E. (1979). *The Maximally Discriminative Facial Movement Coding System (MAX).* Newark: Office of Academic Computing and Technology, University of Delaware.

Izard, C.E., & Malatesta, C.Z. (1987). Perspectives on emotional development I: Differential emotions theory of early emotional development. In J.D. Osofsky (Ed.), *Handbook of infant development* (2nd ed., pp. 494–554). New York: Wiley.

Jaedicke, S., Storoschuk, S., & Lord, C. (1994). Subjective experience and causes of affect in high-functioning children and adolescents with autism. *Development and Psychopathology, 6,* 273–284.

Jennings, W.B. (1973). *A study of the preference for affective cues in children with autism.* Unpublished doctoral dissertation, Memphis State University, Memphis, TN.

Kanner, L. (1943). Autistic disturbances of affective contact. *Nervous Child, 2,* 217–250.

Kasari, C., Freeman, S., Sigman, M., & Mundy, P. (1995). Attention regulation by children with Down syndrome: Coordinated joint attention and social referencing. *American Journal on Mental Retardation, 100,* 128–136.

Kasari, C., Hughes, M., & Freeman, S. (1994, June). *Emotion recognition in children with Down syndrome.* Paper presented at the International Conference on Behavioral Development, Amsterdam.

Kasari, C., Mundy, P., & Sigman, M. (1990, April). *Empathy in toddlers with Down syndrome.* Paper presented at the Society for Research in Child Development, Seattle, WA.

Kasari, C., Mundy, P., Yirmiya, N., & Sigman, M. (1990). Affect and attention in children with Down syndrome. *American Journal on Mental Retardation, 95,* 55–67.

Kasari, C., & Sigman, M. (in press). Linking perceptions to interactions in young children with autism. *Journal of Autism and Developmental Disabilities.*

Kasari, C., Sigman, M., Baumgartner, P., & Stipek, D. (1993). Pride and mastery in children with autism. *Journal of Child Psychology and Psychiatry, 34,* 353–362.

Kasari, C., Sigman, M., Mundy, P., & Yirmiya, N. (1990). Affective sharing in the context of joint attention interactions. *Journal of Autism and Developmental Disabilities, 20,* 87–100.

Kasari, C., Sigman, M., Yirmiya, N., & Mundy, P. (1993). Affective development and communication in young children with autism. In A. Kaiser & D. Gray (Eds.), *Enhancing children's communication: Research foundations for intervention* (pp. 201–222). New York: Brookes.

Klinnert, M., Campos, J., Sorce, J., Emde, R.N., & Svejda, M. (1983). Emotions as behavior regulators: Social referencing in infancy. In R. Plutchik & H. Kellerman (Eds.), *Emotion: Theory, research, and experience* (pp. 57–86). New York: Academic Press.

Knieps, L.J., Walden, T.A., & Baxter, A. (1994). Affective expressions of toddlers with and without Down syndrome in a social referencing context. *American Journal on Mental Retardation, 99,* 301–312.

Kubicek, L.F. (1980). Organization in two mother-infant interactions involving a normal infant and his fraternal twin brother who was later diagnosed as autistic. In T. Field, S. Goldberg, D. Stern, & A. Sostek (Eds.), *High-risk infants and children: Adult and peer interactions* (pp. 99–110). New York: Academic Press.

Landry, S.H., & Chapieski, M.L. (1990). Joint attention of six-month-old Down syndrome and preterm infants: I. Attention to toys and mothers. *American Journal on Mental Retardation, 94,* 488–498.

Lewis, M. (1993). Self-conscious emotions: Embarrassment, pride, shame, and guilt. In M. Lewis & J.M. Haviland (Eds.), *Handbook of emotions* (pp. 563–573). New York: Guilford.

Lewis, M., & Michalson, L. (1983). *Children's emotions and moods: Developmental theory and measurement.* New York: Plenum.

Loveland, K., & Landry, S. (1986). Joint attention and language in autism and developmental language delay. *Journal of Autism and Developmental Disorders, 16,* 335–349.

Malatesta, C.Z., & Haviland, J.M. (1982). Learning display rules: The socialization of emotion expression in infancy. *Child Development, 53,* 1001–1003.

Mauer, H., & Newbrough, J.R. (1987). Facial expressions of mentally retarded and nonretarded children: I. Recognition by mentally retarded and nonretarded adults. *American Journal on Mental Retardation, 91,* 505–510.

McAlpine, C., Kendall, K.A., & Singh, N.N. (1991). Recognition of facial expressions of emotion by persons with mental retardation. *American Journal on Mental Retardation, 96,* 29–36.

Mundy, P., Kasari, C., & Sigman, M. (1992). Nonverbal communication, affective sharing, and intersubjectivity. *Infant Behavior and Development, 15,* 377–381.

Mundy, P., Sigman, M., Ungerer, J., & Sherman, T. (1986). Defining the social deficits of autism. The contribution of nonverbal communication measures. *Journal of Child Psychology and Psychiatry, 27,* 657–669.

Ornitz, E. M., Guthrie, D. & Farley, A.J. (1978). The early symptoms of childhood autism. In G. Serban (Ed.), *Cognitive defects in the development of mental illness* (pp. 24–42). New York: Brunner/Mazel.

Osterling, J., & Dawson, G. (1994). Early recognition of children with autism: A study of first birthday home videotapes. *Journal of Autism and Developmental Disorders, 24,* 247–257.

Ozonoff, S., Pennington, B., & Rogers, S. (1990). Are there emotion perception deficits in young autistic children? *Journal of Child Psychology and Psychiatry, 31,* 343–361.

Ricks, D.M., & Wing, L. (1975). Language, communication, and the use of symbols in normal and autistic children. *Journal of Autism and Childhood Schizophrenia, 5,* 191–221.

Rutter, M. (1985). Infantile autism and other pervasive developmental disorders. In M. Rutter & L. Hersov (Eds.), *Child and adolescent psychiatry: Modern approaches* (pp. 545–566). Oxford: Blackwell Scientific.

Sigman, M., Kasari, C., Kwon, J. H., & Yirmiya, N. (1992). Responses to the negative emotions of others by autistic, mentally retarded and normal children. *Child Development, 63,* 796–807.

Sigman, M., Mundy, P., Sherman, T., & Ungerer, J. (1986). Social interactions of autistic, mentally retarded and normal children and their caregivers. *Journal of Child Psychology and Psychiatry, 27,* 647–655.

Smiley, P., & Huttenlocher, J. (1989). Young children's acquisition of emotion concepts. In C. Saarni & P.L. Harris (Eds.), *Children's understanding of emotion* (pp. 27–49). New York: Cambridge University Press.

Snow, M.E., Hertzog, M.E., & Shapiro, T. (1987). Expression of emotion in young autistic children. *Journal of the American Academy of Child and Adolescent Psychiatry, 26,* 836–838.

Sorce, J.F., & Emde, R.N. (1982). The meaning of infant emotional expressions: Regularities in caregiving responses in normal and Down's syndrome infants. *Journal of Child Psychology and Psychiatry, 23,* 145–158.

Stipek, D. (1983). A developmental analysis of pride and shame. *Human Development, 26,* 42–54.

Stipek, D., Recchia, S., & McClintic, S. (1992). Achievement-related self-evaluation in young children. *SRCD Monographs, 57.*

Termine, N.T., & Izard, C.E. (1988). Infants' responses to their mothers' expressions of joy and sadness. *Developmental Psychology, 24,* 223–229.

Walden, T.A., Knieps, L.J., & Baxter, A. (1991). Contingent provision of social referential information by parents of children with and without developmental delays. *American Journal on Mental Retardation, 96,* 177–187.

Walden, T.A., & Ogan, T.A. (1988). The development of social referencing. *Child Development, 59,* 1230–1240.

Weeks, S.J., & Hobson, R.P. (1987). The salience of facial expression for children with autism. *Journal of Child Psychology and Psychiatry, 28,* 137–151.

Yirmiya, N., Kasari, C., Sigman, M., & Mundy, P. (1989). Facial expression of affect in autistic, mentally retarded, and normal children. *Journal of Child Psychology and Psychiatry, 30,* 725–735.

Yirmiya, N., Sigman, M., Kasari, C., & Mundy, P. (1992). Empathy and cognition in high-functioning children with autism. *Child Development, 63,* 150–160.

Zahn-Waxler, C., Friedman, S.L., & Cummings, E.M. (1983). Children's emotions and behaviors in response to infants' cries. *Child Development, 54,* 1522–1528.

– 7 –

Inhibited Children Talk About Themselves: Self-Reflection on Personality Development and Change in 7-Year-Olds

Nathan A. Fox
Ana Sobel
University of Maryland

Susan Calkins
University of North Carolina, Greensboro

Pamela Cole
Pennsylvania State University

The study of behavioral inhibition, like the study of so many other developmental phenomena, is one that involves describing continuities and discontinuities of behavior over time. Children who as toddlers appear to be fearful and vigilant when confronted with mild stress or novelty may, when seen during the preschool years, behave no differently than other children their age. Alternatively, they may continue to exhibit patterns of withdrawal and anxiety that characterize them as reticent, inhibited preschoolers. A good deal of research has been completed on children who display behavioral inhibition, describing the patterns of continuity or change as well as understanding the possible factors that may mediate these changes. For example, Kagan, Reznick, Snidman, Gibbons, and Johnson (1988) reported that more than 60% of children identified as behaviorally inhibited during the toddler years continue to exhibit signs of inhibition and social reticence as preschoolers. The remaining 40% of behaviorally inhibited children were no longer inhibited when assessed during the preschool period.

Rubin and Lollis (1988) speculated about the factors that may mediate these patterns of continuity and discontinuity. They argued that the quality of the relationship between mother and child, the degree of stress in the family, and the pattern of childrearing will all have important effects on the child's developing personality. Temperamentally inhibited children who have secure relationships with their parents and who grow up in low stressful and supportive households are less likely to display continuity of anxious and inhibited behaviors. Rubin and Lollis also argued that differences in personality style will ultimately affect child self-concept and contribute to the continuity or discontinuity of such styles over time. Evidence from a number of longitudinal studies seems to support the notion that the interaction of familial, relationship, and environmental factors with temperamental style together account for the multiple pathways that children take in personality development (Rubin & Lollis, 1988).

These studies have all assessed, via questionnaire or via behavioral observation, changes in child behavior, in family functioning, and/or in environmental context. Few studies have asked children about their own views of changes in their lives or about their own personality development. That is, how do behaviorally inhibited children feel about their own behavior patterns or personality? Do they recognize themselves as shy or anxious? What are the self-perceptions of children who change their pattern of behavior over time? Do these children recognize the change in themselves and perhaps also the reasons for that change?

These questions about the lives of inhibited children raise even broader questions about what children in general understand about their own personality development. Adults seem to have specific notions about the stability or instability of specific personality factors over time. Ross (1989) found, for example, that adults describe the factor of ability as having an inverted U shape function over age, signifying that ability improves from an early age to some high point after which it begins to decrease. Other aspects of personality (such as sociability) were described as having stable characteristics over time. Ross argued that the manner in which people view a particular trait will influence the way in which they report their relation to that trait. So, for example, individuals who view shyness as a stable trait may understand their own behavior from a characterological point of view. Alternatively, if one viewed such traits as modifiable by the environment or subject to change, one may look for instances in one's own experience that verify such discontinuities.

Another way to understand this issue is to view these individual theories as the end state of the developmental history of the individual reflecting not so much an abstract theory of development but rather reflecting the history of change or stability that has occurred over time to the individual. Thus, one's view of shyness as either a stable trait or a changing quality may be a function of one's individual history. For those individuals who have experienced and perceived self-change, their views of traits will be different than for those who have not experienced change. These personal views of shyness are therefore important in terms of understanding the individual's behavior and perception of that behavior.

Obviously, children's perceptions of these personality dispositions, their notion of them as being stable or changing, and their notion of their potential for change with age or development may influence their own attitude toward their personality. Thus, it seems worthwhile to interview children about their personalities and the possible changes or lack of changes that occur over time.

Interviewing children about themselves, particularly with regard to their personal selves, acknowledges some level of self-understanding by the child. Questions about the self over time, about changes in the self, and about characteristics of the self all involve a particular level of knowledge and understanding. This knowledge has often been studied by those interested in the development of self-concept.

An important facet of the development of the self-concept involves the ability to look upon the self as an object, or view oneself from the perspective of another person (Lewis, 1992). According to Piaget (1937/1954), this ability to "decenter" from one's egotistical point of view occurs during the preoperational period of development, between the ages of 2 and 6. Numerous theorists attribute the emergence of this decentration to the experience of social learning and interaction (Cooley, 1909/1962; Mahler, Pine, & Bergman, 1975; Mead, 1934/1972). The recognition that others possess their own points of view toward oneself is a necessary, but not a sufficient capability to experiencing self-conscious emotions (Harter, 1983). It is necessary that this understanding exists not only when others are present and reactive, but also that it be internalized and can be conceptualized in the absence of others (Harter, 1983).

The ability to infer the evaluation of others is strongly linked to another milestone in the development of the self-concept. This is the understanding that people have stable and enduring psychological qualities. Researchers have found that as children increase in age so does their ability to describe themselves and others in regard to feelings, thoughts, and interest rather than merely by overt behaviors (Perry & Bussey, 1984; Rosenberg, 1979). Young children grasp notions of constancy and invariance in people, in the external, observable domain before the psychological domain. They first attain the awareness that a child cannot change into an animal, a child of the opposite gender, or another child before they comprehend that the psychological traits of individuals can endure through time and different situations (Guardo & Bohan, 1971). The dual knowledge that individuals are evaluated by others and that they and their evaluators possess consistent personality dispositions, enables individuals to make social comparisons with others (Eder, 1990).

These capabilities are fundamental to experiencing self-conscious emotions, defined by researchers as embarrassment, pride, shame, and guilt (Lewis, 1992). However, a third element is necessary before these emotions are fully realized. This third element is the acceptance of rules and standards for socially acceptable behavior. Once children have an internalized set of principles they can make value judgments concerning their self-worth in comparison to others based on measures they deem important (Lewis, 1992). An individual with a developed self-concept has the capability to describe him or herself as shy. As consistent with the cognitive definition of shyness, shy children may realize that they are not as sociable as their peers or as they would like themselves to be. They may also fear social situations and the opportunities these situations present for the negative evaluation by others.

Children who have mastered the developmental stages necessary for self-reflection, and who view themselves as shy in comparison to their peers, have been found to evaluate their competencies negatively and to possess low self-esteems. Socially inhibited children as young as 7 display poorer self-concepts and were more depressed and anxious than their more sociable peers (Rubin & Lollis, 1988). Children who exhibited a low frequency of social interaction at this age also self-assessed social, cognitive (Moskowitz & Schwartzman, 1989), and physical attributes negatively (Rubin, 1985). In the fourth grade, children observed to be socially withdrawn perceived themselves as lacking in social skills and attempting to avoid peer interactions (Rubin & Lollis, 1988).

Researchers speculate that the negative self-perceptions experienced and the inhibited behavior displayed by shy children cyclically influence one other. Thus, shy children withdraw from their peers, which in turn may cause increased social isolation and more inhibited behaviors (Rubin & Lollis, 1988). Furthermore, socially reticent children who expect their interactions with peers to have negative outcomes may be creating a self-fulfilling prophesy (Hymel, Franke, & Friegang, 1985). Low academic expectations found among withdrawn children may also be hampering their future scholastic achievement (Moskowitz & Schwartzman, 1989).

It seems clear, then, that shy and socially withdrawn children are at some risk for developing a negative self-concept and experiencing negative peer-social interaction. These self-evaluations and negative social experiences come at a time when the child is able to articulate notions about who he or she is with regard to the personal self. These self-evaluations may influence the formation of perceptions of the personal self.

Since 1987, we have been studying a group of children and their families with an interest toward describing both the temperamental and familial factors that influence variation in social competence. The children were randomly chosen from a local university hospital neonatal unit. The major selection criterion was lack of medical problems during the prenatal and immediate postnatal period. The children and parents visited our laboratory when the children were 5 months old, 14 months old, 24 months old, and again when they were 4 and 7 years of age. At age 24 months, we assessed behavioral inhibition by observing each individual child in a playroom (with mother present) during the following situations: a free-play period, interaction with an unfamiliar adult, presentation of a toy robot, presentation of a plastic tunnel through which the child was asked to crawl and retrieve a toy, and interaction with a clown. We coded the child's behavior on videotapes for such measures as latency to talk to the adult, latency to touch the novel object, and proximity to mother, and we computed a standardized index of inhibition. At age 4, the children returned to our laboratory for a same-gender quartet play session. At age 7, children again returned and again same-gender quartets were formed (different in composition from those formed at age 4). Children were videotaped interacting with their same-age same-gender peers at age 7. The 4- and 7-year play quartet sessions were coded for the type and maturity of play of each child as well as the role relationships that were established during the session (Coplan, Rubin, Fox, Calkins, & Stewart, 1984; Rubin, 1989). At age 7, we computed a measure of reticence (social withdrawal) based on the child's behavior during the quartet session. This variable consisted of the amount of time the child spent unoccupied and onlooking during the play session as well as the frequency of anxious behaviors exhibited during the session.

At age 7, each child returned individually to the laboratory for a visit during which he or she was interviewed. An experimenter informed the child that he or she would view a series of videotapes and then would be asked questions concerning what he or she saw in the videotapes. We presented the children with videotapes of 2-year-olds of the same gender who reflected extreme examples of social behavior. One videotape showed a fearful 2-year-old in our laboratory situation (being presented with the robot and clown). The child stayed close to her mother, buried her head in her mother's lap, and cried during the episodes. The second videotape showed an exuberant and highly social child in the same laboratory situation (robot and clown). This child immediately approached and touched the robot and approached and interacted with the clown. Our goal was to have each child watch these tapes and then, via interview, talk about the behavior of the child in the tape. We reasoned that presenting these tapes would elicit language about the feeling state of temperamentally different children and would prepare our target children for questions that we would ask them about themselves. After watching the video of the inhibited 2-year-old, the 7-year-olds were asked what they thought the toddler in the videotape was feeling. They were also asked to describe their own emotions while watching the tape. After watching the second videotape of the uninhibited toddler, the study subjects were again asked the same series of questions regarding the feeling state of the child on the tape as well as their own affective responses to watching the tape.

Prior to seeing the third videotape, the study subjects were asked if they, as 7-year-old children, were more like the uninhibited child (named Julia for the girls and Sam for the boys) or more like the inhibited child (named Megan for the girls and Brock for the boys). The experimenter next asked the children which child seen in the videotape they were more like when they were 2. The subjects were then informed that they had been filmed when they were 2 with the robot and the clown under similar circumstances and that they were going to watch themselves at age 2. They then watched the videotapes of themselves and were asked about what they thought they were feeling in the videotape and how they felt currently as they watched themselves. In addition, the experimenter asked the subjects to state which of the children from the previous films they more closely resembled at age 2. At the conclusion of the interview, the children were given the opportunity to discuss discrepancies between their conjectured behavior and their actual behavior and between their levels of inhibition at 2 and at 7.

Research indicates that at about age 7, an important shift occurs in the children's understanding that people behave in consistent and predictable ways (Rholes & Ruble, 1984). In addition, around age 7 children's ability to make dispositional inferences increases (Eder, 1989). There has been a tendency among theorists to underestimate the level of awareness that children below the age of 7 possess concerning the internal nature of individuals and to limit the understanding of younger children of others to observable, external factors (Miller & Aloise, 1989). However, studies reveal that children as young as 3 and 4 understand that behavior is determined by psychological factors such as emotions, knowledge, intentions, and motives (Eder, 1989, 1990; Miller & Aloise, 1989). Thus, younger children acknowledge that people experience changing internal states, but it is not until about the age of 7 that they understand that these traits are stable over time and situation and can be used to differentiate and evaluate the self and others (Eder, 1990; Rholes & Ruble, 1984). Thus, around age 7 there is an important transition in both self-knowledge and access to that knowledge regarding the stability of one's personal self over time. The 7-year assessment that took place during our study offered us a unique opportunity to examine the emergence of children's personal selves. Children were given the opportunity to reflect on their past behavior and compare it to their perception of their current behavior. In that manner, we hoped to examine their understanding of continuity or discontinuity of personal self over time.

In order to accomplish this goal, we asked children to speculate about the factors that might have accounted for change or continuity in their behavior over time. They offered a wide variety of explanations when asked about the factors that led to changes in their behavior from age 2 to age 7. This variability is consistent with the research findings that important shifts in the causal understanding of behavior occur at about age 7. Examination of their responses led us to categorize these answers into five major categories: physical, experience, knowledge, psychological states, and psychological traits.

Responses were categorized as physical when the study subjects described the changes in themselves since they were 2 as being externally observable. For example, a 7-year-old boy ascribed changes in his behavior to differences in his appearance and dress: "I had short hair when I was littler, and I have different sneakers now, too." A 7-year-old girl similarly noted changes in her behavior, "[At 7] I go up and see new things. I don't go to my mom anymore."

A number of children ascribed changes in their behavior to experiences that they had which they felt had caused changes in their behavior. A typical response of this nature was, "I've seen things more and more often so now I'm less and less afraid of them," or "Maybe I'm less scared of clowns cause I went to the circus and I know what they look like." In these instances, the children often described events or series of events that they felt were influential in modifying their behavior.

Some subjects attributed the changes they observed in themselves between the ages of 2 and 7 to their increased knowledge. These knowledge responses included such statements as, "At first I was kinda young and I didn't know stuff as well and now I know stuff better and it's easier to understand" and "Right now I know that that's only a robot and a clown and not something that wants to get me." The increase in their ability to understand the world and make sense of their environment and the novel and sometimes threatening stimuli in it was reason in some children's mind for a change in their behavior over time. They no longer feared novelty because they were able to understand it.

A number of children provided responses that were based on the quality of emotions children felt were elicited both previously and currently by novel or threatening stimuli. These responses, categorized as psychological states, consisted of an awareness of differing emotions that was the result of specific situations. For example, one child stated, "When I was younger I was really kinda scared when I saw those things. Now they aren't scarry." Another child said "[At 7] I'm happy when I see clowns but when I was a baby, robots and clowns made me sad." The same event at two different age points elicited different emotions and the child's personal self was defined by the quality of these emotions.

A number of children were able to articulate answers to the interview that indicated their ability to reflect on changes in the trait-like aspect of their personal selves. These responses were categorized as psychological traits, specifically when dispositional characteristics were discussed. For example, a 7-year-old girl explained the change in her behavior since age 2 through the statement, "I'm not shy anymore," and a 7-year-old boy attributed his behavior change to being "braver" and desiring "to have fun and not be embarrassed." In both instances, the children utilized trait-like terms to describe their previous behavior and their current status as well.

These examples demonstrate that 7-year-old children are capable of describing notions about their personal selves and notions about change in that self over time. These descriptions varied in their content and in the structure that was used to describe that content. Explanations varied from physical changes to changes in personal traits. Did these explanations vary as a function of the child's actual behavior as observed in our study? In the next section of this chapter we investigate this question.

CHILDREN'S RESPONSES AS A FUNCTION OF THEIR OBSERVED SOCIAL BEHAVIOR

Of the 46 seven-year-old children who were interviewed, 36 (20 females) had scores on the inhibition index at 24 months of age as well as scores on the reticence measure at 7 years of age. High inhibition scores were correlated with specific anxious behaviors, unfocused behavior, and passive observation of peers.

Four categories of children were defined based on their inhibition scores: Group 1—children who were uninhibited at both 2 and 7 years, Group 2—children who were inhibited at 2 years and uninhibited at 7 years, Group 3—children who were uninhibited at 2 years and inhibited at 7 years, and Group 4—children who were inhibited at both 2 and 7 years. Table 7.1 illustrates the number of subjects in each of the categories. The children in each of the four groups tended to share common intragroup personality traits. The descriptions here are provided to give a sense of the type of child represented in each of the four groupings.

TABLE 7.1
The Four Categories of Children Based on
Their Inhibition Scores at Age 2 and Age 7

		Level of Inhibition at 7 Years	
		Uninhibited	*Inhibited*
Level of Inhibition at 2 Years	Uninhibited	Group 1: 12 Children 8 Females 4 Males	Group 3: 6 Children 1 Female 5 Males
	Inhibited	Group 2: 12 Children 8 Females 4 Males	Group 4: 6 Children 2 Female 4 Males

Group 1: Uninhibited at 2 Years and 7 Years

Twelve children were evaluated as uninhibited at both 2 and 7 years of age. This group was comprised of 8 females (40% of the female subjects) and 4 males (25% of the male subjects).

Mary L. was highly representative of the children in this group. At 2 years of age, Mary's exploratory nature was evident. While in a free-play session with her mother, she spent the majority of her time investigating the various toys in the room. When she was later exposed to an unfamiliar experimenter, as well as a clown and a toy robot that moved and made noises, she spoke happily to the experimenter and, without hesitation, to the clown and touched and smiled at the robot.

Mary communicated often with her mother, although she did not spend time in close proximity to her. When her mother attempted to exit the room, Mary followed her and grasped her hand at first, but shortly thereafter resumed playing with her toys and allowed her mother to leave. Throughout the time Mary was at the laboratory, she seemed to be enjoying her activities and smiled frequently at her mother as well as at the experimenters she met.

When Mary was 4 years old, she again presented the image of a highly uninhibited child. Of the four children in the room during the free-play session, she most frequently spoke to her peers as well as to the experimenter who periodically entered the room. She spent the majority of her time playing with at least one other child. When Mary was not involved in a game with the others, she either joined them or invited them to join her. In one instance, when Mary desired a play companion, she told a peer whose mother had not yet left the room, "Come here. Your mother will come, too."

Mary expressed a willingness to engage in the new activities the experimenter introduced. Several times after the experimenter described the next activity that was to take place, she exclaimed excitedly, "I'm ready." Mary was also the first to volunteer when the experimenter requested that someone initiate the activity.

When Mary was 7 years old, she exhibited an even more distinctly uninhibited personality than she had when she was 4. In comparison to the peers with whom she was engaged in a free-play session, Mary spoke the most often and took the role of the leader of the group. She frequently addressed all the other children at once by prefacing her statements with, "Hey guys. . . ." She also successfully organized games in which she did not exclude any of the group members. However, in a few instances she criticized her peers and attempted to direct their behavior through such statements as, "You're not doing it right, it's my turn again."

The responses that Mary offered during her individual interview session were highly representative of the manner in which the uninhibited children in the study discussed shyness. Although Mary was uninhibited at both 2 and 7 years of age, she was not unaware of the concept of shyness. She described the inhibited 2-year-old seen in the videotape as shy, and acknowledged her own capacity to feel shy at times. However, Mary clearly expressed that she more strongly identified with the uninhibited child. This was reflected in statements such as, "[At 2], sometimes I would be shy, but Megan was shyer than me and I'm not shy anymore," and "[At 7], I am like Julia because she was the one that wasn't scared."

Mary believed that being inhibited could lead to experiencing negative emotions. When asked how Megan was feeling, she remarked, "She was sad because she was shy." She also stated that she "felt sorry" for Megan.

Mary offered a brief and superficial response when questioned about changes she noted since she was 2. She explained her developmental change as, "When I growed I got a bigger brain, so now my head is bigger than it was when I was 2." She addressed notions of change over time from a physical point of view but perceived her own personal self as remaining unchanged over time. This was a personal self, suffused with positive emotion and approach-oriented behaviors.

A final point of interest concerning Mary's interview was the excitement that she expressed when she discovered that she would be given the opportunity to observe herself at 2, and the enjoyment she felt while viewing the videotape of herself. When asked how she felt while watching herself, Mary responded with a big smile, "Really, really, really happy."

Group 2: Inhibited at 2 Years, Uninhibited at 7 Years

Twelve children were scored as inhibited as 2 years and uninhibited at 7 years of age. This group consisted of 9 girls (45% of the female subjects) and 3 boys (19% of the male subjects).

Jill S. most strongly typified the behaviors and personalities of the children in this group. At age 2, during the free-play session with her mother, Jill explored the toys in the room, however, she did not approach the robot or the strangers or communicate to them.

During the majority of her 2-year visit, Jill displayed negative affect. She used an anxious tone of voice when conversing with her mother both when they were alone and when they were in the company of the unfamiliar experimenters. When Jill's mother exited the room, Jill cried, and ran to hug her when she returned.

At 4 years of age, Jill demonstrated both inhibited and uninhibited behaviors throughout a free-play session with peers. During the first few minutes of the session, Jill's mother remained in the room upon her daughter's urging. She even informed the experimenter, "It would be fun if my mom played, too." After Jill's mother left, she spent most of her free-play time playing by herself or with one other peer. As she became more comfortable with the group situation, she spoke freely to the other group members and smiled and laughed with them.

Although Jill was not the first to participate spontaneously in the new activities that the experimenter introduced, she did so when it was her designated turn. Furthermore, when asked to speak in front of her peers, Jill did so at length.

At 7 years, Jill seemed to have virtually nothing in common with the anxious toddler she once was. Jill was friendly and talkative with the other children during the free-play session. She primarily spent her time playing with another girl who was also highly sociable, but in several instances she joined a quieter peer who was playing alone.

Jill expressed self-confidence in her ability to play a variety of games. This was evident in her willingness to take active roles at play and from comments that directly addressed her competence. While engaged in a board game with the others, she said with a smile, "Let's play that whoever wins gets to play again, which means that I'll always get to play."

In Jill's 7-year individual interview, she personified the children in the study who had changed in their behavior over time. Jill recognized her own shyness at age 2, but seldom described the children in the other videotapes as inhibited. She also noted shy aspects of herself at age 7. Although she stated that she more closely identified with the uninhibited 2-year-old both at 2 and at 7 prior to watching the videotape of herself, she did express the opinion that commonalities existed between herself and the inhibited child. For example, she remarked, "I am kind of like Megan because when I was little I was scared of those things, but now that I'm older, I'm not."

Jill perceived her own inhibition as a highly negative quality. She expressed embarrassment when asked about how she felt while watching the videotape of herself. She told her interviewer, "I felt like I was a total idiot then."

Jill attributed her change from a shy 2-year-old to an uninhibited 7-year-old to increased knowledge and experience. She explained, "When I was little my mom took me to a lot of places so I learned a lot of new stuff so now I'm not as scared as I was when I was a baby." Jill later showed a strong capacity for self-reflection when she remarked, "I've gotten older and I don't want to be embarrassed."

Group 3: Uninhibited at 2 Years, Inhibited at 7 Years

Six children were categorized as belonging in Group 3. The group consisted of five boys (31% of the male subjects) and 1 girl (5% of the female subjects).

Steven K. strongly represented the characteristics of the children in this category. At 2, he conducted himself in much the same way that Mary did. He did not remain in close proximity to his mother during the free-play session, but instead explored the many toys scattered throughout the room. Steven was quick to speak to the unfamiliar adults who entered the room and approached the robot after only 20 seconds of hesitation.

When Steven was in the room with his mother he spoke to her often about the toys with which he was playing. He watched as she exited the room as she had been instructed to do, but soon resumed his play. Steven's mother was told to knock and call out her son's name upon entering. When she did this, Steven did not demonstrate any negative affect at having been left alone but instead responded, "I'm in here."

At 4, the picture Steven presented was somewhat different. He was reluctant to let his father leave the free-play room, but was able to remain without him at the start of his session with three peers. During the free-play time, he played with and conversed with the other children, but also spent much of his time passively watching them. In general, Steven was among the quieter children, but he did participate fully in the activities that the experimenter led.

While in a free-play session with his peers at age 7, Steven exhibited many of the same behaviors he did when he was 4. He again was among the quieter group members who watched his peers often. Steven did, however, laugh along with the other children in many instances. Interestingly, Steven was highly aware that the free-play session was being videotaped. He informed his peers that there was a one-way mirror in the room and pointed out the microphone to them as well.

During Steven's interview, he presented the image of a thoughtful child who offered detailed, self-reflective answers. He indicated that he shared personality traits with both the uninhibited and inhibited 2-year-old children. He asserted, "When I saw new people I was more like Brock, but when I saw new things I was more like Sam."

Like Jill, Steven voiced strong negative sentiments concerning his own inhibition. When asked how he felt while watching himself, he told his experimenter that he could not answer that question without saying a bad word but said that it was "close to mad." He later told her, "I did not like how unintelligent I was acting."

When asked to comment on how he had changed since he was 2, he offered a sophisticated response that involved an analysis of his traits, behaviors, and experiences. He explained, "I know that I changed more than I stayed the same. I'm braver now and I'm used to things." When asked if anything else had changed, he said, "I treat animals different, I don't tell lies anymore, and I'm used to meeting new people."

Group 4: Inhibited at 2 Years and 7 Years

Six children were categorized as in Group 4, 4 males (25% of the male subjects) and 2 females (10% of the female subjects).

Paul R. was highly representative of the inhibited children in the study. At 2, he cried and climbed into his mother's lap when the clown and the unfamiliar experimenter with the robot entered the room. When alone with his mother, he played with the toys in the room. When she left the room, his concern about being alone was made clear through his actions. He did not cry, but shouted out for his mother about 10 times. He also tried to leave the room to find her by bringing a chair over to the door in order to reach the knob.

At 4, Paul demonstrated great difficulty in remaining in the room with his peers. Although he played with the other children, he asked his experimenter several times when he could go see his mother. He participated in some of the activities that the experimenter led, but during other activities he told her, "I'm just gonna watch." When asked to speak in front of his peers he complied, but was very quiet and was requested by two of his peers to speak louder.

During the free-play session with his peers at 7 years of age, Paul primarily played either with one other peer or alone. He spoke in a quiet tone of voice, but did converse with his peers in many instances. Paul initially expressed hesitancy about participating in each new activity that was introduced by offering such statements as, "I don't feel well," but eventually joined each one.

Paul seemed to allow his peers to dictate his role in several of the games. For example, he did not resist when a peer told him that he had to go last. In one telling instance, while Paul was sitting alone playing with a toy, he said to his peers, "Raise your hand if you're my friend."

Like the other inhibited children, Paul did not use the word shy while participating in his interview session, either to describe himself or the toddlers in the videotapes. He did, however, express embarrassment when asked about his emotions while watching the tape of himself. Paul's reaction when he was informed that he and the experimenter would watch the videotape of himself was highly indicative of the embarrassment he was feeling. He asked her if anyone else had seen the videotape and then requested that she close her eyes while he was viewing it.

Before watching the videotape of himself, Paul expressed little identification with the inhibited toddler aside from, "I am sometimes like Brock when they won't let me play." He did, however, acknowledge that he more closely resembled Brock after watching the tape.

In general, Paul offered brief responses to the interview questions. He also joked with his experimenter about "sneaking out" of the room so as to end the interview session early. Paul did not directly answer the question about what factors contributed to changes in his personality since he was 2, but did share some personal information with his experimenter such as, "I was a mischievous 2-year-old and now I am a mischievous 7-year-old."

SUMMARY

A number of striking issues emerged from the interviews with the children in our study. First, it was apparent that, at least for some children, there was a clear recognition of their personal self and the changes that they have gone through. This was most apparent from the interviews with the children who changed in personal style over the period of study. Interestingly, there was a high degree of self-reflection in the children who changed. This included those who at age 2 were inhibited and were at age 7 no longer so, as well as those children who were not inhibited at age 2 and were at age 7, reticent in their behavior during the peer session. Children who remained either inhibited/reticent across the 5-year span or were not inhibited at either age were less reflective about their personal selves.

The second issue to emerge across all four groups of children was their ability to understand and characterize the affective and social consequences of social withdrawal and shyness. All four groups of children associated shyness and withdrawal with negative affect or negative mood state. Children who were in the change group (either direction) in addition, framed these affective states around self-conscious emotions (embarrassment, shame), whereas children who remained stable in trait over time (either inhibited or not) were more likely to describe these states in nonself oriented emotions (fear, scared).

There were interesting differences in the reflective descriptions of the children who changed over the study period. The children who were inhibited at age 2 and were now uninhibited provided explanations of that change in their behavior. Many of the responses suggested that this change in their personal selves occurred as a function of parental caregiving behavior. For example, children reported that parents often slowly introduced their child to novel and mildly stressful events, providing them with the opportunity to experience these events within safe environments. This systematic desensitization seemed particularly successful for the inhibited toddlers. On the other hand, children who at age 2 had not seemed inhibited but who were now shy were more self-critical about their behavior than any of the other children. Their behavior seemed particularly associated with self-presentation within the social group.

The emergence of this self-conscious shyness among a group of children who were not necessarily inhibited as toddlers raises the issue first addressed by Buss (1984) in his dual theory of shyness. Buss proposed that there are two main forms of shyness: fearful shyness and self-conscious shyness. He maintained that fearful shyness, characterized by wariness and stranger anxiety, appears early in life, and that self-conscious shyness, discernable by feeling "conspicuous and psychologically unprotected," emerges later (Buss, 1984). Crozier and Burnham (1990) suggested that the development of self-conscious shyness does not displace fearful shyness, but rather, emerges independently in the elementary school years. Thus, an older child can manifest both forms of the trait. Alternatively, self-conscious shyness could emerge as an outgrowth of fearful shyness exhibited during the infancy period. The fact that we identified a group of children who were not fearfully shy as toddlers but were self-consciously shy as elementary school children would argue that the two forms of shyness may be independent, at least in some individuals.

There are far too few studies that ask children to reflect on their social and emotional behaviors. In contrast, the study of theory of mind has seen a resurgence recently in an attempt to gain access to the reasoning strategies of children about the manner in which they solve problems. The current study might serve as an example of the means by which children's theory of mind regarding their personal selves may be explored. It may help produce an understanding of the manners in which the continuities and discontinuities in their social lives occur and are perceived by children during the developmental process.

ACKNOWLEDGMENT

The research reported on in this chapter was funded by a grant from the National Institutes of Health (HD#17899) to Nathan A. Fox.

REFERENCES

Buss, A. H. (1984). A conception of shyness. In J.A. Daly & J.C. McCroskey (Eds.), *Avoiding communication: Shyness, reticence and communication apprehension.* London: Sage.

Cooley, C. H. (1962). *Social organization: A study of the larger mind.* New York: Schocken. (Original work published 1909)

Coplan, R. J., Rubin, K. H., Fox, N. A., Calkins, S. D., & Stewart, S. (1994). Being alone, playing alone and acting alone: Distinguishing reticence and passive and active solitude in young children. *Child Development, 65,* 129–137.

Crozier, W. R., & Burnham, M. (1990). Age-related differences in children's understanding of shyness. *British Journal of Developmental Psychology, 8,* 179–185.

Eder, R. A. (1989). The emergent personologist: The structure and content of 3 1/2-, 5 1/2-, and 7 1/2-year olds' concepts of themselves and other persons. *Child Development, 60,* 1218–1228.

Eder, R. A. (1990). Uncovering young children's psychological selves: Individual and developmental differences. *Child Development, 60,* 849–863.

Guardo, C. J., & Bohan, J.B. (1971) Development of sense of self-identity in children. *Child Development, 42,* 1909–1921.

Harter, S. (1983). Developmental perspectives on the self-system. In P.H. Mussen (Series Ed.) & E. M. Hetherington (Vol. Ed.), *Handbook of child psychology 4: Vol. 4. Socialization, personality, and social development* (4th ed.). New York: Wiley.

Hymel, S., Franke, S., & Friegang, R. (1985). Peer relationships and their dysfunction: Considering the child's perspective. *Journal of Social and Clinical Psychology, 3*(4), 405–415.

Kagan, J., Reznick, J. S., Snidman, N., Gibbons, J., & Johnson, M. (1988). Childhood derivatives of inhibition and lack of inhibition to the unfamiliar. *Child Development, 59,* 1580–1589.

Lewis, M. (1992). *Shame: The exposed self.* New York: The Free Press.

Mahler, M. S., Pine, F., & Bergman, A. (1975). *The psychological birth of the infant.* New York: Basic Books.

Mead, G. H. (1972). *Mind, self, and society.* Chicago: University of Chicago Press. (Original work published 1934)

Miller, P. H., & Aloise, P. A. (1989). Young children's understanding of the psychological causes of behavior: A review. *Child Development, 60,* 257–285.

Moskowitz, D. S., & Schwartzman, A. E. (1989). Painting group portraits: Studying life outcomes for aggressive and withdrawn children. *Journal of Personality, 57*(4), 723–743.

Perry, D. G., & Bussey, K. (1984). *Social development.* Englewood Cliffs, NJ: Prentice-Hall.

Piaget, J. (1954). *The construction of reality in the child* (M. Cook, Trans.). New York: Basic Books. (Original work published 1937)

Rholes, W. S., & Ruble, D. N. (1984). Children's understanding of dispositional characteristics of others. *Child Development, 55,* 550–560.

Rosenberg, M. (1979). *Conceiving the self.* New York: Basic Books.

Ross, M. (1989). Relation of implicit theories to the construction of personal histories. *Psychological Review, 96,* 341–357.

Rubin, K. H. (1985). Socially withdrawn children: An "at risk" population? In B. Schneider, K. H. Rubin, & J. Ledingham (Eds.), *Children's peer relationships: Issues in assessment and intervention* (pp. 125–140). New York: Springer-Verlag.

Rubin, K. H. (1989). *The play observation scale.* Waterloo, Ontario: University of Waterloo.

Rubin, K. H., & Lollis, S. P. (1988). Origins and consequences of social withdrawal. In J. Belsky & T. Nezworski (Eds.), *Clinical implications of attachment* (pp. 219–253). Hillsdale, NJ: Lawrence Erlbaum Associates.

Attributional Beliefs of Persons With Mild Mental Retardation

Lisa A. Turner

University of South Alabama

For some time, research in the area of mental retardation (MR) has focused on cognitive deficits. These deficits, as measured by IQ, are one of the defining features of MR. Numerous studies have identified the cognitive deficits (e.g., Ellis, 1970), developed procedures to remediate them (e.g., Brown & Barclay, 1976), and suggested methods to promote generalization of newly trained skills (e.g., Turner, Dofny, & Dutka, 1994). Although this focus on cognitive skills has been fruitful, the larger social and emotional experience of persons with MR has often been ignored. If the question, "Do we want smart kids or happy kids?" was asked, a review of the research literature would imply that we are most interested in smart kids.

However, recently, it has become clear that a child's cognitive skills are not independent of his or her social and emotional experience. An influential link between cognition and emotion is an individual's beliefs about the self. A person's belief in his or her ability to impact outcomes influences cognitive activities such as task selection (Elliot & Dweck, 1988), strategy use (Turner, Dofny, & Dutka, 1994), and persistence (Andrews & Debus, 1978). These attributional beliefs also influence the self-conscious evaluate emotions of pride and shame (Lewis, 1993). An individual who experiences success and attributes that success to factors within his or her control will experience pride. However, if success is attributed to factors outside of the individual, pride will not be the resultant emotion.

Although attributional beliefs are an influential factor in cognition and emotion, there have been few theoretical attempts to integrate these constructs in the study of persons with MR. One exception is a metacognitive model developed by Borkowski and colleagues that integrates attributions and cognition.

METACOGNITIVE MODEL

The metacognitive model developed by Pressley, Borkowski, and O'Sullivan (1985) and Borkowski, Johnston, and Reid (1986) describes strategic behavior as dependent on cognitive strategies, executive processes, and motivation. The model includes three interrelated components. The first is specific strategy knowledge, which refers to the individual cognitive strategies that each child has available in his or her repertoire for use. Metamemory acquisition procedures include the higher level skills used to detect and fill in missing information in a cognitive situation. Regulatory skills important for monitoring, evaluating, and revising strategies are also included in metamemory acquisition procedures. Finally the component that is central to the work discussed here is general strategy knowledge, which includes the motivation and beliefs that may influence a child's decision to behave strategically.

Strategies are effortful behaviors, therefore the child's belief in the effectiveness of his or her efforts is important for strategy use. Children who believe that effort is important and that their efforts are effective are likely to engage in activities that are strategic. In addition, they are likely to select tasks or to be assigned tasks that will lead to more knowledge about strategic activities.

Borkowski et al. (1986) suggested that when faced with a difficult problem, a child relies on his or her beliefs about the workings of the world (e.g., "When I work hard, things go well"; "When I work hard, it does not make a difference"). This concept has been supported by research with normally developing children. Kurtz and Borkowski (1984) found that the maintenance and transfer of trained strategies was correlated with effort-related attributional beliefs. Other investigators have reported the relation of attributions and self-efficacy to achievement-related behaviors. Elliot and Dweck (1988) found that children who thought they had the ability to perform a task were likely to engage in mastery-oriented behaviors such as persistence. Similarly, children who believed that intelligence was something that changes and can be developed through effort engaged in more achievement-related behaviors (Cain & Dweck, 1989).

MOTIVATIONAL BELIEFS OF PERSONS WITH MR

In comparison to the wealth of research on motivational beliefs of students without retardation, there is relatively little corresponding information on students with MR. Because of the combined experiential and developmental factors that form motivational beliefs, it cannot be assumed that the motivational beliefs of students with retardation are the same as either children without retardation of the same chronological age or the same mental age. For example, a 12-year-old student with a mental age of 6 years, who has been in school for 6 years has had more opportunity for failure and feedback than the normally developing child of the same mental age who is just beginning school. Children with and without retardation of the same chronological age are also likely to differ in ways that influence motivational beliefs. For example, the cognitive skills used to evaluate one's efforts and related performance are likely to differ between a 12-year-old with retardation and a 12-year-old without retardation. Therefore, one cannot assume that the research on motivational beliefs of students without MR generalizes completely to persons with MR.

The research on motivational beliefs among students with MR includes several studies on attributional beliefs. For some time, researchers interested in MR have suggested that these attributional beliefs and/or locus of control are likely related to achievement behaviors (Cromwell, 1963; Hale & Borkowski, 1991; Zigler, 1969).

Attributional Beliefs

The study of attributional beliefs can be traced to the locus of control literature (e.g., Rotter, 1966). Persons with an internal locus of control believe that outcomes are due to factors within the persons such as effort or ability. In contrast, external locus of control refers to the belief that forces outside of the individual control outcomes. Individuals who attribute success to internal sources have been reported to engage in achievement-oriented behaviors more frequently than their peers with an external locus of control (Rotter, 1966).

In a comparison of 14-year-olds with MR, students with learning disabilities, and students identified as at risk for school failure, Wehmeyer (1994) found that locus of control was more external for the students with retardation than for students at risk for school failure. These external beliefs did not appear to dissipate with time. Locus of control was investigated cross-sectionally from ages 13 to 18 and was found to remain stable. Wehmeyer suggested that external beliefs undermined the individual's self-determination in adulthood.

Attributing outcomes to external factors may be an adaptive, self-preserving mechanism in the case of failure. For instance, if a child is prevented from completing a task, it is adaptive to attribute that failure to the force that intervened and interrupted work on the task. However, persons with MR appear to often attribute failure to themselves. MacMillan (1969) reported that when prevented from completing a task, students with MR blamed themselves in contrast to students without MR who attributed the outcome to external causes. Similarly, Chan and Keogh (1974) reported that males with retardation were likely to attribute success to external causes and failure to internal causes. It appears that persons with retardation, rather than developing a protective bias, develop a bias that undermines self-confidence.

Further delineation of the locus of control construct was made by Weiner (1985) who determined that causal factors varied along three dimensions: stability (stable/unstable), controllability (controllable/uncontrollable), and locus (internal/external). For example, the internal characteristics of effort and ability differ in that ability is often seen as stable and uncontrollable, whereas effort is viewed as controllable and unstable. An individual who attributes failure to ability would have little hope of performing better in the future. Yet, if failure is attributed to a lack of effort the reasonable course of action would be to try harder to perform better in the future.

In an attempt to determine the attributional beliefs of 10-year-olds with mild MR, Turner, Hale, and Borkowski (1993) asked children to identify the likely causes of academic outcomes such as performing well (or poorly) in math and spelling. Students with MR were less likely to attribute success to effort than were their peers without MR. In failure situations, students with MR were more likely to attribute failure to ability and less likely to attribute failure to luck than were their peers without MR.

The tendency to attribute failure to ability is likely to undermine efforts to perform well. Ability is usually seen as an enduring, stable characteristic of the self. Therefore, failure would be expected to reoccur and to be outside of the control of the individual. Clearly, these beliefs are likely to result in maladaptive behaviors.

The data reviewed to this point indicate that students with MR report relatively negative attributional beliefs. If these students perceive ability as uncontrollable, then they see their behaviors as having little impact in academic situations.

Attributional Beliefs and Beliefs About Control

The assumption that students with retardation view effort as within their control and ability as outside of their control deserves consideration. Nicholls (1978) demonstrated that young students without MR focus on effort as the primary cause of ability and of outcomes. That is, they reported that if someone tries hard that person is also smart and will perform well. This failure to differentiate effort and ability suggests that young children view ability as somewhat within their control. Nicholls (1990) suggested that students with this level of reasoning will be less impaired (than those who differentiate effort and ability) by information that indicates they are low in ability. According to Nicholls, it is when ability is differentiated from effort and is seen as capacity that we will "have less faith in the power of effort to raise our performance relative to others" (p. 26).

In an effort to determine if students with retardation perceived ability and intelligence as within their control, Hale, Turner, and Borkowski (1989) measured theories of intelligence among 10-year-olds with and without MR. According to Cain and Dweck (1989), children without MR differ in their theories of intelligence. Those with an incremental view of intelligence report that intelligence (smartness) increases with experience and effort. In contrast, those with an entity view report that intelligence is stable and cannot be altered through individual effort. Hale et al. found that students with MR were more likely to ascribe to an entity view of intelligence than were their peers without MR. It is likely that the belief that "smartness is stable" and cannot be increased through effort undermines the child's motivation to work hard in challenging situations.

Turner, Pickering, and Matherne (1994) also assessed control beliefs of persons with MR. Turner et al. administered the Students' Perception of Control Questionnaire (SPOCQ; Wellborn, Connell, & Skinner, 1989) to 11- and 17-year-old African Americans with MR and 11-year-old African Americans without MR. The SPOCQ is a unique attributional measure in that it does not assume that some characteristics are seen by the child as inherently controllable. Instead, the SPOCQ assesses the degree to which a child believes he or she has control over a given characteristic.

Three constructs are addressed in the 60-item questionnaire: control beliefs, strategy beliefs, and capacity beliefs. Control beliefs refer to one's ability to reach a desired goal (e.g., "I can do well in school, I can learn something hard when I want to"). These control beliefs are similar to self-efficacy (Bandura, 1989). Strategy beliefs refer to the means deemed necessary to reach a goal. Five strategies are included in the SPOCQ: effort, attributes (e.g., ability), luck, powerful others, unknown factors. Finally, capacity beliefs reflect the students' belief in their access to the strategies of effort, ability, luck, and powerful others. For example, a student may indicate that effort is very important for academic success (effort strategy) but report that he or she is unable to try hard (effort capacity). By assessing these three constructs—control, strategies, and capacity—a relatively complete picture of the child's beliefs can be portrayed.

The 11- and 17-year-old students with MR responded similarly on the SPOCQ but differed significantly from the 11-year-old students without MR. In comparison to the students without MR, the students with MR scored lower on control beliefs and rated the strategy of effort as less influential in academic outcomes. In contrast, the strategies of luck, powerful others, and unknown factors were rated as more influential by the students with MR in comparison to those without MR.

Capacity beliefs reflect the perceived access a student has to the identified strategies. Students with MR scored lower than their peers without MR on several capacity beliefs. The students with MR rated themselves as less capable of behaving effortfully, being smart, and being lucky.

It appears that students with MR have developed beliefs that are likely to undermine achievement-related behaviors. The intellectual challenges of these students may be especially difficult in light of these negative beliefs. If failures are perceived as uncontrollable, individual effort appears fruitless. This perception and the resultant passive behaviors and failures may result in outcomes that extend far beyond school failure. This cycle of experiences and beliefs is likely to result in painful emotional experiences, reduced self-esteem, and a reduced quality of life.

ATTRIBUTIONAL BELIEFS AND EMOTION

According to Lewis (1993), self-conscious evaluative emotions are linked to attributional beliefs. For example, attributing failure to an enduring characteristic of the self is likely to result in feelings of shame. Attributing this failure to a more specific (and controllable) aspect of the self is likely to result in guilt, but also direct a course of action that may be taken to relieve the guilt.

The self-conscious evaluative emotions of pride, shame, and guilt begin to emerge around 24 to 30 months of age (Lewis, 1993). These emotions are dependent on the child's evaluation of him or herself. It has been demonstrated that children as young as 2 to 3 years of age recognize and respond emotionally to failure (Lewis, Alessandri, & Sullivan, 1992; Stipek, Recchia, & McClintic, 1992). As children develop, the cognitive complexity of their self-evaluations is likely to increase. They will begin to consider a wider array of possible causes and the possibility of multiple causes.

Unfortunately, there is no research with mentally retarded persons that addresses the relationship of attributions and emotions. In fact, there is very little research focusing on the emotional life of mentally retarded persons. (See Whitman, O'Callaghan, & Sommer, in press, for a recent exception.) Until further information is gathered on attributions and emotions including persons with MR, one must rely on the evidence available from research on persons without retardation.

Numerous studies have obtained support for the link between emotions and attributions in samples without MR. Developmental research that required children to rate the controllability of a cause (attribution) and the intensity of an emotion indicated that the link between emotions and attributions emerged around age 5 to 6 and increased until 10 to 11 years of age (Graham, 1988).

Heyman, Dweck, and Cain (1992) found that a subset of 5- and 6-year-olds attributed criticism on a school task to internal characteristics of the self. These children concluded that they were not nice, good children. In turn, they experienced more sadness and anger, and less happiness than their peers who did not receive criticism. The children receiving criticism also rated their work more poorly than their peers. Apparently, these children evaluated themselves poorly and experienced related emotions.

In research with adults, Nurmi (1991) reported that undergraduate students who attributed success to internal factors such as effort and ability experienced more pride than those who attributed the success to external factors. Failure attributed to a lack of effort (an internal, controllable cause) resulted in shame and guilt. Similarly, Zaleski (1988) reported that among college students, internal attributions for successfully reaching goals were related to pride and internal attributions for failure were related to guilt and shame.

There is some evidence that females may be less likely to experience pride than males. Stipek and Gralinski (1991) reported that females were more likely than males to attribute success to external factors and were less likely than males to experience pride as a result of their accomplishments. The tendency to attribute success to factors beyond their control could have caused these females to devalue their achievement and therefore experience less pride and less sense of accomplishment. It is likely that this phenomena occurs with persons with MR to an even greater degree.

The research cited with persons without MR supports the relationship of attributions and emotions. Yet the question remains "What processes contribute to the experience of failure and the tendency to attribute failure to uncontrollable causes?" In the following section, possible developmental explanations for individual differences in attributional beliefs are considered.

DEVELOPMENT OF ATTRIBUTIONAL BELIEFS

It is likely that the processes that operate to produce a cycle of failure, negative attributions for failure, and related feelings of shame are the same for persons with and without MR. However, persons with MR are likely at greater risk of experiencing this negative cycle of failure because of both individual and social factors.

The cognitive deficits that many persons with MR experience are related to failure experiences in multiple domains. A child may fail to remember classroom information or to understand the rules of a game. In either case, if the child with MR is expected to perform similarly to his or her peers without retardation (without any support), failures may occur. Without a complete understanding of the cognitive demands of the situation and the effective means to achieve success, a child may quickly assume that his or her effort does not matter; failure appears inevitable and beyond his or her control.

There are many social factors that may contribute to the belief that outcomes are beyond one's control. Persons with MR may be the target of open discrimination and derogatory remarks (Jones, 1972) suggesting that they are unable to succeed. In a more subtle manner, the tendency to consistently prevent an individual from making choices and acting on those choices often suggests that the individual's choices and actions would be inappropriate and ineffective. If an individual without MR continually intervenes and acts on the part of the individual with MR, outcomes will likely be attributed to the power and activities of the person without MR.

Similarly, important persons in the environment may respond to an individual's efforts and related failures with pity, implying that the person is unable to succeed at the task in question (Graham, 1984). Weisz (1981) reported that adults tend to overextend the mental retardation label and use it to explain failures that are within the child's ability range and use the label to discount the role of effort.

The development of negative beliefs and painful emotional experiences is not inevitable. If expectations are matched to ability and effective means are made available to an individual, his or her efforts are likely to become very effective and successful. These successful experiences will likely result in internal attributions and feelings of pride.

However, success experiences are probably not sufficient to change negative attributional beliefs once these beliefs are in place. Diener and Dweck (1980) reported that persons with learned helplessness underestimate their successes and attribute success to external factors. To change a negative attributional system, success must be paired with the understanding that the success is under the individual's control. For example, Turner, Dofny, and Dutka (1994) reported that students with mild MR generalized an effective strategy only when strategy training was paired with attributional information. Students who received strategy training in isolation abandoned the effective strategy. It is likely that the successful strategy was not considered to be controllable by the individual. Neither attributional training nor cognitive training appears to be optimally successful in isolation; persons with mental retardation need to experience success and understand that success is within their control.

IMPLICATIONS FOR MILD MR

As one begins to consider research on cognitive activities, attributional beliefs, and emotional experience, it becomes clear that these constructs are inextricably related in the life of a child with mild MR. This interrelationship is reflected in the American Association on Mental Retardation's new definition of MR (Luckasson et al., 1992), which includes deficits in self-direction as a characteristic of MR. Self-direction includes the cognitive skills to identify choices and make decisions, and the attributional belief system to empower one to risk making decisions rather than relying on others. It appears that the attributional beliefs of persons with retardation are not empowering. The tendency of persons with retardation to attribute success to factors outside of their control and failures to a lack of ability undermines self-direction and promotes dependency (Wehmeyer, 1994).

To promote self-direction and optimal development, persons with MR must develop necessary cognitive skills and understand that those skills are within their control. Successes would then be attributed to the self and result in feelings of pride and accomplishment. This approach requires an acknowledgment and understanding of the interrelationships of attributions, cognition, and emotion.

REFERENCES

Andrews, G. R., & Debus, R. L. (1978). Persistence and the casual perception of failure: Modifying cognitive attributions. *Journal of Educational Psychology, 70,* 154–166.

Bandura, A. (1989). Regulation of cognitive processes through perceived self-efficacy. *Developmental Psychology, 25*(5), 729–735.

Borkowski, J. G., & Dukewich, T. L. (1994, March). *Environmental covariations and intelligence: How attachment influences self-regulation.* Paper presented at the Gatlinburg Conference on Mental Retardation, Gatlinburg, TN.

Borkowski, J. G., Johnston, M. B., & Reid, M. K. (1986). Metacognition, motivation, and the transfer of control processes. In S. J. Ceci (Ed.), *Handbook of cognitive, social, and neuropsychological aspects of learning disabilities* (pp. 147–173). Hillsdale, NJ: Lawrence Erlbaum Associates.

Brown, A. L., & Barclay, C. R. (1976). The effects of training specific mnemonics on the metamnemonic efficiency of retarded children. *Child Development, 47,* 71–80.

Cain, K. M., & Dweck, C. S. (1989). The development of children's conceptions of intelligence: A theoretical framework. In R. J. Sternberg (Ed.), *Advances in the psychology of human intelligence* (pp. 47–82). Hillsdale, NJ: Lawrence Erlbaum Associates.

Chan, K. S., & Keogh, B. K. (1974). Interpretation of task interruption and feelings of responsibility for failure. *Journal of Special Education, 8*(2), 175–178.

Cromwell, R. L. (1963). A social learning approach to mental retardation. In N. R. Ellis (Ed.), *Handbook of mental deficiency* (pp. 41–91). New York: McGraw-Hill.

Diener, C. I., & Dweck, C. S. (1980). An analysis of learned helplessness: II. The processing of success. *Journal of Personality and Social Psychology, 39*, 940–952.

Elliot, E. S., & Dweck, C. S. (1988). Goals: An approach to motivation and achievement. *Journal of Personality and Social Psychology, 54*, 5–12.

Ellis, N. R. (1970). Memory processes in retardates and normals. In N. R. Ellis (Ed.), *International review of research in mental retardation* (Vol. 4, pp. 1–32). New York: Academic Press.

Graham, S. (1984). Communicating sympathy and anger to black and white students: The cognitive (attributional) consequences of affective cues. *Journal of Personality and Social Psychology, 47*, 40–54.

Graham, S. (1988). Children's developing understanding of the motivational role of affect: An attributional analysis. *Cognitive Development, 3*, 71–88.

Hale, C. A., & Borkowski, J. G. (1991). Attention, memory, and cognition. In J. L. Matson & J. A. Mulick (Eds.), *Handbook of mental retardation* (2nd ed., pp. 505–528). New York: Pergamon Press.

Hale, C. A., Turner, L. A., & Borkowski, J. G. (1989, March). *Attributional beliefs in mildly retarded adolescents.* Paper presented at the Gatlinburg Conference on Mental Retardation, Gatlinburg, TN.

Heyman, G. D., Dweck, C. S., & Cain, K. M. (1992). Young children's vulnerability to self-blame and helplessness: Relationship to beliefs about goodness. *Child Development, 63*, 401–415.

Jones, R. L. (1972). Labels and stigma in special education. *Exceptional Children, 38*, 553–564.

Kurtz, B. E., & Borkowski, J. G. (1984). Children's metacognition: Exploring relations among knowledge, process, and motivational variables. *Journal of Experimental Child Psychology, 37*, 335–354.

Lewis, M. (1992). The self in self-conscious emotions. In D. Stipek, S. Recchia, & S. McClintic (Eds.), Self-regulation in young children. *Monographs of the Society for Research in Child Development, 57*(1), (Serial No. 226).

Lewis, M. (1993). Self-conscious emotions: Embarrassment, pride, shame, and guilt. In M. Lewis & J. M. Haviland (Ed.), *Handbook of emotions* (pp. 563–573). New York: Guilford.

Lewis, M., Alessandri, S. M., & Sullivan, M. W. (1992). Differences in shame and pride as a function of children's gender and task difficulty. *Child Development, 63*(3), 630–638.

Luckasson, R., Coulter, D. L., Polloway, E. A., Reiss, S., Schalock, R. L., Snell, M. E., Spitalnik, D. M., & Stark, J. A. (1992). *Mental retardation: Definition, classification, and system of supports.* Washington, DC: American Association on Mental Retardation.

MacMillan, D. L. (1969). Motivational differences: Cultural-familial retardates vs. normal subjects on expectancy for failure. *American Journal of Mental Deficiency, 74*(2), 254–258.

Nicholls, J. G. (1978). The development of the concepts of effort and ability, perception of own attainment, and the understanding that difficult tasks require more ability. *Child Development, 49*, 800–814.

Nicholls, J. G. (1990). What is ability and why are we mindful of it? A developmental perspective. In R. J. Sternberg & J. Kolligan (Eds.), *Competence considered* (pp. 11–40). New Haven, CT: Yale University Press.

Nurmi, J. E. (1991). The effect of others' influence, effort, and ability attributions on emotions in achievement and affiliative situations. *The Journal of Social Psychology, 131*(5), 703–715.

Pressley, M., Borkowski, J. G., & O'Sullivan, J. T. (1985). Children's metamemory and the teaching of memory strategies. In D. L. Forrest-Pressley, G. E. MacKinnon, & T. G. Waller (Eds.), *Metacognition, cognition, and human performance* (Vol. 1, pp. 111–153). New York: Academic Press.

Rotter, J. B. (1966). Generalized expectancies for internal versus external control of reinforcement. *Psychological Monographs, 80* (1, Whole No. 609).

Stipek, D. J., & Gralinski, J. H. (1991). Gender differences in children's achievement-related beliefs and emotional responses to success and failure in mathematics. *Journal of Educational Psychology, 83*(3), 361–371.

Stipek, D., Recchia, S., & McClintic, S. (1992). Self-evaluation in young children. *Monographs of the Society for Research in Child Development, 57*(1), (Serial No. 226)

Turner, L. A., Dofny, E. M., & Dutka, S. (1994). Effect of strategy and attribution training on strategy maintenance and transfer. *American Journal on Mental Retardation, 98*(4), 445–454.

Turner, L. A., Hale, C. A., & Borkowski, J. G. (1993). *Components of memory performance in children as a function of intelligence.* Unpublished manuscript.

Turner, L. A., Pickering, S., & Matherne, J. L. (1994, March). *Attributional beliefs of students with and without mental retardation.* Paper presented at the Gatlinburg Conference on Research in Mental Retardation, Gatlinburg, TN.

Wehmeyer, M. L. (1994). Perceptions of self-determination and psychological empowerment of adolescents with mental retardation. *Education and Training in Mental Retardation and Developmental Disabilities,* 9–21.

Weiner, B. (1985). An attributional theory of achievement motivation and emotion. *Psychological Review, 92*(4), 548–573.

Weisz, J. R. (1981). Effects of the "mentally retarded" label on adult judgments about child failure. *Journal of Abnormal Psychology, 90,* 371–374.

Wellborn, J. G., Connell, J. P., & Skinner, E. (1989). *Students' Perception of Control Questionnaire.* Rochester, NY: University of Rochester.

Whitman, T. L., O'Callaghan, M., & Sommer, K. (in press). Emotion and mental retardation. In W. McLean (Ed.), *Handbook of mental deficiency: Psychological theory and research* (3rd ed.). Hillsdale, NJ: Lawrence Erlbaum Associates.

Zaleski, Z. (1988). Attributions and emotions related to future goal attainment. *Journal of Educational Psychology, 80*(4), 563–568.

Zigler, E. (1969). Developmental versus difference theories of mental retardation and the problem of motivation. *American Journal of Mental Deficiency, 73,* 536–556.

Emotional Competence in Children With Externalizing and Internalizing Disorders

Rita J. Casey
Wayne State University

Children who manifest psychopathology are commonly spoken of as having "emotional problems" or as being "emotionally disturbed." Theoretical work linking psychopathology to emotion processes as well as clinical observation of expressive behavior also suggest that emotion has an important role in childhood psychopathology. For example, anger, resentment, sadness, and fear can be diagnostic markers of different psychiatric disorders (American Psychiatric Association, 1994). Nevertheless, little clinical research has explicitly focused on emotional characteristics of children with psychiatric disorders, or on how emotional aspects of development are involved in childhood psychopathology. Perhaps this is because some clinicians believe that the emotions expressed by children who have psychiatric disorders are not central to their difficulties, or that there are no discernible patterns in emotion processes that would provide insight into the children's psychopathology. Others suggest that the role of emotion goes well beyond being an expressive sign of difficulty (e.g., Cicchetti & Schneider-Rosen, 1984; Cole, Michel, & Teti, 1994; Gray, 1987). Rather, they see emotion processes as fundamental aspects of certain kinds of psychopathology .

Outside the arena of clinical research, particularly in the study of human and infrahuman development, there has arisen a rich literature examining individual differences as well as normal characteristics of emotional development. This body of work may have clear implications for clinical research, even though developmental researchers do not typically focus on clinical populations. To cite just one example, Eisenberg's empirical and theoretical work on emotion and self-regulation in children could easily be used to inform the study of disruptive behavior disorders in children (e.g., Eisenberg & Fabes, 1992).

The purpose of this chapter is to set forth a preliminary model linking emotion processes to some common forms of childhood psychopathology, and to present some findings that are consistent with such a model. In brief, I propose that children with certain internalizing and externalizing disorders manifest characteristic patterns in several aspects of their emotional functioning that differentiate them from normal children. Of course, it is not necessarily unusual or noteworthy to find that behavior-disordered children differ from nondisordered children. Such differences are common in a variety of domains, including academic performance, and social behavior. However, there is evidence to suggest that there may be characteristic of the emotional function of children with clinical disorders that involve systematic patterning according to type of psychopathology, rather than simple differences from nondisordered children.

The theoretical context for this working model is an integration of bioevolutionary and social constructivist theories about emotion development, in which the social context and history of the child serve to organize and mediate the child's use of biologically based expressive and receptive emotion systems. These emotion systems are seen in children's expressive behavior, in their appraisal of emotion, and in their regulation of emotion, aspects of emotion that are similar to what Salovey and Mayer (1990) called *emotion skills* or *emotional intelligence.* Saarni (1990), speaking from a developmental perspective, provided a more detailed description of a similar set of skills that she called *emotional competencies.* These include several aspects of emotion expression and understanding as well as management of internal emotion experience and expressive behavior. Competency in emotion expression includes socially and culturally appropriate and accurate use of patterns of facial expression; vocal qualities that convey emotion, such as pitch, rhythm, and prosody of sound; emotion words and phraseology; and other nonverbal behavior that communicates emotion, including gestures, movement, and posture. Competence in appraisal includes recognition and understanding of bodily expression as well as internal experience of one's own as well as other's emotions, and accurate appraisal of emotionally relevant aspects of the social context. Regulation of emotion involves the most complex set of competencies, a partial list might include management of emotion expression in oneself and in others; management of internal emotion states, and use of emotion in planning and executing plans.

These skills or competencies are not separate but, rather, interrelated. Their relations are hierarchical (Fischer, 1980), in that acquisition of skills in emotion expression and appraisal may precede competency in some forms of emotion regulation. They also develop laterally in that expression, appraisal, and regulation of simple emotions, in familiar social contexts, occurs before more complex emotions, emerging in more ambiguous or unfamiliar social situations, can be regulated.

In this view, a child's immediate social context elicits emotion appraisal and expression that can help the child manage his or her emotional response to the situation. This management includes the modulation of emotion expression and internal feelings, but also extends to guidance of cognitive processes and behavioral action tendencies appropriate to the situation (Campos, Campos, & Barrett, 1989). For example, a child's initial appraisal of his or her social context can include identification of emotion signals in the environment, such as positive and negative stimuli, and expressive behavior of others, as well as his or her own emotions and emotion signals. The child's initial expressive response may be nearly automatic, such as matching another person's emotion expression. In addition, a child's expression may reflect more subtle influences that are cognitively mediated. Deliberate suppression of display or maintenance of a nonthreatening display may reflect the child's understanding of her emotions within the situation. For instance, one child in explaining why she might not respond to praise with a smile, said, "I'm not sure if she's teasing me or saying something nice—I better not show how I feel until I'm sure." Such managed expression may assist the child by providing controlled emotion cues to others in the situation or allowing time for the child to make further appraisal of the situation. In this fashion, children's initial appraisal, expression, and understanding of emotion serve adaptive functions, guiding children's interpretation and responses to social interactions.

Children who are high in emotional competence are aware of their own and other's emotion, express emotion appropriately, and can control their emotions during social and cognitive tasks in ways that facilitate performance on those tasks. Therefore, children's strengths and weaknesses in emotion competencies should predict their success in social interactions and in other arenas, such as school performance, particularly when those circumstances require management of emotions and/or good social relations. I propose that certain psychological disorders that emerge during childhood are characterized by particular patterns of emotional competence. The disorders in which emotion skills are likely to be most important are those having a strong affective component. Externalizing disorders, such as disruptive behavior disorders, which often involve difficulties with anger, irritability, and a lack of positive affiliation with other people, are one example. Internalizing disorders, particularly depression and anxiety that are defined in part by the presence of specific kinds of affective behavior, are clearly another example. Such disorders, involving deficits in inhibition of aggression and excess of internally focused sadness or guilt, have been posited to be at their core disturbances of emotion regulation. Children with these serious problems may demonstrate inadequate or dysfunctional use of their emotion skills. Weaknesses in emotional competence, in turn, may be responsible in part for the complex behavior problems observed in these children, such as poor relations with peers, teachers, and parents.

In the adult clinical literature, many recent studies have focused on emotion processes in persons with psychiatric disorders or symptoms. These include several disorders or types of symptoms and many aspects of emotion, ranging from examination of expressed emotion in schizophrenia (e.g., Mueser et al., 1993) to emotion recognition in depression (e.g., Persad & Polivy, 1993). Little is known, however, about emotion appraisal, emotion expression, and regulation of emotion in clinically disordered children. P. Cole et al. (1994) suggested that when dysregulation of emotion becomes a characteristic style for children, that they are at risk for psychopathology. Selman (1976) proposed that aggressive behavior seen in disturbed children is a reflection of general developmental delay in understanding of interpersonal relationships, including the emotions that children and their peers exhibit. If this is true, externalizing children, relative to normal children, would demonstrate gross deficiencies in many of their emotion skills.

Most studies of emotional characteristics of behavior-disordered children have examined emotion expression or appraisal rather than general deficiencies in emotional competence. For example, Zabel (1979) compared accuracy of emotion recognition in normal and emotionally disturbed elementary and junior high children. Although a majority of the emotional disturbed children (a mixture of externalizing and socially withdrawn students) could correctly recognize six basic emotion expressions, they performed consistently worse than the other students. Walker (1981) reported that a mixed group of clinically diagnosed children were deficient at recognition of emotions. Taylor and Harris (1983) found that boys attending schools for maladjusted children were essentially the same as other boys in their knowledge about ways in which emotions influenced memory. However, the maladjusted group demonstrated less understanding of display rules. Another study found emotion expression or appraisal weaknesses in children with depression (Altmann & Gotlib, 1988). Finally, children with learning disabilities have been found to have some weakness in emotion-related tasks (Loveland, Fletcher, & Bailey, 1990; Rourke, 1988).

Perhaps the most extensive attention to emotional development and specific forms of psychopathology has focused on autistic children. Several studies have found that autistic persons have difficulties or deficiencies in some aspects of emotion. For example, autistic children have been found to be deficient in expressing or imitating emotion, compared to children with Down syndrome or nondisordered children (Loveland et al., 1994; Yirmiya, Kasari, Sigman, & Mundy, 1989) and less likely to use positive expression contingently (Dawson, Hill, Spencer, Galpert, & Watson, 1988; Snow,

Hertzig, & Shapiro, 1987). Autistic children have difficulty appraising emotion expressions in others and in using emotion in communication with others (Hobson, Ouston, & Lee, 1988; Loveland et al., 1994; Snow et al., 1987; Weeks & Hobson, 1987).

With the exception of the studies of autistic children, much of the existing literature fails to specify the kinds of disturbances manifested by potential subjects. There is little or no research examining emotion skills in children with the more common forms of childhood disorders, such as attention deficit hyperactivity disorder (ADHD), oppositional defiant disorder (ODD), or depression, even though these disorders include emotional behavior as diagnostic markers. In addition, many studies focus only on a few aspects of emotion, which does not permit the examination of patterns in emotional competence.

In contrast, this chapter includes research findings obtained from four studies in which my students and I explored several aspects of the emotional behavior of children ages 6 through 14 who were diagnosed with one or more common childhood behavior disorders. Although these projects were not originally intended to produce or test a model linking emotional competence and psychopathology, the emotion skills examined in these studies are consistent with that idea. Rather than detailing each of these studies and their overall findings, the focus here is on what data they present that deal with emotion expression, appraisal, and regulation among specific diagnostic groups of children. Finally, some conclusions and recommendations are suggested concerning emotional competence and childhood psychopathology.

METHOD

Subjects

Children in these four studies were recruited through a common set of procedures. A general invitation was issued to parents of all public school children in two southeastern counties in Iowa, to participate in a subject registry for research in developmental psychology. More than 500 children in this registry were identified for further participation as being high or low in behavior problems on the basis of Child Behavior Checklist (CBCL; Achenbach & Edelbrock, 1983) responses obtained from their parents. *High* was defined as being at or above the 90th percentile in Externalizing or Internalizing subscales, whereas *low* was identified as being at or below the 60th percentile on these same subscales. Children identified as high or low were invited to participate for further screening in the form of diagnostic interviews with the parents, according to the requirements of the particular study. All of the diagnoses were obtained or ruled out based on structured parental interviews adapted from the K-SADS (Orvaschel & Puig-Antich, 1987) to meet *DSM–III–R* diagnostic criteria for childhood behavior disorders (American Psychiatric Association, 1987). Interviews were conducted by advanced graduate students in clinical psychology who were trained in administering diagnostic interviews. Reliability was obtained by having one third of the interviews audited by a second trained interviewer; kappas for diagnoses ranged from .68 to 1.00, *M* = .87. Diagnostic interviewers were unaware of what specific study the children were participating in, and all experimenters within the studies were blind to the diagnostic status of the subjects.

None of the children bearing a diagnosis had ever been hospitalized for their problems; indeed, only about 20% of the diagnosed children had been or were receiving treatment for their problems at the time they served as subjects. In most cases where children were not in treatment, parents were aware that their child had problems, but they had not necessarily known how to describe their child's difficulties, or they were not sure whether and how to seek treatment. Therefore, although clinical subjects were selected for exhibiting a clear diagnosis, they were unlikely to demonstrate extreme levels of a disorder, and were not so severely impaired that they could not go to school or carry on most of their day-to-day activities.

Almost all subjects in these studies were on grade level for their age, with just four diagnosed children and six diagnosis-free children having repeated Grades 1 or 2. Potential subjects were excluded on the basis of mental retardation, pervasive developmental disorders, or physical condition such as blindness that made it difficult for them to engage in the tasks of the studies. Based on cognitive ability estimates obtained from WISC-III Vocabulary and Block Design subscale scores, the diagnosed children did not differ in cognitive performance from the nondiagnosed children.

In each of these studies, a proportion of the diagnosed children exhibited more than one diagnosis, for example, ADHD and depression. In order to explore possible patterns in emotion competencies within diagnostic groupings, this chapter focuses on those subjects within each study who had only one kind of diagnosis. Because the numbers of children with a single diagnosis is small, only descriptive statistics are reported here.

Study 1

In this study (Casey & Schlosser, 1994), clinical subjects were 30 diagnosed aggressive children ages 7 to 14. Mean age was 10.6. Subjects were selected for this study based on having scores at or above the 96th percentile on the CBCL Aggression subscale and a diagnosed externalizing disorder. All but 4 of the aggressive children were diagnosed with ODD, three of the exceptions had ADHD, and one had ADHD and major depressive disorder

(MDD), although 19 also carried a second diagnosis. The purpose of the study was to assess diagnosed aggressive children's understanding of their own emotions in response to a positive social situation.

Procedure. Subjects were exposed to positive peer feedback from a same-gender, same-age, unfamiliar peer who was visible on a video monitor while subjects played a shape-sorting game. This child, actually videotaped in advance, responded affirmatively to an experimenter's request to play the game with the target subject, saying "yes [assenting to play with the subject], he looks nice, he looks friendly, I like the way he plays the game." The target subject's responses were compared to those of 30 age- and gender-matched nondiagnosed subjects who received the same feedback, and to another group of 30 nondiagnosed subjects who received neutral feedback: "Maybe OK, he was looking at me, he looks familiar, he thought of a different way to play the game."

Emotion Measures. Subjects' facial expressions during the 2-minute period beginning with the start of the peer feedback peer interaction were videotaped and coded, using Izard's (1980) AFFEX system for coding facial expressions. Duration of discrete emotions was combined to obtain percent of time spent in positive display, and in two kinds of negative display. These were externalizing of hostile display, such as anger and contempt, and display of internalizing emotion, including sadness, fear, shyness, and pain. Children's initial verbal response to the feedback was rated for expressiveness and negativity of expression. Children were also interviewed following the game session, and were asked to recall the emotion-eliciting stimulus, and to report what emotions they felt in response to peer feedback. Measures of self-understanding of felt emotions and accuracy in report of expressive display in response to the stimulus were also obtained. Reliability of measures was estimated based on recoding or rescoring of tapes and interviews of one third of the subjects by a second rater or coder. Reliability was maintained at or above .82 for all measures (coefficient kappa or intra-class correlations), with average reliability of .89.

Results. Diagnosed children typically reported a positive response to peer compliments, however, they displayed more hostile and surprised emotions than the nondiagnosed subjects. Diagnosed children recalled fewer details of the emotion stimulus, were less sophisticated in self-understanding of their emotions, and were less accurate in reporting their facial display compared with the nondiagnosed children. The 14 children with a single diagnosis (ODD = 11, ADHD = 4) generally conformed to the pattern established in the comparisons of the complete sample of diagnosed to nondiagnosed children.

Children diagnosed with ODD displayed hostile emotion for a mean of 10 seconds (SD = 2.41 seconds), contrasting with a mean of 0.67 seconds (SD = 0.58 seconds) among ADHD children, and just 1.2 seconds (SD = 1.83 seconds) in nondiagnosed comparison children. Display of surprise averaged 5.72 seconds (SD = 2.53 seconds) in ODD subjects, 4.73 seconds (SD = 2.41 seconds) in ADHD subjects, and 3.3 seconds (SD = 2.47 seconds) in nondiagnosed children. Negativity and expressivity of diagnosed children's verbal responses to positive feedback also appeared to differ from that of nondiagnosed comparison subjects. Based on Likert-type ratings of expressivity and negativity with 1 being *not at all expressive or negative*, and 5 being *very expressive or negative*, ODD children averaged ratings of 2.00 (SD = 0.81) and 3.18 (SD = 1.33), respectively, for expressiveness and negativity. Children with ADHD, on the other hand, received ratings of 3.60 (SD = 0.58) for expressiveness and 1.33 (SD = 0.58) for negativity. In contrast, the nondiagnosed comparison subjects received mean ratings of 3.18 (SD = 0.81) for expressiveness, and 1.18 (SD = 0.40) for negativity.

Appraisal of emotion was assessed through measures of recall of the stimulus, recall of facial display, and self-understanding of children's internal emotional response to the stimulus. Children with ODD or ADHD were similar in recalling less of the emotion stimulus than their comparison subjects. Respective means for recall were 1.33 (SD = 0.27) for ADHD children, 1.51 (SD = 0.18) for children diagnosed as ODD and 1.96 (SD = 0.17) for nondiagnosed subjects. Most of the diagnosed children were inaccurate in reporting (or showing us by demonstration) what they had shown facially in response to the stimulus, with none of the ADHD children and only 2 of the ODD children accurately reporting their display. The nature of their inaccurate reports was most commonly to state they had displayed nothing (N of ADHD = 1, N of ODD = 6) when they had shown a distinct facial response, or to state that they did not know what they had displayed (N of ADHD = 2, N of ODD = 3). In contrast, a majority of the comparison children were accurate in reporting their facial response to the stimulus.

Children's explanations for how they knew they felt their particular emotional response to the stimuli were coded for the kinds of explanations that they gave. All 3 of the ADHD children and most of the children with ODD (N = 6) said that they could not explain how they knew they were feeling they way they did. The explanations given by the other 5 ODD children were simple restatements of their feeling (N = 3; e.g., "I just felt happy") or referred to some aspect of the stimulus as how they knew the way the felt (N = 2; e.g., "He said I looked nice"). Only one of the comparison children could not state how he knew his feelings, and comparison children's reactions were about evenly distributed across a variety of explanations, including referring to their facial or bodily reaction to the stimulus (e.g., "I smiled") and generalizing beyond the immediate situation (e.g., "I've always been a friendly person") as well as relying on aspects of the stimulus and simple restatements of what they had felt.

Two of the measures, gaze at video partner before and during feedback and reported control over facial expression, may be related to emotion regulation. Duration of gaze at the partner was measuring beginning 20 seconds before the onset of the stimulus and continuing until the stimulus ended, about 35 seconds total. Children diagnosed as ODD looked directly at their video partner an average of just 7 seconds (SD = 2.5 seconds) and the ADHD children looked at their partner an average of 22.3 seconds (SD = 14.6 seconds). In contrast, comparison nondiagnosed children watched the video partner 29.4 seconds (SD = 8.2 seconds) during this period. Children with ODD were most likely to state that they either did or could have controlled their expressive display in response to the stimulus (N = 8), whereas none of the ADHD children and fewer than a fourth of the nondiagnosed comparison subjects expressed this degree of control over their expression of emotion.

It is interesting that the ODD children, although displaying hostile expressions, nevertheless reported feelings about the peer feedback that were positive. These children also observed the video peer less than other children did, which may had contributed to their inaccurate appraisal of their partner's expression. This gaze aversion, in combination with expression that doesn't match internal feelings, places these children at particular risk for being perceived negatively by their peers.

Study 2

The second study (Casey & Murphy, 1991; Casey, Murphy, & Nelson, 1993) examined the emotional and behavioral responses of diagnosed aggressive children to background anger. Subjects were 118 children, selected for their level of aggression. Aggressive subjects scored at or above the 95 percentile on the CBCL Externalizing subscale (Achenbach & Edelbrock, 1983), and were typically diagnosed as having ODD. Nonaggressive children had no diagnoses and scored at or below the 60th percentile.

Procedure.   In two conditions, pairs of unacquainted same-age and same-gender children played a building game while witnessing live emotional or neutral simulations. Two groups of children were exposed to a background anger simulation. One of these groups was composed of a set of 19 diagnosed aggressive children paired with 19 nondiagnosed children, and another group consisted of 20 nondiagnosed pairs of children. Two additional groups received a neutral background simulation. One of these groups was made up of 8 aggressive children paired with 8 nonaggressive children, the second group was composed of 12 pairs of nonaggressive children.

Children were introduced to their partners, but were not told to expect the background interactions. The room was divided by some open shelves with the subjects at one end of the room. The other end of the room, where the emotional simulations occurred, looked like a waiting area. Subjects were given a cooperative building game to work on, which involved pulling pieces out of the bottom of a tower and putting them on top. As the pair played the game, they were exposed to one of the emotion simulations.

Each of these conditions consisted of six scripted 3-minute episodes. The background anger condition involved three persons: a child (an actor), his mother (actually a lab assistant), and an experimenter. Period 1 consisted of positive interaction between the experimenter and child; Period 3 involved the angry interaction of the mother and child, focused on where the child and the mother expected to find each other following the experiment; and Period 5 was the reconciliation of the parent–child differences. Periods 2, 4, and 6 involved no emotional interaction or conversation. The neutral background simulation involved two experimenters, with neutral interactions in Periods 1, 3, and 5 consisting of discussion of work and leisure activities occurring, and no interactions occurring in Periods 2, 4, and 6. Both conditions were similarly executed in the presence of the children, with equal amounts of conversation and movement.

Emotion Measures. Several measures were coded from videotapes of children's behavior during the simulations. The number of aggressive acts made by each subject was counted, including knocking down the building, hitting toys, verbal aggression (e.g., "I want to knock this down") and competitive remarks (e.g., "I'm going to win, you'll lose"). Duration and direction of gaze behavior was measured for looking at the partner, looking at the actors, or looking at other things, such as the game. Rule infractions were counted, including touching the game with both hands, playing with toys other than the game, and touching a piece and not pulling it out. Off-task, out-of-seat behavior was also measured (e.g., wandering around the room). Contingencies in the emotional organization of children's interactions with their partner were also measured by coding each subject's behavior for emotional tone (positive, negative, and neutral) and organizational quality (regulated, disregulated/disorganized, or immobilized). This coding was based on judgments of the facial, gestural, and vocal behavior of the child, using a scoring system adapted from affect scoring systems developed by Izard (1980) and P. Cole (1990; Casey, Witherington, Witherington, & Murphy, 1992). The organizational quality of the social interaction and/or activity was coded as regulated, dysfunctional/disorganized (e.g., behavior not related to game, such as playing some other game with building blocks or walking away from the game), or immobilized (e.g., "freezing"). A trained rater independently counted or applied each of these coding systems. Reliability was checked by use of a second trained coder who also rated one fourth of the pair interactions, selected at random. Inter-rater reliabilities were calculated using intraclass correlations or coefficient kappa, according to the type of measure. Reliability was maintained at or above .80 for all measures; average reliability was .88.

A structured clinical interview following the simulations assessed under-standing and report of emotions in self and in the child actor, recall of the background stimulus, and strategies for dealing with the angry interchange. Children were asked what the child in the argument could have done to feel better, and what they themselves would like to have done in intervene in the angry interchange. Suggested interventions were coded for avoiding the angry exchange, minimizing the negative interaction, helping (giving sug-gestions, offering advice, arbitrating a difference, etc.), verbal nurturance (offering reassurance, reasoning with target child, talking problems over, telling jokes, etc.), or social nurturance (inviting target child to do some-thing, playing with target child, etc.), using a coding system developed by McCoy and Masters (1985). Reliability of interview rating was checked by use of a second trained coder who also rated the interview responses. Inter-rater reliability was calculated using coefficient kappa, which assessed relia-bility corrected for the probability of chance agreement. Reliability was maintained at or above kappa = .93 for all items; average kappa was .98.

Results. Overall, there were marked differences in children's responses to the angry versus neutral background simulations, with aggressive acts and negative affect increasing following the angry but not the neutral back-ground. Among the 19 aggressive children who received the background anger condition were 14 children diagnosed solely with ODD. Except where indicated otherwise, the ODD children are compared with age- and gender-matched nondiagnosed children who had a nondiagnosed partner. The expressive behavior of these children did not differ from the nondiag-nosed children in that negative affect and aggressive acts rose sharply among both groups in the episodes following the angry parent–child interaction. Children's appraisal of emotion, however, did appear to differ by diagnostic status. Children diagnosed as having ODD recalled more details of the background anger simulation (Mean recall score = 2.4, SD = 1.1) than did the nondiagnosed comparison subjects who had another nondiagnosed partner (Mean recall score = 1.6, SD = 0.9). More of the ODD children (78%) labeled the child's emotion as being some form of negative feeling than did the non-ODD comparison children (28.6%).

Measures of emotion regulation included the organizational quality of the children's interactive behavior, conformity to game rules throughout the simulation, gaze at the simulation during the game, and suggested strategies for intervention in the angry situation. The quality of ODD children's

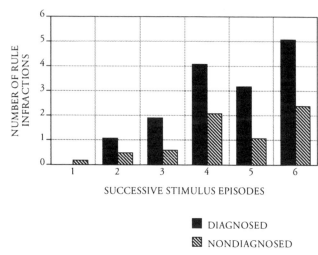

FIG. 9.1.   Rule infractions by episode for diagnosed and nondiagnosed children.

behavior showed less organization than was the case among the comparison children. This disorganization typically consisted of freezing (immobilization) or disintegration of activities into forbidden or off-task actions, seen in 86.7% of the ODD children as compared to 40% of the comparison subjects. Similarly, the number of rule infractions among all children rose following the angry parent–child interaction, however the rise was more pronounced among the ODD children than the non-ODD children (see Fig. 9.1). Children with ODD were less likely to avoid watching the angry simulation than were the comparison children, with ODD children watching on the average 58.2% ($SD = 10.1\%$) of the anger simulation, versus a mean of 35.7% of the anger simulation among the comparison subjects.

   In the postgame interview, ODD children were more likely to suggest an intervention that would have avoided the negative interaction in the first place, often quite unrealistically (e.g., "he could take a trip to the zoo instead of coming here" : 29%), or which involved an immediate physical response the interaction (e.g., "he should kick her in the stomach" : 64%). Comparison children, although also reporting similar strategies (21% and 7%, respectively, for avoidance and physical response), suggested as well strategies to minimize the negative aspects of the immediate situation (e.g., "I'd apologize right off, and tell her I was sorry" : 57%).

   The aggressive children in this study appeared to be drawn into the angry interchange at the other end of the room more so than the nonaggressive children. They spent more time watching the parent and child, and played the game less well, breaking more rules and becoming more aggressive.

Their memory of the stimulus was stronger than that of nonaggressive children with nonaggressive partners, and they were apt to think of intervention of an "all or none" sort, such as never experiencing the angry interchange, or resolving it with an act of aggression. It is interesting to note that the nondiagnosed partners of the ODD children also showed higher recall of the anger simulation (Mean recall = 2.3, *SD* = 1.3), which suggests that having an aggressive partner may alter children's recall of certain situations.

Study 3

The purpose of the third study was to explore the social and emotional behavior of children with ADHD as a function of different degrees of structure during peer interaction, comparing them to children with other clinical problems as well as to normal children (Casey, Loge, Schatz, Whitmore, & Schumacher, 1991). Subjects were children ages 7 through 14 (*M* = 10.5 years), approximately one third of the children in each clinical group were female. Forty met *DSM–III–R* criteria for ADHD. Of these children, 22 also met criteria for other disorders, most typically ODD, conduct disorder (CD), or MDD, 21 met *DSM–III–R* criteria for ODD but not ADHD, and 18 met *DSM–III–R* criteria for MDD but not ADHD. Each diagnosed subject was paired with a same-age, same-gender unfamiliar peer partner who was without diagnosis. Another 20 children without diagnoses served as a comparison group. These children were selected to represent the age and gender distribution of the diagnosed subjects; they also were paired with a matching peer partner who had no diagnosis.

Procedure. Peer interaction between paired children was observed during three successive episodes: (a) a 5-minute get-acquainted period; (b) a 5-minute art activity (designing a tee-shirt logo); and (c) a puzzle game of four rounds, with subjects alternating in two roles, coach and player, as easy and hard puzzles were assembled. As the player, children assembled a puzzle concealed from view inside a box. As the coach, children could see into the box and direct their partner's performance. Afterward, each child was interviewed concerning his own and his partner's performance during these activities. Participants also completed measures of self-perception and mood.

Emotion Measures. Several aspects of subjects' emotional expression and behavior were measured, including duration of expression during the three episodes, number of changes in expression, and ratings of vocal expressivity and negativity. Duration and changes in facial expression were coded using Izard's (1980) AFFEX system. Duration was measured as percent of time in emotion display, and frequency of change was transformed into *z* scores based on the mean and standard deviation of changes in the nondiagnosed subjects, because of differing length of the puzzle box episode from subject to subject. Children's vocal expressiveness was rated during the get-acquainted episode and each round of the puzzle box, using a Likert-type scale, ranging from 1 (*not at all expressive*) to 5 (*very expressive*). In addition, the negativity of children's vocalizations during the puzzle box episode was also rated on a scale ranging from 1 (*not at all negative*) to 5 (*very negative*). Also coded were children's gaze during the get-acquainted episode (duration of gaze at partner and away from partner), and their contingent display of emotion, defined as emotion display that followed and matched the valence of partner's display.

In the interview following the peer interaction, subjects were asked to describe their own and their partner's expressive behavior at the point where their difficult puzzle rounds ended, in the player's role. Children were scored as being accurate if they described or demonstrated facial expression of the same valence (or lack of expression) consistent with what was demonstrated on the child's video record of that point in the procedure. Interrater reliability for each of these measures was calculated from a second coding of the videotapes and interviews from one third of the children, with reliability being maintained at or above .80 (kappas or intraclass correlations as appropriate to the particular measure) for these measures; average index of reliability for these measures was .84.

Results. Children belonging to a single diagnostic group included 18 children with ADHD, 18 children with ODD, and 15 children with MDD.

Emotion Expression. Children with ADHD tended to show more facial affect than normal children (41.3% vs. 30% across all episodes), with more frequent changes in facial expression as well ($z = 3.1$ for ADHD). In contrast, ODD children showed much less facial expression (22.7%), with fewer changes as well ($z = -1.1$). Like ODD children, depressed children showed little facial expression (21.3% of the time), however, they demonstrated changes in expression similar in number to nondiagnosed subjects ($z = -0.2$).

Emotion Appraisal. Children with ADHD were the least accurate in reporting their own and their partner's expressive behavior, as only 11% of the group were accurate in appraising their own emotion, and 11% were accurate in judging their partner's expression. In contrast, many more of the children with MDD or with no diagnosis were accurate in judging their own emotions (53.3% of the MDD group and 50% of the nondiagnosed group). Children in these two groups were also the most accurate in assessing the emotion expression of their partners (73.3% of the MDD group, and 55% of the nondiagnosed group). Children with ODD appeared to be slightly better at appraising their own emotion expression (38.9% were accurate) than they were at appraising their partner's expression (22.2% were accurate). When children judged their partner's expression, the errors of the groups were somewhat different, in that ODD and MDD children who were wrong tended to state that their partners had shown a negative expression or no expression, whereas ADHD children typically were wrong by asserting that their partners had shown a positive expression. Nondiagnosed children as a group had no pattern to their errors.

Emotion Regulation. Four measures obtained during the study may tap aspects of emotion regulation. These included children's tendency to become more expressive across the four box puzzle rounds, the negativity of statements made in the coach role during the puzzle box game, display of emotion contingent on the previous expression of a partner, and gazing at the partner during the initial get-acquainted session (which makes emotion appraisal possible and also is necessary for contingent facial expression).

Depressed children appeared to avoid gaze toward their partners (only 8% of the episode), and demonstrated little use of contingent display, as just 11% of their display during the first episode was contingent display. Children with ODD watched their partners somewhat more, about 16% of the time, and used contingent display for about 23% of their expressive behavior. The ADHD children looked at their partners most of all groups (43% of the time), however, little of their display was contingent, just 11%. Nondiagnosed children watched their partners 32% of the time, and 43% of their display was contingent on their partner's display.

Children in all groups became more expressive with each successive round of the puzzle box game (see Fig. 9.2), however MDD children appeared to be much less expressive than other children until the final round, and ADHD and ODD children rose to somewhat higher levels of expressivity faster than the other groups. Children in the ODD group were the most negative of all as they coached their partners through the puzzle box game, M negativity rating = 4.0 (SD = .88). Negativity for other groups was M = 2.0 (SD = 1.3) for ADHD children; M = 1.1 (SD = .58) for MDD children; and M = 1.5 (SD = .67) for nondiagnosed children.

The emotional characteristics of the diagnosed children changed somewhat across episodes, suggesting that the particular social context and its requirements plays a major role in how children express, appraise, and regulate their emotions. For example, depressed children avoided looking at their partners in the first episode, but in the puzzle box procedure, where they were face to face with their partners, they had to see their partners, and they were as good as nondiagnosed children in remembering their partners expressive response. Their own expressive response changed markedly in that episode, as well. All of the children responded strongly to the build-up of excitement in the third (puzzle box) episode of the study. ODD children

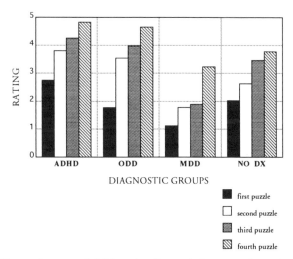

FIG. 9.2. Expressiveness of children by diagnosis in successive episodes of puzzle game.

became increasingly more aggressive, whereas ADHD children became more and more happy and excited, compared to normal children. Depressed children appeared initially to be "slow to warm up," but by the end of the puzzle series, they behaved similar to normal children, suggesting that the activity helped overcome their typically slow motoric and emotional responses.

Study 4

In the fourth study (Casey, Hill, Witherington, Wiecek, & Greer, 1994), children with and without a variety of disorders were studied to determine their ability to identify emotions present in common childhood situations that typically elicit happiness, sadness, anger, fear, or a combination of emotions. Subjects were 7- to 12-year-old children, 14 diagnosed as having ADHD, 14 children with a disruptive behavior disorder (ODD or CD), and 22 children with a combination of disorders. In addition, 58 age- and gender-matched children without disorders were also included.

Children were presented with 15 vignettes of situations describing commonly occurring childhood events likely to elicit one or more emotions. Each vignette was read aloud and shown in print, along with a picture of the situation, with the face of the central character turned away from view. Subjects were asked to state how the central character would be likely to feel. When children voiced a particular feeling, they were asked if there was any other way the character might feel, or if their first choice was the only likely possibility. Next, subjects were asked to choose from an array of pictured facial expressions the one closest to how the person would be likely to feel. For each choice, 14 pictured expressions (5 pure expressions and 9 blends of expressions) were shown to the children in three randomly ordered sets of 4 or 5. Children selected the best picture of each subset, which was placed in front of the child. Then children were asked to pick the best overall expression picture from the three they had initially selected.

The vignettes had been written based on the kinds of situations that children commonly report as eliciting emotions, and confirmed by the ratings of 25 adults as consistently depicting either one particular emotion or a combination of two emotions (consistency estimates for all vignettes exceeded .85). Five vignettes depicted single emotion situations (happy, surprised, angry, fearful, and sad), and 10 vignettes depicted situations where two of these emotions were likely to be elicited (e.g., surprised and fearful, happy and sad). The facial expressions were line drawings of children's faces, based on photographs of prototypical facial expressions of a moderate level of expression of an emotion or blend of emotion (Ekman, 1982; Ekman & Friesen, 1975) but drawn to reflect facial proportions of children (Enlow, 1982). These faces were also rated by 40 adults unfamiliar with the purposes of this study, with consistency of ratings of each face being above .85.

Results. Twenty-eight children in this study were diagnosed with a single disorder, 14 with ADHD, and 14 with ODD. Overall, although there were no differences in children's ability to recognize versus label emotions, children were less accurate in recognition and labeling of blended emotions than single emotions, $M = 1.66$ ($SD = 0.38$) for single emotions, $M = 0.97$ ($SD = 0.69$) for mixed emotions. There were differences in children's accuracy for appraising single versus mixed emotions, depending on children's diagnostic status. Children with ADHD were relatively better at recognition and labeling of emotion in nonsocial situations, $M = 1.55$ ($SD = 0.43$) for nonsocial versus 1.05 ($SD = 0.63$) for social, whereas nondiagnosed children were better and recognition and labeling of emotions within a social context, $M = 1.59$ ($SD = 0.43$) for social, $M = 1.19$ ($SD = 0.49$) for nonsocial. Children with ODD scored between the nondiagnosed children and the ADHD group, with no difference in social versus nonsocial situations, $M = 1.24$ ($SD = .75$) for social vignettes, $M = 1.25$ ($SD = .80$) for nonsocial vignettes.

DISCUSSION

Overall, these studies suggest a pattern of strengths and weaknesses in emotion skills that differentiates diagnosed and nondiagnosed children. Effect sizes for several emotion skills were calculated by subtracting the difference

TABLE 9.1
Emotion Expression Effect Sizes by Diagnostic Group

	Diagnosis		
Kind of Emotion Expression	ADHD	ODD	MDD
Amount of facial display	0.45	1.40	−0.13
Changes in facial display	3.10	−1.10	−0.20
Vocal negativity	−0.37	5.00	—
Vocal expressivity	0.52	−1.46	—

Note. Effect sizes are averaged across studies, based on means and standard deviations obtained from comparison children, who were matched to diagnosed children by age and gender. ADHD = attention deficit hyperactivity disorder, ODD = oppositional defiant disorder/conduct disorder, MDD = major depressive disorders.

between the mean of each diagnostic group and the mean of the nondiagnosed group, and dividing by the mean of the nondiagnosed group. This permits aggregation of findings across different studies in a manner that permits comparison of specific areas of competence for each group. Skill differences are found in all three areas of competence: expression, appraisal, and regulation of emotion. It also appears that some skills may distinguish internalizing children, in this case children with depression, from externalizing children with attention deficit or oppositional problems

For expressive behavior, children with ADHD demonstrated the most use of facial expression, with the most changes in facial display (see Table 9.1). Their expressed emotion tended to be more positive than that of other diagnosed children. In contrast, the ODD children were more typically negative in their vocal expression. Depressed children could be compared to other groups in only one study, in which they showed less facial display than any other group of children.

Perhaps the most consistent characteristic of the emotion skills of externalizing children was their weakness in emotion appraisal. Table 9.2 summarizes appraisal skills. In contrast, nondiagnosed and depressed children were similar in their ability to appraise emotion. Externalizers also demonstrated quite different patterns from internalizers in using emotions during social approach and task performance. Children with ADHD and ODD did not look at their partners as much as depressed or nondiagnosed children, and they were much less likely to use contingent expression of emotion. However, this finding must be considered in light of the expressive characteristics of the children, as ADHD children did a lot of noncontingent smiling, whereas ODD children displayed little emotion other than brief hostile displays following positive peer feedback, or strongly negative expression during the puzzle box activity.

TABLE 9.2
Emotion Appraisal Effect Sizes by Diagnostic Group

	Diagnosis		
Kind of Emotion Expression	ADHD	ODD	MDD
Own expression	−1.01	−0.64	0.07
Own emotion	−1.43	−0.51	—
Others	−0.97	0.07	0.37
Context	−3.83	−0.87	—

Note. Effect sizes are averaged across studies, based on means and standard deviations obtained from comparison children, who were matched to diagnosed children by age and gender. ADHD = attention deficit hyperactivity disorder, ODD = oppositional defiant disorder/conduct disorder, MDD = major depressive disorders.

Depressed versus externalizing children demonstrated very different responses to emotion contagion (see Table 9.3). In the context of background anger or game play, ODD children became increasingly negative in expression. ADHD children and depressed children, observed only in the puzzle game context, also became more expressive during the game, but more positively so. Children with ODD report that they have a great deal of control over their expressive behavior, in contrast to ADHD children who do not feel much sense of control. Perhaps the gaze avoidance and use of hostile display are part of how ODD children control their emotion display, but it may also be the case that they wish to deny any lack of control.

Why are these patterns present? It may be that emerging psychopathology disrupts normal patterns of emotional development by producing delayed or dysfunctional acquisition and use of emotion competencies. Alternately, problems in emotional development may be precursors to

TABLE 9.3
Emotion Regulation Effect Sizes by Diagnostic Group

	Diagnosis		
Kind of Emotion Expression	ADHD	ODD	MDD
Contingent expression and gaze	−0.70	−1.26	0.08
Response to emotion contagion	1.30	0.79	−1.30
Self-perception of control	−0.52	1.33	—
Emotional tone in cognitive tasks	−0.74	−3.73	0.60

Note. Effect sizes are based on means and standard deviations obtained from comparison children, who were matched to diagnosed children by age and gender. ADHD = attention deficit hyperactivity disorder, ODD = oppositional defiant disorder/conduct disorder, MDD = major depressive disorders.

psychopathology. It is also possible that psychopathology and problems with emotional competence arise independently and more or less simultaneously, but I doubt it. I suspect that the emergence of psychopathology and emotional development are complexly interrelated, including important contributions from biological aspects of a child's functioning, particularly through temperament and maturation.

I expect, in particular, that the temperamental characteristics of vulnerability to anxiety, impulsivity, and inhibition of responses may be related to children's emotional expressiveness and to their regulation of emotion. If so, temperamental influences on emotional competence may be an important link between children's emotions and the emergence of childhood psychopathology. It is also likely that the socialization children experience, particularly from their parents, has a lot to do with their emotional competence (e.g., Eisenberg et al., 1991). If parents themselves have psychiatric problems, the quality of parent socialization may be particularly disturbed (e.g., Goodman et al., 1993)

There are marked limitations to these findings. Some important aspects of children's emotional function were not considered, such as the biological substrate of emotion. Other factors, such as gender and age, were given scant attention. For purposes of this chapter, age differences were ignored, although some were found. These results, by themselves, do not compare emotional competence to other aspects of the children's functioning, so they do not tell us whether emotion processes are central to the psychopathology that these children have. Temperament, attachment, cognitive development, and socialization of the children should be examined. These domains are known to play an important role in children's emotional development and are also considered to contribute to the emergence of psychopathology.

We cannot say whether it is accurate to speak of a pattern of differences from nondiagnosed children as deficits, as I have done here. Nevertheless, one approach to conceptualizing psychopathology in children is to view it in terms of competence, as D. Cole (1991) has done. Other domains of functioning, such as the cognitive or social, have a longer history of interest and research to help determine what is and is not evidence of competence. We are just beginning to explore these ideas in the arena of emotional development. Also, most previous studies, including my own, relate emotion skills to *concurrent* social adjustment or psychopathology. Clearly, developmental differences in emotion skills are to be expected in that children are likely to possess skill with simpler emotions while they are in the process of acquiring skills in expressing, appraising, and regulating more complex emotions, such as guilt or envy.

In summary, I have presented a pattern of emotion skills observed in diagnosed children that suggests there may be systematic differences in expression, appraisal, and regulation of emotion according to the type of psychopathology that children have. The presence of patterns in these emotion skills, rather than simple differences between nondiagnosed and diagnosed children, may indicate that emotion processes are important components of children's functioning. Emotional development may be altered by psychopathology, or atypical emotional development may contribute to the occurrence of psychopathology. The origin of these patterns, and possibly their relation to the children's psychopathology and other areas of functioning, present compelling hypotheses to be explored concerning the relations between the emergence of childhood behavior disorders and the course of emotional development.

ACKNOWLEDGMENTS

Support from the National Institute for Mental Health via PHS grant MH49229 is gratefully acknowledged. My thanks also to members of the emotional development labs at the University of Iowa and Wayne State University for their assistance with this research, and to Carolyn Saarni, Nancy Eisenberg, and Susanne Denham for previous discussions that contributed to my thinking.

REFERENCES

Achenbach, T. M., & Edelbrock, C. S. (1983). *Manual for the Child Behavior Checklist and Revised Child Behavior Profile*. Burlington: Department of Psychiatry, University of Vermont.

Altmann, E. O., & Gotlib, I. H. (1988). The social behavior of depressed children: An observational study. *Journal of Abnormal Child Psychology, 16*, 29–44.

American Psychiatric Association. (1987). *Diagnostic and statistical manual of mental disorders* (3rd ed., rev.). Washington, DC: Author.

American Psychiatric Association. (1994). *Diagnostic and statistical manual of mental disorders* (4th ed.). Washington, DC: Author.

Campos, J. J., Campos, R. G., & Barrett, K. C. (1989). Emergent themes in the study of emotional development and emotion regulation. *Developmental Psychology, 25*, 394–402.

Casey, R. J., Hill, K., Witherington, D., Wiecek, K., & Greer, A. E. (1994). *Behavior-disordered children recognize pure and blended emotions*. Unpublished manuscript.

Casey, R. J., Loge, D. V., Schatz, J., Whitmore, E., & Schumacher, E. (1991, April). *Social interactions of children with attention deficit disorder: The role of emotions and self-control*. Paper presented at the biennial meeting of the Society for Research in Child Development, Seattle, WA .

Casey, R. J., & Murphy, B. C. (1991, April). *Emotional and behavioral effects of background anger on aggressive children*. Paper presented at the biennial meeting of the Society for Research in Child Development, Seattle, WA.

Casey, R. J., Murphy, B. C., & Nelson, P. Y. (1993, June). *Emotional organization and childhood psychopathology.* Nag's Head Conference on Emotion and Cognition, Boca Raton, FL.

Casey, R. J., & Schlosser, S. (1994). Emotional responses to peer praise in children with and without a diagnosed externalizing disorder. *Merrill-Palmer Quarterly, 40,* 60–81.

Casey, R. J., Witherington, D., Witherington, R. S., & Murphy, B. C. (1992, March). *Emotional organization: Assessing relations between affect and behavioral regulation.* Paper presented at the biennial meeting of the Southwest Society for Research in Human Development, Tempe, AZ.

Cicchetti, D., & Schneider-Rosen, K. (1984). Toward a transactional model of childhood depression. In D. Cicchetti & K. Schneider-Rosen (Eds.), *Childhood depression* (pp. 5–27). San Francisco: Jossey-Bass.

Cole, D. A. (1991). Preliminary support for a competency-based model of child depression. *Journal of Abnormal Psychology, 100,* 181–190.

Cole, P. M. (1990). *Cole affect coding scheme.* Bethesda, MD: Author.

Cole, P. M., Michel, M. K., & Teti, L. O. (1994). The development of emotion regulation and dysregulation: A clinical perspective. In N. A. Fox (Ed.) *The development of emotion regulation: Biological and behavioral considerations: Monographs of the Society for Research in Child Development (Serial No. 240), 59*(2), 73–100.

Dawson, G., Hill, D., Spencer, A., Galpert, L., & Watson, L. (1988). Affective exchanges between young autistic children and their mothers. *Journal of Abnormal Child Psychology, 18,* 335–345.

Eisenberg, N., & Fabes, R. A. (1992). Emotion, self-regulation, and the development of social competence. In M. S. Clark (Ed.), *Emotion and social behavior: Vol. 14. Review of personality and social psychology* (pp. 119–150). Newbury Park, CA: Sage.

Eisenberg, N., Fabes, R A., Schaller, M., Carlo, G., & Miller, P. A. (1991). The relations of parental characteristics and practices to children's vicarious emotional responding. *Child Development, 62,* 1393–1408.

Ekman, P. (Ed.). (1982). *Emotion in the human face* (2nd ed.). Cambridge: Cambridge University Press.

Ekman, P., & Friesen, W. V (1975). *Unmasking the face.* Englewood Cliffs, NJ: Prentice-Hall.

Enlow, D. (1982). *Handbook of facial growth* (2nd ed.). Philadelphia: Saunders.

Fischer, K. (1980). A theory of cognitive development: The control and construction of hierarchies of skills. *Psychological Review, 87,* 477–531.

Goodman, S. H., Brogan, D., Lynch, M. E., & Fielding, B. (1993). Social and emotional competence in children of depressed mothers. *Child Development, 64,* 518–531.

Gray, J. A. (1987). *The psychology of fear and stress* (2nd ed.). Cambridge: Cambridge University Press.

Hobson, R. P., Ouston, J., & Lee, A. (1988). What's in a face? The case of autism. *British Journal of Psychology, 79,* 441–451.

Izard, C. E. (1980). *Affex: A system for identifying affect expression by holistic judgments.* Newark, DE: Author.

Loveland, K., Fletcher, J. M., & Bailey, V. (1990). Verbal and nonverbal communication of events in learning-disability subtypes. *Journal of Clinical and Experimental Neuropsychology, 12*, 433–447.

Loveland, K., Tunali-Kotoski, B., Pearson, D. A., Brelsford, K. A., Ortegon, J., & Chen, R. (1994). Imitation and expression of facial affect in autism. *Development and Psychopathology, 6*, 433–444.

McCoy, C. L., & Masters, J. C. (1985). The development of children's strategies for the social control of emotion. *Child Development, 56*, 1214-1222.

Mueser, K. T., Bellack, A. S., Wade, J. H., Sayers, S. L., Tierney, A., & Haas, G. (1993). Expressed emotion, social skill, and response to negative affect in schizophrenia. *Journal of Abnormal Psychology, 102*, 339–351.

Orvaschel, H., & Puig-Antich, J. (1987). *Schedule for affective disorder and schizophrenia for school-age children.* Pittsburgh, PA: Author.

Persad, S. M., & Polivy, J. (1993). Differences between depressed and nondepressed individuals in the recognition of and response to facial emotional cues. *Journal of Abnormal Psychology, 102*, 358–368.

Rourke, B. P. (1988). Socioemotional disturbances of learning disabled children. *Journal of Consulting and Clinical Psychology, 56*, 801–810.

Saarni, C. (1990). Emotional competence: How emotions and relationships become integrated. In R. A. Thompson (Ed.), *Socio-emotional development. Nebraska Symposium on Motivation, 1988* (pp. 115–182). Lincoln, NE: University of Nebraska Press.

Salovey, P., & Mayer, J. D. (1990). Emotional intelligence. *Imagination, Cognition, and Personality, 9*, 185–211.

Selman, R. L. (1976). Toward a structural analysis of developing interpersonal relations concepts: Research with normal and disturbed preadolescent boys. In A. Pick (Ed.), *Minnesota Symposium on Child Psychology* (Vol. 10, pp. 113–147). Minneapolis: University of Minnesota Press.

Snow, M. E., Hertzig, M. E., & Shapiro, T. (1987). Expression of emotion in young autistic children. *Journal of the American Academy of Child and Adolescent Psychiatry, 26*, 836–838.

Taylor, D. A., & Harris, P. L. (1983). Knowledge of the link between emotion and memory among normal and maladjusted boys. *Developmental Psychology, 19*, 832–838.

Walker, E. (1981). Emotion recognition in disturbed and normal children: A research note. *Journal of Child Psychology and Psychiatry, 22*, 263–268.

Weeks, S. J., & Hobson, R. P. (1987). The salience of facial expression for autistic children. *Journal of Child Psychology and Psychiatry and Allied Disciplines, 28*, 1237–152.

Yirmiya, N., Kasari, C., Sigman, M., & Mundy, P. (1989). Facial expressions of affect in autistic, mentally retarded and normal children. *Journal of Child Psychology and Psychiatry and Allied Disciplines, 30*, 725–735.

Zabel, R. H. (1979). Recognition of emotions in facial expressions by emotionally disturbed children and non-disturbed children. *Psychology in the School, 16*(1), 119–126.

— 10 —

Development of the Self-Conscious Emotions in Maltreated Children

Steven M. Alessandri
Medical College of Pennsylvania

Michael Lewis
*University of Medicine and Dentistry
of New Jersey*

The study of emotional development has important implications for understanding the development and organization of processes underlying personality functioning and psychopathology. Research on the developmental sequelae of child maltreatment is important because it can contribute to our understanding of human development through the provision of information about the impact of punitive caregiving environments on the developing child. It is important to determine how children who have experienced extended interpersonal interactions in abusive familial environments construct, interpret, and structure their social world. Knowledge of emotional and self-development in maltreated children offers an opportunity to examine parental behaviors that influence these domains and about socialization processes in general.

Although considerable effort has been invested in the study of the primary emotions, those that occur in the first half year of life (e.g., anger, joy, interest, disgust, fear, and sadness), less attention has been paid to the development and measurement of the self-conscious emotions M. Lewis, 1993). It is widely believed that this set of emotions first emerges in the second year of life, consisting first of embarrassment and later pride, shame, and guilt. Most theories about the development of the self-conscious emotions assume that these emotions are derived, in part, from the child's developing cognitive capacities (Heckhausen, 1987a; M. Lewis, 1992; M. Lewis, Alessandri, & Sullivan, 1992, M. Lewis, Sullivan, Stanger, & Weiss, 1989; Weiner, 1986) and from the child's socialization experiences (Alessandri & Lewis, 1993; Campos & Barrett, 1984; Stipek, 1993; Stipek, Recchia, & McClintic, 1992). The cognitive capacities that are likely to be prerequisites for the self-conscious emotions, particularly shame and pride, are the ability to mentally represent standards for comparison (Kagan, 1981), objective self-awareness and self-evaluation (M. Lewis, 1992; M. Lewis et al., 1992), as well as the ability to reflect on and attribute outcomes to personal competence (Dweck & Leggett, 1988; Heckhausen, 1984). Research indicates that these cognitive abilities are in place by 2 to 2½ years of age (M. Lewis et al., 1992).

Empirical study of the self-conscious emotions, particularly the measurement of shame and pride, has recently appeared (Alessandri & Lewis, 1993; Heckhausen, 1988; M. Lewis et al., 1989; M. Lewis et al., 1992). Heckhausen (1984, 1987a, 1987b, 1988) and M. Lewis et al. (1992) observed shame and pride in reaction to success and failure on achievement tasks. In these studies, when children are successful, they show pride. However, if they fail, they show shame. Pride and shame are measured by facial and bodily action. In general, the expressions of pride are observed earlier than the expressions of shame (Geppert & Gartmann, 1993) and girls show more shame than boys (M. Lewis et al., 1992). The cognitive and expressive environments provided by parents partially account for individual differences in children's emotional expression (Camras et al., 1990; Halberstadt, 1991). The emotions children experience are likely to reflect, therefore, both their developing cognitive skills and their changing social environment (Alessandri & Lewis, 1993; M. Lewis, 1992).

Given our understanding of the cognitive and social factors that underlie emotional functioning in normal children, we would expect that abusive socialization practices would play an important role in the development of the self and self-conscious emotions and that maltreated children are likely to be compromised in these domains. In this chapter, recent theory and research findings are examined as they concern the development of the self and self-conscious emotions in maltreated children. The chapter is divided into three sections. We begin with an examination of theoretical models that contribute to our understanding of the processes that influence the course of self-development and self-conscious emotions in maltreated children. Research from studies on both normal and maltreated children are then reviewed. Finally, we conclude by speculating on the implications of this research for the understanding of the intergenerational transmission of abuse and child and adult psychopathology.

THEORETICAL MODELS

Psychodynamic and Attachment Perspective

Recent theory and research on the caregiver–infant relationship proposes that "working models" of the self are an important socioemotional factor that influences children's subsequent development (Cassidy, 1988; Crittenden, 1990; Sroufe, 1983). According to Bowlby (1973), an infant learns a prototype of self and interpersonal relationships through interaction with a primary caregiver and that internal models of the self develop in parallel with working models of attachment figures. These working models or unconscious mental representations of the world and one's relation to it are constructed out of children's own actions and the actions of caregivers. The psychological unavailability of parents for extended periods of time can affect a powerful influence on emotional functioning and self-development (Bowlby, 1973; Cummings & Cicchetti, 1990).

According to this perspective, the experience of maltreatment during childhood may lead to the development of negative representational models of attachment figures, the self, and the self in relation to significant others (Cicchetti, 1991; Crittenden & Ainsworth, 1989). Children with sensitive caregivers learn to view themselves as worthy of care and as lovable. To the child, the secure attachment relationship brings a sense of "felt security" which is related to feelings of confidence and mastery. Beginning in infancy, maltreated children consistently evidence a greater percentage of insecure attachment relations with their primary caregivers than do nonmaltreated infants (Cicchetti & Barnett, 1991; Crittenden, 1988). Typically, these early insecure attachments are "disorganized" in nature (Carlson, Cicchetti, Burnett, & Braunwald, 1989). Representational models derived from these early relationships are internalized and may affect self-development and the process of self-evaluation. Maltreated children's self-esteem, self-attributions, and sense of competence can be compromised when exposed to an early relationship that communicates rejection, fear, and humiliation. Maltreated children with unresponsive or punitive caregivers are likely to construct a working model of attachment figures who are unavailable and, in turn, of the self as not worthy of being loved. Moreover, maltreated children are likely to experience internal conflict about interpersonal relationships; on the one hand they desire closeness from an adult, on the other, the object of that desire happens to be the source of pain (Crittenden & Ainsworth, 1989). Thus, maltreated children are likely to have representational models of the self and interpersonal relationships as negative, conflict-ridden, and unpredictable. The child's internal working model of his or her attachment relationship is an important organizational construct that provides us with a better theoretical understanding of the intrapersonal processes that affect maltreated children's sense of self and emotional functioning.

Deviant Parenting and Socialization Factors

Another theoretical perspective is that maltreatment is a marker for other deviant parenting behaviors that are likely to have impact on negative child outcomes. The role of socialization in the development of the self and self-conscious emotions can be seen in several ways. First is the internalization of parental values that children infer from parents' evaluative feedback (Alessandri & Lewis, 1993; Barrett & Campos, 1987; Campos & Barrett, 1984). External evaluation in the form of praise or disappointment from significant others may promote self-evaluations in children by focusing their attention on the social value of particular outcomes. Thus, the very act of interpretation and evaluation by the social environment provides the rules by which children learn to evaluate and interpret their own experiences.

Moreover, the socialization of affective expression (e.g., the behavioral, communicative aspects of affective states) is another source of influence on children's self and emotional functioning. Children learn much from parents regarding the nature of emotional expressions, their intensity, and the situations that might elicit them (Halberstadt, 1986, 1991). Emotion-related parental didactic practices or disciplinary encounters, parental reactions to their children's emotions, and parents' own expression of emotion are likely to be related to children's emotional functioning. The emotional culture of the family can encourage the child to maintain affective states that are either of a positive or negative nature (Malatesta-Magai, 1991; Tomkins, 1962, 1963). According to Tomkins (1963), rewarding socialization of affect is fostered when caregivers assist children in maintaining positive affect and help children to reduce negative affect. Punitive socialization of affect, on the other hand, occurs when parents amplify or maximize the negative affect experienced by the child. For example, matching anger with anger produces a spiral of angry interchanges or responding to a child's pain by behaving angrily when the child is sad. Thus, the child's emotional functioning depends, in part, on the expressive environment provided by the family. Parents serve as important models of emotion that can influence both directly and indirectly their children's emotional behavior.

Praise and criticism from parents are important factors in the development of pride and shame because these evaluations focus the child on the reasons for their success or failure. The experience of shame and pride would be particularly affected by maladaptive parent–child interactions. Abnormalities in the development of affective communication between maltreated infants and their caregivers have been studied. The maltreating mother–infant dyad is characterized by decreased responsiveness and reciprocal interactions, negative styles of affective displays (e.g., anger and sad facial expressions), and deviations in the capacity to express emotional states (Crittenden & Ainsworth, 1989; Gaensbauer, Mrazek, & Harmon, 1981; Gaensbauer & Sands, 1979). Aragona and Eyberg (1981) found that in a laboratory play session, neglecting mothers gave less verbal praise and acknowledgment and more criticism and commands than did mothers of behavior problem, nonmaltreated children. Burgess and Conger (1978), in a home study, reported that neglectful and abusive mothers were more negative, more controlling, and less positive than the nonmaltreating mothers in their verbalizations. Moreover, abusive parents show fewer physical and positive behaviors and less positive affect during interactions with their children (Alessandri, 1992; Bousha & Twentyman, 1984; Lahey, Conger, Atkeson, & Treiber, 1984). These negative maternal behaviors may act as potent influences on the child's emotional expression.

If parental blame and praise are likely to be one of the prerequisites for the development of shame and pride, and given that maltreated children receive more negative evaluative and emotional feedback from their parents, one would expect more shame and less pride in maltreated, relative to nonmaltreated, children. One would assume that the development of pride would be hampered in a child whose family rarely responds to him or her with social approval or acknowledges personal accomplishments. Similarly, one would expect that children, when exposed to high levels of negative evaluative and emotional feedback, might be predisposed to experiencing shame (M. Lewis, 1992; Morrison, 1989).

Maltreating parents are likely to amplify or maximize the negative affect experienced by the child which in turn may bias the child toward the development of an anxious, hostile, and shamed affective organization. When recurrent and unremitting exposure to shame and contempt becomes the primary mode of relation, the outcome may be shame toward the self (Tomkins, 1963). Thus, maltreated children are exposed to specific patterns of emotional expressivity that may influence the development of their own emotional styles. In addition to being the victim of physical and/or sexual abuse, and/or experiencing pronounced psychological abuse or emotional neglect from caregivers, maltreated children are likely to experience a family structure that fails to provide appropriate emotional socialization experiences and, instead, serves to disrupt and interfere with normal developmental processes in both subtle and blatant ways (Wolfe, 1987).

Cognitive and Attributional Influences

Another socialization perspective focuses on the cognitive, specifically attributional, climate of the family. Studies have shown that attributions influence our emotional functioning (Weiner, 1980), our attitudes toward other persons (Peevers & Secord, 1973) and, more important, our conceptions of ourselves (Harter, 1986; Weiner, 1980). Children's evaluative processes play an important role in their experience of the self-conscious emotions (M. Lewis, 1992; M. Lewis et al., 1992). Shame is most likely to occur when children fail an easy rather than difficult task. The reverse is true of pride. These findings suggest that children evaluate task difficulty, and that this evaluation involves both the nature of the task itself and one's attribution of success or failure at it.

Individual differences in children's attributional style related to their success or failure have been observed. Dweck and her colleagues (Diener & Dweck, 1978, 1980; Dweck, 1975; Dweck & Leggett, 1988; Dweck & Reppucci, 1973; Smiley & Dweck, 1994) identified two distinct attributional patterns. Children who attribute their failure to global or uncontrollable factors such as lack of ability tend to show negative self-cognitions, negative affect, and decreased task persistence. These children are termed *helpless*. In contrast, children who attribute failure to specific or controllable factors such as effort tend to show positive self-cognitions, positive affect, and maintain or improve their performance in the face of failure. These children are described as "mastery-oriented."

Very little is known about the origin of these differences. Although several studies of teacher influence have emerged (Brophy & Good, 1974; Wilkinson & Marrett, 1985), there have been few studies of the attributions parents make about their children and how these attributions are related to children's self-attributions. Since prior to school, children are socialized within the family, parents serve as the primary agents of influence and evaluation. It may be that the helpless and mastery-oriented patterns seen in children have their developmental origins within the family. Differential socialization experiences are likely to account for whether children adopt a helpless or mastery-oriented attributional style.

Studies with both children and adults support the notion that people tend to adopt attributions received during social interaction. For example, children whose sharing is attributed by an adult to altruistic dispositions subsequently share more than children whose sharing is attributed to external pressures (Dienstbier, Hellman, Lehnhoff, Hillman, & Volkenar, 1975; Grusec, Kuczynski, Rushton, & Simutis, 1978). Miller, Brickman, and Bolen (1975) found that labeling children neat or able tended to increase neatness and ability, an effect observed as well for cooperativeness and competitiveness by Jensen and Moore (1977). Parents also react to their children's achievement outcomes and either explicitly or implicitly supply causes as to why such outcomes were achieved. Empirical evidence indicates that parents ascribe causes to the successes and failures of their children and directly communicate their attributions to their children as well (Alessandri

& Lewis, 1993; Bar-Tal & Guttman, 1981; Beckman, 1976). All of this work suggests that children's attributions are suggestible and highly sensitive to the verbal input of others within a social context. Like overt acts, children's beliefs about the meaning of their behavior may be influenced and shaped by early social experiences.

Studies examining the cognitions of maltreating parents have shown that they are likely to interpret age-appropriate behavior as "willful" disobedience or intentional behavior when the child's actions opposes the parent's commands (Bauer & Twentyman, 1985; Helfer, Mckinney, & Kempe, 1976; Twentyman & Plotkin, 1982). Abusive parents are likely to interpret noncompliant behavior as an indication of the child's "bad" disposition (Azar, Robinson, Hekimian, & Twentyman, 1984; Rosenberg & Reppucci, 1983). Moreover, maltreating parents tend to appraise their children's dispositions globally through such negative terms as stubborn, unloving, or spoiled (Steele, 1970). Such cognitive patterns are likely to have important attributional implications.

Negative global attributions on the part of maltreating parents could very well lead their children to see themselves as less competent across a variety of domains and predispose them toward a "helpless" orientation. Such experiences, in turn, can result in learning an expectation of future helplessness whereby the child comes to believe that there is little that one can do to prevent or gain control over stressful situations. In this way, maltreated children are likely to develop a sense of overall negative self-evaluation, including feelings of shame, inadequacy, and inferiority. In contrast, nonmaltreated children move toward focusing on the positive in their self-understanding. A child who is highly regarded and treated well develops positive self-esteem, including a general bias toward the positive in self-evaluation (Harter, 1986). This positive bias becomes part of the child's personality structure and continues throughout adulthood. The attributions children adopt for themselves, therefore, are likely to be related to the attributions parents offer them early in life. Children's negative evaluations of themselves, their family, and the world in general is of primary interest since their future behavior may be largely affected by such viewpoints.

EFFECTS OF MALTREATMENT ON THE SELF AND SELF-CONSCIOUS EMOTIONS

Given the punitive familial environments in which maltreated children are raised and that they are likely to experience problems with attachments, one would expect that maltreated children's sense of self and emotional functioning might be impaired. Existing research seems to support this view. Several studies have demonstrated a link between maltreatment and children's self-concept and self-esteem. Maltreated toddlers express negative affect in visual self-recognition tasks, use less internal state language, and talk less about themselves relative to nonmaltreated children (Cicchetti & Beeghly, 1987; Coster, Gersten, Beeghly, & Cicchetti, 1989; Schneider-Rosen & Cicchetti, 1984). Maltreated children are also more likely to be rated by teachers as less competent and lacking self-esteem (Allen & Tarnowski, 1989; Vondra, Barnett, & Cicchetti, 1989). Maltreated children seem to have a core model of themselves as unworthy and of others as unavailable, rejecting, and exploitive.

With regard to emotional functioning, maltreated children are less accurate in their recognition and deliberate posing of emotional expressions than nonmaltreated children (Camras, Grow, & Ribordy, 1983; Camras et al., 1988). This depends, in part, on the expressive environment provided by mothers (Camras et al., 1990). Recently a study in which the expressions of shame and pride were examined in maltreated children found that maltreated girls showed significantly more shame compared to nonmaltreated girls (Alessandri & Lewis, in press). They also showed significantly less pride. It seems that maltreated girls are characterized by a disturbance in their development of pride and shame. Maltreated boys, on the other hand, show less shame and pride than nonmaltreated boys. These findings may have important implications for the development of maltreated children. It has been documented that the degree of positive affect that children feel about their own performance is important, not only in maintaining positive attitudes toward school learning, but also in promoting feelings of competence and self-worth (Aber & Allen, 1987; Cassidy, 1988). That maltreated girls showed few pride behaviors and more shame in achievement situations suggests that they are at risk for problems in motivation, school achievement, and self-concept.

If negative global attributions underlie shame (M. Lewis, 1992), maltreated girls are likely to see themselves as less competent across a variety of domains that might predispose them toward a "helpless" orientation (Abramson, Seligman, & Teasdale, 1978). Such experiences, in turn, can result in learning an expectation of future helplessness, whereby the girl comes to believe that there is little that she can do to prevent or gain control over stressful situations. In this way, maltreated girls are likely to develop a sense of overall negative self-evaluation, including feelings of low self-esteem. Dialogues with women who were abused as children support this contention of learned helplessness, indicating that many victims express feelings of shame, insecurity, and self-doubt across a diversity of situations (Brown & Finkelhor, 1986; Kilpatrick, Best, & Veronen, 1978; Veronen & Kilpatrick, 1980). Gold (1986) found that women who were sexually abused in childhood and who reported psychological distress and low self-esteem were likely to display an attributional style marked by internal, stable, and global attributions for bad events.

It appears that for girls, maltreatment, particularly sexual abuse, results in emotional partitioning and configuration of self in which negative rather than positive attributions become central (Calverley, Fischer, & Ayoub, 1994). Thus, shame may be mediated by internal attributions of responsibility that lead to self-blame (Celano, 1992). Girls are more likely to blame themselves for the abuse (e.g., "I am a bad person who brings trouble to my family"), may feel guilty if they enjoyed aspects of it and, in the case of incest, may feel that their disclosure has caused the destruction of their families. They are also likely to see their situation as not amenable to change (e.g., "There is little that can be done to prevent this from happening again"). Guilt and shame are likely to intensify over time as children gain a clearer understanding of cultural norms. In addition, there is coalescing evidence which suggests a relation between maltreatment and depression, particularly in females (Allen & Tarnowski, 1989; Kashani, Shekim, Burk, & Beck, 1987; Kazdin, Moser, Colbus, & Bell, 1985). Thus, these findings underscore the effects of maltreatment on the developing sense of self in girls and the contributory role that this may play in either current or later psychopathology.

Maltreated boys, on the other hand, did not show the same emotional pattern as maltreated girls in our study. They show less self-evaluative emotions. The reasons for this are unclear. One possibility is that maltreated males, unlike females, do not make internal attributions about their achievement behavior but rather explain their successes and failures in terms of factors external to their own efficiency. Although boys, as opposed to girls, are more likely to do this for failures than successes, it appears that maltreated males may do this for both failures and successes. Boys are, therefore, less likely to attribute their abuse and emotional discomfort to their own fallibilities. They are more likely to attribute blame to persons or circumstances external to the self (e.g., parents, teachers, siblings). For boys, maltreatment results in the reduction of self-conscious evaluative emotions, whereas in girls it results in more shame and less pride. Although the underlying mechanism for the self-conscious emotional differences can be only inferred, the results are consistent with other findings.

Maltreated boys also may show less emotional expression because of cultural expectations that boys should be tough and strong and, therefore, able to resist victimization. These social messages are likely to encourage boys to avoid reference to their maltreatment and to suppress emotional expression of their trauma. In addition to the denial of their abuse, boys are more prone to greater intellectualization of their experience (Briere, Evans, Runtz, & Wall, 1988). Thus, for boys the tendency to deny, suppress, or intellectualize their maltreatment has obvious effects on their ability to express feelings. This may, in turn, reduce the amount of emotional insight achieved during treatment. Given the general tendency of action over affect in males (Gold, 1986), acting out or impulsive responses to long-standing problems may be seen. One therapeutic goal for boys would be to facilitate the expression of feelings such as shame regarding the abuse. Interestingly, boys and men in our society are less likely to be punished for anger or expressions of hostility (Briere, 1989). Anger often becomes the only emotion available for expression in males. Feelings of fear, guilt, and shame are often fused into a single affect of rage that can be elicited by a variety of interpersonal stimuli. Such emotional behavior is consistent with narcissistic-like personality disorders, the cause of which is due to shame proneness (Morrison, 1989).

Girls who experience too much shame, on the other hand, respond with depression, often blaming themselves for failure and not crediting themselves for success. Such an account with modification for gender differences is in keeping with Rose and Abramson (1993). They proposed a model linking cognition regarding abuse with hopelessness and depression. We believe that maltreatment leads to shame through an attributional process in which girls attribute their interpersonal difficulties to internal, negative characteristics of the self. For boys, shame leads to attributional strategies that result in a reduction of self-conscious evaluative emotions and to defenses such as denial and acting-out behavior.

IMPLICATIONS

The study of the self-conscious emotions has important ramifications in the etiology, course, and sequelae of many forms of psychopathology. H. B. Lewis (1971, 1987) and M. Lewis (1992) suggested that shame is frequently the core of psychopathology, especially in depression. Kohut (1971) believed that shame is intimately connected with narcissistic disturbances in borderline personality disorders. It is generally recognized that aberrations in self-development and emotional functioning in the early years of life can result in the emergence of later forms of adult psychopathology, such as borderline and narcissistic disorders (Lewis, 1992; Morrison, 1989). Support for this hypothesis has been derived mostly from retrospective studies from adults who recalled abusive experiences during childhood or from clinical reports of childhood experiences (Kilpatrick et al., 1978; Veronen & Kilpatrick, 1980). In this regard, research examining the self-conscious emotions in maltreated children can have important implications for understanding the developmental sequelae of maltreatment and, in particular, early emotion and self-perturbations that might reflect current maladaptation and/or future psychopathology.

As we have seen, maltreated children are likely to have dysfunctional internal working models, both in relationships with primary caregivers and with regard to self, deviations in self-development, and a disturbance in emotional functioning. Such disturbances place maltreated children at risk for poor future adaptation. Although not all maltreated children will develop psychopathological disorders (Cicchetti & Garmezy, 1993; Cicchetti, Rogosch, Lynch, & Holt, 1993), later disturbances in functioning are likely to occur with the resolution of stage-salient developmental issues. For example, it may be difficult for maltreated children to develop effective coping strategies for dealing with frustration and conflict later in life due to chronic exposure to inadequate and negative parenting. The principle that is implied by these developmental sequelae is that issues at one developmental period lay the foundation for subsequent issues (Sroufe & Rutter, 1984). That is, the child who fails to develop an attachment to others, peer relationships, and self-control, common themes that pervade the literature on maltreated children, has missed important socialization experiences that may interfere with adult functioning. The child's inability to successfully adapt to environmental demands at one point in time may later compromise the child's future adjustment.

Deviant socialization processes in maltreating families play an important role in the development of the self and the self-conscious emotions and may contribute to the intergenerational transmission of negative affect, particularly shame. When trying to understand how this contributes to the child's emotional and self-development, the role of representational models in conjunction with punitive cognitive and affective socialization practices, and the inferences that maltreated children make about such interpersonal events must be taken into consideration. Given this level of complexity, prevention and intervention strategies need to be multidisciplinary and multicontextual in their focus.

The goals of therapy should be to assist the child in healing from the actual experience, to prevent or reverse the development of shame and stigma, to support the development of emotional intimacy and other age-appropriate skills, and to empower the child to become a survivor. Cognitive therapeutic approaches that include the articulation and modification of faulty or destructive belief systems, such as attributions and self-blame, are likely to be helpful. Childhood messages and familial beliefs are often entrenched because of strong reinforcement and modeling when the child was young and impressionable. These can usually be modified with repeated challenge and reinforcement with alternative beliefs and messages resulting in greater empowerment (Beck, 1976). Such an approach is important given that revictimization is considered to be related to helplessness and powerlessness (Briere & Runtz, 1988), perceived vulnerability (Marhoefer-Dvorak, Resick, Hutter, & Girelli, 1988), and low self-esteem (Maltz & Holman, 1987). Play, dyadic, and family therapies are additional treatment modalities that may be useful in working with maltreated children. Through continued exploration of therapeutic interventions we may learn more about the underlying mechanisms in the development of the self-conscious emotions as well as the means of helping children from abusive families to better adjust to their emotional lives and concept of themselves.

ACKNOWLEDGMENTS

The work described in this chapter was supported by an MCP grant awarded to Steven M. Alessandri and grants from the William T. Grant Foundation and National Science Foundation awarded to Michael Lewis.

REFERENCES

Aber, J.L., & Allen, J.P. (1987). The effects of maltreatment on young children's socioemotional development. An attachment theory perspective. *Developmental Psychology, 23,* 406–414.

Abramson, L.Y., Seligman, M.E.P., & Teasdale, J. D. (1978). Learned helplessness in humans: Critique and reformulation. *Journal of Abnormal Psychology, 87,* 49–74.

Alessandri, S.M. (1992). Mother-child interactional correlates of maltreated and nonmaltreated children's play behavior. *Development and Psychopathology, 4,* 257–270.

Alessandri, S.M., & Lewis, M. (1993). Parental evaluation and its relation to shame and pride in young children. *Sex Roles, 29,* 335–343.

Alessandri, S.M., & Lewis, M. (in press). Differences in pride and shame in maltreated and nonmaltreated children. *Child Development.*

Allen, D., & Tarnowski, K. (1989). Depressive characteristics of physically abused children. *Journal of Abnormal Child Psychology, 17,* 1–11.

Aragona, J.A., & Eyberg, S.M. (1981). Neglected children: Mothers' report of child behavior problems and observed verbal behavior. *Child Development, 52,* 596–602.

Azar, S.T., Robinson B.R., Hekimian, E., & Twentyman, C.T. (1984). Unrealistic expectations and problem-solving ability in maltreating and comparison mothers. *Journal of Consulting and Clinical Psychology, 52,* 687–691.

Barrett, K.C., & Campos, J.J. (1987). Perspectives on emotional development II. A functionalist approach to emotions. In J.D. Osofsky (Ed.), *Handbook of infant development* (2nd ed., pp. 555–578). New York: Wiley.

Bar-Tal, D., & Guttman, J. (1981). A comparison of pupils', teachers' and parents' attributions regarding pupils' achievement. *British Journal of Education Psychology, 51,* 301–311.

Bauer, W.D., & Twentyman, C.T. (1985). Abusing, neglectful, and comparison mother's responses to child-related and non-child related stressors. *Journal of Consulting and Clinical Psychology, 53,* 335–343.

Beck, A. (1976). *Cognitive therapy and the emotional disorder.* New York: International Universities Press.

Beckman, L.J. (1976). Causal attributions of teachers and parents regarding children's performance. *Psychology in the Schools, 13,* 212–218.

Bousha, D.M., & Twentyman, C.T. (1984). Mother–child interactional style in abuse, neglect, and control groups: Naturalistic observations in the home. *Journal of Psychology, 93,* 106–114.

Bowlby, J. (1973). *Attachment and loss (Vol. 2): Separation.* New York: Basic Books.

Briere, J. (1989). *Therapy for adults molested as children.* New York: Springer.

Briere, J., Evans, D., Runtz, M., & Wall, T. (1988). Symptomology in men who were molested as children: A comparison study. *American Journal of Orthopsychiatry, 58,* 457–461.

Briere, J., & Runtz, M. (1988). Symptomatology associated with childhood sexual victimization in a nonclinical adult sample. *Child Abuse & Neglect, 13,* 65–75.

Brophy, J.E., & Good, T. (1974). *Teacher-student relationships: Causes and consequences.* New York: Holt, Rinehart & Winston.

Brown, A., & Finkelhor, D. (1986). Impact of child sexual abuse: A review of the research. *Psychological Bulletin, 99,* 66–77.

Burgess, R.L., & Conger, R.D. (1978). Family interaction in abusive, neglectful, and normal families. *Child Development, 49,* 1163–1173.

Calverley, R.M., Fischer, K.W., & Ayoub, C. (1994). Complex splitting of self-representations in sexually abused adolescent girls. *Development and Psychopathology, 6,* 195–213.

Campos, J.J., & Barrett, K.C. (1984). A new understanding of emotions and their development. In C.E. Izard, J. Kagan, & R. Zajonc (Eds.), *Emotions, cognition, and behavior* (pp. 229–264). New York: Cambridge University Press.

Camras, L., Grow, G., & Ribordy, S. (1983). Recognition of emotional expressions by abused children. *Journal of Clinical Child Psychology, 12,* 325–328.

Camras, L.A., Ribordy, S., Hill, J., Martino, S., Sachs, V., Spaccarelli, S., & Stefani, R. (1990). Maternal facial behavior and the recognition and production of emotional expression by maltreated and nonmaltreated children. *Developmental Psychology, 26,* 304–312.

Camras, L.A., Ribordy, S., Hill, J., Martino, S., Spaccarelli, S., & Stefani, R. (1988). Recognition and posing of emotional expressions by abused children and their mothers. *Developmental Psychology, 24,* 776–781.

Carlson, V., Cicchetti, D., Burnett, D., & Braunwald, K. (1989). Disorganized/disoriented attachment relationships in maltreated infants. *Developmental Psychology, 25,* 525–231.

Cassidy, J. (1988). Child–mother attachment and the self in six-year olds. *Child Development, 59,* 121–134.

Celano, M. (1992). A developmental model of victims' internal attributions of responsibility for sexual abuse. *Journal of Interpersonal Violence, 7,* 57–69.

Cicchetti, D. (1991). Fractures in the crystal: Developmental psychopathology and the emergence of the self. *Developmental Review, 11,* 271–287.

Cicchetti, D., & Barnett, D. (1991). Attachment organization in pre-school aged maltreated children. *Development and Psychopathology, 3,* 397–411.

Cicchetti, D., & Beeghly, M. (1987). Symbolic development in maltreated young-sters: An organizational perspective. In D. Cicchetti & M. Beeghly (Eds.), *New directions for child development* (Vol. 36, pp. 47–67). San Francisco: Jossey-Bass.

Cicchetti, D., & Garmezy, N. (Eds.). (1993). Milestones in the development of resilience [Special issue]. *Development and Psychopathology, 5,* 497–502.

Cicchetti, D., Rogosch, F.A., Lynch, M., & Holt, K. (1993). Resilience in maltreated children: Processes leading to adaptive outcome. *Development and Psychopathology, 5,* 629–647.

Coster, W., Gersten, M., Beeghly, M., & Cicchetti, D. (1989). Communicative functioning in maltreated toddlers. *Developmental Psychology, 25,* 1020–1027.

Crittenden, P.M. (1988). Relationships at risk. In J. Belsky & J. Nezworski (Eds.), *Clinical implications of attachment theory* (pp. 136–174). Hillsdale, NJ: Lawrence Erlbaum Associates.

Crittenden, P.M. (1990). Internal representational models of attachment relation-ships. *Infant Mental Health Journal, 11,* 259–277.

Crittenden, P.M., & Ainsworth, M. (1989). Attachment and child abuse. In D. Cicchetti & V. Carlson (Eds.), *Child maltreatment: Research and theory on the consequences of child abuse and neglect* (pp. 432–463). New York: Cambridge University Press.

Cummings, E.M., & Cicchetti, D. (1990). Attachment, depression, and the trans-mission of depression. In M.T. Greenberg, D. Cicchetti, & E.M. Cummings (Eds.), *Attachment during the pre-school years* (pp. 339–372). Chicago: Univer-sity of Chicago Press.

Diener, C.I., & C.S. Dweck (1978). An analysis of learned helplessness: Continu-ous changes in performance, strategy, and achievement cognitions following fail-ure. *Journal of Personality and Social Psychology, 36,* 451–462.

Diener, C.I., & Dweck, C.S. (1980). Analysis of learned helplessness: II. The processing of success. *Journal of Personality and Social Psychology, 39,* 940–952.

Dienstbier, R.A., Hellman, D., Lehnhoff, J., Hillman, J.H., & Volkenar, M.C. (1975). An emotion-attribution approach to moral behavior: Interfacing cogni-tive and avoidance theories of moral development. *Psychological Review, 82,* 299–315.

Dweck, C. (1975). The role of expectations and attributions in the alleviation of learned helplessness. *Journal of Personality and Social Psychology, 31,* 674–685.

Dweck, C.S., & Leggett, E.L. (1988). A social-cognitive approach to motivation and personality. *Psychological Review, 25,* 256–273.

Dweck, C.S., & Reppucci, N.D. (1973). Learned helplessness and reinforcement responsibility in children. *Journal of Personality and Social Psychology, 25,* 109–116.

Gaensbauer, T., Mrazek, D., & Harmon, R. (1981). Emotional expression in abused and/or neglected infants. In N. Frude (Ed.), *Psychological approaches to child abuse* (pp. 120–135). Totowa, NJ: Rowman & Littlefield.

Gaensbauer, T., & Sands, K. (1979). Distorted affective communication by abuse/neglected infants and their potential impact on caretakers. *Journal of the American Academy of Child Psychiatry, 18,* 236–250.

Geppert, U., & Gartmann, D. (1983). *The emergence of self-evaluative emotions as consequences of achievement actions.* Extended version of a poster presented at the seventh biennial meetings of the International Society for the Study of Behavioral Development, Munchen.

Gold, E. R. (1986). Long-term effects of sexual victimization in childhood: An attributional approach. *Journal of Consulting and Clinical Psychology, 54,* 471–475.

Grusec, J., Kuczynski, L., Rushton, J., & Simutis, Z. (1978). Modeling, direct instruction, and attributions: Effects on altruism. *Developmental Psychology, 14,* 51–57.

Halberstadt, A. (1986). Family socialization of emotional expression and nonverbal communication styles and skills. *Journal of Personality and Social Psychology, 51,* 827–836.

Halberstadt, A. (1991). The ecology of expressiveness: Family expressiveness in particular and a model in general. In R.S. Feldman & B. Rime (Eds.), *Fundamentals in nonverbal behavior* (pp. 106–162). Cambridge, U.K.: Cambridge University Press.

Harter, S. (1986). Processes underlying the construction, maintenance, and enhancement of the self-concept in children. In J. Suls & A. Greenwald (Eds.), *Psychological perspectives on the self* (Vol. 3, pp. 137–181). Hillsdale, NJ: Lawrence Erlbaum Associates.

Heckhausen, H. (1984). Emergent achievement behavior: Some early developments. In J. Nicolls (Ed.), *The development of achievement motivation* (pp. 1–32). Greenwich, CT: JAI Press.

Heckhausen, H. (1987a). Causal attribution patterns for achievement outcomes: Individual differences, possible types, and their origins. In F.E. Wienert & R.H. Kluwe (Eds.), *Metacognition, motivation, and understanding* (pp. 143–184). Hillsdale, NJ: Lawrence Erlbaum Associates.

Heckhausen, H. (1987b). Emotional components of action: Their ontogeny as reflected in achievement behavior. In D. Gorlitz & J.F. Wohlwill (Eds.), *Curiosity, imagination and play: On the development of spontaneous cognitive and motivational processes* (pp. 326–348). Hillsdale, NJ: Lawrence Erlbaum Associates.

Heckhausen, H. (1988). Becoming aware of one's competence in the second year: Developmental progression within the mother-child dyad. *International Journal of Behavioral Development, 11,* 305–326.

Helfer, R.E., McKinney, J., & Kempe, R. (1976). Arresting or freezing the developmental process. In R.E. Helfer & C.H. Kempe (Eds.), *Child abuse and neglect: The family and the community.* Cambridge, MA: Ballinger.

Jensen, R., & Moore, S. (1977). The effect of attribute statements on cooperativeness and competitiveness in school-age boys. *Child Development, 48,* 305–307.

Kagan, J. (1981). *The second year: The emergence of self-awareness.* Cambridge, MA: Harvard University Press.

Kashani, J.H., Shekim, W.O., Burk, J.P., & Beck, N.C. (1987). Abuse as a predictor of psychopathology in children and adolescents. *Journal of Clinical Child Psychology, 16,* 43–50.

Kazdin, A., Moser, J., Colbus, D., & Bell, R. (1985). Depressive symptoms among physically abused and psychiatrically disturbed children. *Journal of Abnormal Psychology, 94,* 298–307.

Kilpatrick, D.G., Best, C.L., & Veronen, L.J. (1978). The adolescent rape victim. In K.K. Krentner & D.R. Hollingsworth (Eds.), *Adolescent obstetrics and gynecology* (pp. 325–357). New York: Yearbook Medical.

Kohut, H. (1971). *The analysis of the self.* New York: International Universities Press.

Lahey, B., Conger, K., Atkeson, B., & Treiber, F. (1984). Parenting behavior and emotional status of physically abusive mothers. *Journal of Consulting and Clinical Psychology, 52,* 1062–1071.

Lewis, H.B., (1971). *Shame and guilt in neurosis.* New York: International Universities Press.

Lewis, H.B. (Ed.). (1987). *The role of shame in symptom formation.* Hillsdale, NJ: Lawrence Erlbaum Associates.

Lewis, M. (1993). The self-conscious emotions: Embarrassment, pride, shame, and guilt. In M. Lewis & J. Haviland (Eds.), *Handbook of emotions* (pp. 563–575). New York: Guilford.

Lewis, M. (1992). *Shame, The exposed self.* New York: The Free Press.

Lewis, M., Alessandri, S.M., & Sullivan, M.W., (1992). Differences in pride and shame as a function of children's gender and task difficulty. *Child Development, 63,* 630–638.

Lewis, M., Sullivan, M.W., Stanger, C., & Weiss, M. (1989). Self-development and self-conscious emotions. *Child Development, 60,* 146–156.

Maltz, W., & Holman, B. (1987). *Incest and sexuality: A guide to understanding and healing.* Lexington, MA: Lexington Books.

Malatesta-Magai, C. (1991). Emotional socialization: Its role in personality and developmental psychopathology. In D. Cicchetti & S. Toth (Eds.), *Internalizing and externalizing expressions of dysfunction* (pp. 203–224). Hillsdale, NJ: Lawrence Erlbaum Associates.

Marhoefer-Dvorak, S., Resick, P., Hutter, C., & Girelli, S. (1988). Single versus multiple incident rape victims: A comparison of psychological reactions to rape. *Journal of Interpersonal Violence, 3,* 145–160.

Miller, R., Brickman, P., & Bolen, D. (1975). Attribution versus persuasion as a means for modifying behavior. *Journal of Personality and Social Psychology, 31,* 430–441.

Morrison, A.P. (1989). *Shame: The underside of narcissism.* Hillsdale, NJ: The Analytic Press.

Peevers, B.H., & Secord, P.F. (1973). Developmental changes in attribution of descriptive concepts. *Journal of Personality and Social Psychology, 27,* 120–128.

Rose, D.T., & Abramson, L.Y. (1993). Developmental predictors of depressive cognitive style: Research and theory. In D. Cicchetti & S.L. Toth (Eds.), *A developmental approach to depression: Rochester Symposium of Developmental Psychopathology* (Vol. 4). Rochester, NY: University of Rochester Press.

Rosenberg, M.S., & Reppucci, N.D. (1983). Abusive mothers: Perceptions of their own and their children's behavior. *Journal of Consulting and Clinical Psychology, 51,* 674–682.

Schneider-Rosen, K., & Cicchetti, D. (1984). The relationship between affect and cognition in maltreated infants: Quality of attachment and the development of visual self-recognition. *Child Development, 55,* 648–658.

Smiley, P.A., & Dweck, C.S. (1994). Individual differences in achievement goals among young children. *Child Development, 65,* 1723–1743.

Sroufe, L.A. (1983). Infant–caregiver attachment and patterns of adaptation in preschool: The roots of maladaptation and competence. In M. Perlmutter

(Eds.), *Minnesota symposia in child psychology* (Vol. 16, pp. 41–83). Hillsdale, NJ: Lawrence Erlbaum Associates.

Sroufe, L.A., & Rutter, M. (1984). The domain of developmental psychopathology. *Child Development, 54,* 173–189.

Steele, B.F. (1970). Parental abuse of infants and small children. In E.J. Anthony & T. Benedek (Eds.), *Parenthood, its psychology and psychopathology.* Boston, MA: Little, Brown.

Stipek, D.J. (1983). A developmental analysis of pride and shame. *Human Development, 26,* 42–54.

Stipek, D.J., Recchia, S., & McClintic, S. (1992). Self-evaluation in young children. *Monographs of the Society for Research in Child Development, 57* (1, Serial No. 226).

Tomkins, S.S. (1962). *Affect, imagery, consciousness: Vol. I. The positive affects.* New York: Springer.

Tomkins, S.S. (1963). *Affect, imagery, consciousness: Vol. II. The negative affects.* New York: Springer.

Twentyman, C.T., & Plotkin, R. (1982). Unrealistic expectations of parents who maltreat their children: An educational deficit that pertains to child maltreatment. *Journal of Clinical Psychology, 38,* 497–503.

Veronen, L.J., & Kilpatrick, D.G. (1980). Self-reported fears of rape victims: A preliminary investigation. *Behavior Modification, 4,* 383–396.

Vondra, J., Barnett, D., & Cicchetti, D. (1989). Perceived and actual competence among maltreated and comparison school children. *Development and Psychopathology, 1,* 237–255.

Weiner, B. (1980). *Human motivation.* New York: Reinhart & Winston.

Weiner, B. (1986). *An attributional theory of motivation and emotion.* New York: Springer-Verlag.

Wilkinson, L.C., & Marrett, C.B. (1985). *Gender differences in classroom interaction.* New York: Academic Press.

Wolfe, D.A. (1987). *Child abuse.* Newbury Park, CA: Sage.

Emotion Understanding in Maltreated Children: Recognition of Facial Expressions and Integration With Other Emotion Cues

Linda A. Camras
Ellen Sachs-Alter
Sheila C. Ribordy
DePaul University

The study of pathology for the purpose of illuminating normalcy has a long and respected history in the field of psychology (A. Freud, 1965; S. Freud, 1940/1955; Shallice, 1988). Through examination of cognitive, behavioral, or affective deviations, processes responsible for normal functioning can be better understood. With respect to development, this principle is currently a key tenet of developmental psychopathology (Cicchetti, 1993). Advocates of this approach have studied several populations of disordered or high-risk children (e.g., children with Down syndrome, children of depressed mothers, maltreated children) in an effort to generate and confirm hypotheses regarding normal developmental processes. Simultaneously, this research has garnered a greater understanding of these children's competencies and deficiencies, critical to providing them with optimal care and treatment.

With regard to advancing the understanding of emotional development, the study of maltreated children appears to hold particular promise. Childhood maltreatment often involves a severe disruption of the normal mother–child relationship. For example, attachment studies have found insecure and/or disorganized patterns of attachment to be predominant among maltreated infants (e.g., Carlson, Cichetti, Barnett, & Braunwald, 1989). Such findings suggest that maltreated children may be deficient in other aspects of their emotional development.

One aspect of emotional development that is currently receiving considerable attention in studies of normal children is emotion understanding (e.g., Saarni & Harris, 1989). An accurate understanding of other people's emotions is obviously critical for effective social interaction and communication. One important aspect of emotion understanding is the recognition of affective facial expressions. Although numerous studies (see Ekman, 1994) have documented the impressive accuracy with which adults worldwide are able to identify prototypical emotional facial expressions, the ontogenetic origins of this universal ability are poorly understood. Thus, identification and investigation of a population with less-than-average facial expression recognition skill might begin to shed light on the processes underlying its development.

DEVELOPMENT OF EMOTION RECOGNITION SKILL

Beginning with Darwin (1872/1965), two clearly opposing hypotheses regarding the development of expression recognition have continued to be entertained. Reflecting the perpetual tension between nativist and environmentalist viewpoints, one position asserts that emotion recognition is biologically preprogrammed, whereas the second proposes that individuals learn to recognize emotional expression largely through experience.

With relevance to the innateness hypothesis, several investigators (e.g., Caron, Caron, & Myers, 1982; Haviland & Lelwica, 1987) examined young infants' responses to emotional facial expressions. This research has produced convincing data indicating that babies can discriminate and categorize several facial expressions by about 7 months. However, evidence that infants of this age *understand* the emotion meaning of these facial expressions is much more ambiguous (see Nelson, 1987, for review).

By the end of the first year, infants' responses to affective facial expression clearly indicate some degree of emotion understanding. Numerous "social referencing" studies (see Waldren & Ogan, 1988) have found infants to respond with approach to positive facial expressions and to respond with avoidance to negative expressions (e.g., fear or disgust). Differential responsiveness to different negative emotional expressions (e.g., fear vs. disgust) has not been clearly demonstrated, however. Nevertheless, these widely replicated findings indicate that 12-month-old infants consistently comprehend the valence (positive vs. negative) of several emotional facial expressions.

Studies of older children have been able to employ verbal emotion labels, thus circumventing many interpretative difficulties inherent in investigations of linguistically immature infants and children. However, many studies (e.g., Denham, 1986) present both facial and vocal cues to children, precluding definitive conclusions regarding facial expression understanding. Carefully controlled studies of facial expressions alone have found that 4-year-olds can identify six emotional facial expressions with above-chance accuracy (Camras & Allison, 1985) and that further improvement occurs throughout the elementary school years (Izard, 1971).

The gradual refinement of expression recognition skill suggests that experience must play an important role in its development. Among those who accept this environmentalist position, a tacit assumption appears to be that children learn to identify facial expressions by observing other persons produce such expressions in emotion situations. However, this general proposal leaves much unspecified (e.g., the parameters of the expressive environment necessary for observational learning to take place, the processing strategies employed by the learner who is exposed to a particular expressive environment). Investigating expression recognition in maltreated children might lead to a more detailed model of the developmental process.

SOCIAL AND EMOTIONAL CHARACTERISTICS OF MALTREATED CHILDREN

Maltreated children often show behavioral problems that might partly stem from difficulties with emotion recognition. In many studies, physically abused children have been found to display higher levels of aggressive behavior than nonmaltreated children (George & Main, 1979; Haskett & Kistner, 1991; Hoffman-Plotkin & Twentyman, 1984; Klimes-Dougan & Kistner, 1990; Salzinger, Feldman, Hammer, & Rosario, 1993). Both physically abused children and neglected children have been reported to be more withdrawn than their peers (e.g., George & Main, 1979; Haskett & Kistner, 1991; Jacobson & Straker, 1982; Kaufman & Cicchetti, 1989; Klimes-Dougan & Kistner, 1990). In addition, abused and/or neglected children have been reported to be inappropriate in their responses to peer distress (Main & George, 1985), to be less well liked by their peers (Kaufman & Cicchetti, 1989; Rogosch & Cicchetti, 1994; Salzinger et al., 1993), and to have lower self-esteem (Rogosch & Cicchetti, 1994) than their nonmaltreated counterparts. Although these results are not consistently found in all studies (e.g., Egeland, 1991; Howes & Eldredge, 1985; Howes & Espinosa, 1985; Jacobson & Straker, 1982), overall the literature suggests that maltreated children have significant problems with emotion regulation and social interaction.

Information-processing models of social behavior (e.g., Dodge, Pettit, McClaskey, & Brown, 1987) propose that one source of such difficulties can be the misinterpretation of social information, including the emotional expressions of one's cointeractants. Indeed, studies of nonmaltreated aggressive children and children who have difficulties entering social groups have found deficits in these children's reading of social cues (Dodge et al., 1987). With respect to maltreatment, Barahal, Waterman, and Martin (1981) reported abused children to have difficulty identifying emotions presented in the form of audiotaped scenarios. In contrast, Frodi and Smetana (1984) found no differences among physically abused, neglected, and nonmaltreated children who were matched for IQ. However, neither of these investigations focused on the interpretation of facial expressions.

FACIAL EXPRESSION RECOGNITION
BY MALTREATED CHILDREN

To more specifically examine maltreated children's recognition of emotional facial expressions, Camras, Grow, and Ribordy (1983) conducted an initial investigation involving 3- to 7-year-old children. The maltreated subjects, who were all physically abused children, were also neglected in virtually all cases. A group of nonmaltreated children were matched to the maltreatment group for race, socioeconomic status (SES), and age in months. Employing a standard technique used in studies of expression recognition, subjects were told 12 emotion stories and were asked to choose an appropriate facial expression for the story protagonist. The facial expression stimuli were photographs of two child models posing six prototypic facial expressions of emotion: happiness, surprise, anger, sadness, fear, and disgust. These expressions were described by Ekman and Friesen (1975), based on their extensive crosscultural research on emotion recognition.

Results showed that maltreated children were less accurate in their expression recognition than nonmaltreated children. Furthermore, no interaction between expression type and subject group (i.e., maltreated vs. nonmaltreated) was obtained, suggesting that the differences between maltreated and nonmaltreated children were roughly equivalent across the different emotions. Similar results were obtained by During and McMahon (1991) and by Camras et al. (1988) in a replication study that controlled for the effects of verbal competence.

An interesting trend in the data suggested that maltreated children may also have an anger-related attributional bias. When we examined children's response errors in the replication study were examined, nonsignificant tendency was found for maltreated children to mistakenly choose the anger expression more often than did nonmaltreated children. Specifically, 27% of maltreated children's errors were anger misattributions as opposed to only 18% of nonmaltreated children's errors. This pattern of results suggests that overattribution of anger by maltreated children might be demonstrated in further investigations involving a larger number of trials for each emotion.

Given maltreated children's lesser ability to recognize emotional facial expressions, focus was shifted to an investigation of possible sources of this deficiency in their expressive environment. We centered primarily on mothers' behavior between mothers may be assumed to serve as important sources of social and emotional information for their children. Although focusing rather narrowly on facial expressions, our study fits within a larger context of research on the socialization of emotion knowledge.

SOCIALIZATION OF EMOTION KNOWLEDGE

Research on the socialization of emotion understanding typically utilizes measures that amalgamate children's knowledge about emotion elicitation, emotion expressions, and sometimes emotion-coping strategies. Consequently, it has provided little specific data on the development of expression recognition skills. Nevertheless, these studies provide important background information and a useful framework within which to examine the development of facial expression recognition.

A number of processes have been proposed through which adults (particularly mothers) may facilitate the development of emotion knowledge in their children. These include exposure, modeling, coaching or induction, contingent responding, and providing the child with "practice" opportunities (Denham, Zoller, & Couchard, 1994; Halberstadt, 1991; Lewis & Saarni, 1985). Exposure (Gordon, 1989) involves allowing children to witness or even participate in certain types of emotion episodes (e.g., attending a funeral). Through observational learning, sometimes in conjunction with his or her own experience of emotion, the child acquires knowledge about relationships between eliciting situations and emotional responses (including expressive behaviors). *Modeling* refers to the display of emotion by the socialization agent and similarly provides the child with opportunities for observational learning to take place. Although most investigations focus on directly enacted emotions, vicarious exposure and modeling may also be important, such as when adults allow the child to overhear narratives about emotion episodes or when such a narrative is addressed to the child him or herself (Miller & Sperry, 1987).

Coaching or *induction* (Lewis & Saarni, 1985) are terms that describe adults' verbal explanations of emotion to the child. This means of imparting emotion knowledge can occur in conjunction with direct exposure or modeling (e.g., when the parent comments on a witnessed or directly experienced emotion episode by labeling someone's emotion or pointing out the causes or consequences of the emotion). In addition, induction can occur in conjunction with vicarious exposure or modeling, as when an adult's narrated account of an emotion episode includes similar labeling or explanation.

Contingent responding (Denham et al., 1994) refers to the adult's own emotional response to the child's emotion and/or emotional expression (e.g. child angry followed by mother sad). Researchers often assume that positive or negative contingent responses serve to reward or punish the child's expression of emotion (Denham et al., 1994; Tomkins, 1962). However, this assumption is problematic because the meaning of an adult's contingent response may vary considerably across different negative emotions and emotion situations.

Provision of practice opportunities (e.g., teasing the child to provoke mild anger; Miller, 1986) facilitates the child's development of emotion regulation skills. When it occurs in conjunction with adult modeling, induction, and/or contingent responding, practice episodes may also provide the child with information about socially acceptable forms of emotion responding.

Empirical research suggests that some of these socialization mechanisms are more important than others in affecting the child's emotion understanding. In a questionnaire study involving preschoolers and their mothers, Denham and Couchard (1988) found that children with greater emotion knowledge had mothers who both valued emotional expression and endorsed a "rational" approach to childrearing (i.e., involving use of induction). In a laboratory study, Denham et al. (1994) subsequently found that maternal coaching (i.e., induction) and positive contingent responsiveness were positively related to emotion knowledge, whereas maternal negative contingent responsiveness was negatively related to children's emotion knowledge scores. In contrast, mothers' modeling of emotion was generally unrelated to children's emotion knowledge, save that maternal displays of anger were negatively correlated with children's aggregate emotion knowledge scores. Similarly, Cassidy, Parke, Butkovsky, and Braungart (1992) found no relationship between parent expressiveness (i.e., modeling) and their children's emotion knowledge. In summary, these results suggest that modeling alone may have little effect on children's general emotion knowledge, whereas verbal explanations of emotion presented in the context of a positive emotional relationship may facilitate the development of such knowledge.

Extending socialization research outside the laboratory, Dunn, Brown, and Beardsall (1991) studied natural family interactions involving preschool children and their mothers and older siblings. They found a positive relationship between the total amount of emotion talk taking place within the family and children's emotion understanding. More recently, Dunn and

Brown (1994) reported that families with higher levels of negative emotional expression are less likely to discuss emotion causes than are families with lower levels of negative emotional expression. Children in these families also score lower on tests of emotion understanding.

Taken together, the extant research currently suggests that verbal coaching and mothers' positive responsiveness are related to the development of general emotion knowledge. In contrast, family displays of negative emotion are not related to greater understanding despite the fact that negative emotions are overrepresented in emotion knowledge tests. Thus, minimal exposure to negative emotion modeling may be adequate for learning to take place. However, higher levels of negative affect may have undesirable effects that offset the benefits of increased exposure to exemplars of these emotions.

Few studies have examined facial expression recognition independent of other emotion knowledge measures. Such studies are important because socialization practices that facilitate expression recognition may differ from those facilitating other aspects of emotion understanding (e.g., causes and consequences of emotion). In one investigation, Daly, Abramovitch, and Pliner (1980) obtained a positive relationship between maternal expressive behavior and children's recognition skill using a procedure that involved the production and identification of spontaneous expressive behavior. However, Denham et al. (1994) found no relationship between preschoolers' scores on their expression recognition subtest and any of several socialization measures. In addition, Halberstadt (1986) found that college students who reported themselves as growing up in highly expressive families actually did poorer in recognizing spontaneous facial behavior than subjects from less expressive families. Thus, research on the socialization correlates of expression recognition skill has produced inconsistent results so far.

EMOTIONAL AND EXPRESSIVE CHARACTERISTICS OF MALTREATING MOTHERS

Research on maltreated children has not specifically attempted to relate their emotion knowledge to family socialization practices. Nonetheless, studies of maltreating mothers suggest that the emotional and expressive environments they provide their children deviate from the norm in ways that could significantly affect the development of emotion recognition skills in their children. The responses of maltreating mothers on questionnaires measuring family environment and childrearing practices indicate that they are more authoritarian than nonmaltreatment mothers and less encouraging of autonomy (Rogosch & Cicchetti, 1994). In addition, they report enjoying their children less, having more negative affect toward the child, and being less expressive in general than nonmaltreating mothers (Trickett, Aber, Carlson, & Cicchetti, 1991).

Studies in which mother–child interactions have been observed either at home or in the laboratory have found that maltreating mothers display less positive emotion (Bousha & Twentyman, 1984; Bugental, Blue, & Lewis, 1990; Burgess & Conger, 1978; Kavanaugh, Youngblade, Reid, & Fagot, 1988) and/or more negative emotion (Herrenkohl, Herrenkohl, Egolf, & Wu, 1991; Lyons-Ruth, Connell, Zoll, & Stahl, 1987) during interactions with their children. In addition, maltreatment families engage in less talk about emotion than nonmaltreatment families (Cicchetti & Beeghly, 1987).

Distinctions between the behaviors of physically abusive mothers and neglectful mothers have been made in some studies. Findings suggest that abusive mothers may show more negative affect than nonmaltreating mothers, whereas neglecting mothers may be less expressive overall and less engaged with their children than are nonmaltreating mothers (Bousha & Twentyman, 1984; Crittenden, 1981; Egeland, 1991). However, differences between maltreating and nonmaltreating mothers and between abusive and neglecting mothers are not consistently found across all studies (e.g., Mash, Johnston, & Kovitz, 1983).

In summary, the extant research suggests that maltreating mothers may display fewer positive expressions and more negative expressions when interacting with their children than do nonmaltreating mothers. However, only one study (Bugental et al., 1990) specifically examined facial expressions independent from expressive vocalizations. Thus, further research is necessary to determine if maltreating mothers' facial expression modeling is related to their children's expression recognition skill. To explore this issue, we designed a series of investigations to explicitly examine relationships between the posed (i.e., voluntary) and spontaneous facial behavior of maltreating and nonmaltreating mothers and their children's recognition of emotional facial expressions.

MOTHERS' POSED EMOTIONAL EXPRESSIONS

In the course of natural social interaction, both spontaneous and voluntary facial expressions are produced (Ekman, 1984). Voluntary expressions may occur as part of an emoter's efforts at expression regulation (e.g., masking the genuine expression of emotion) or they may be used referentially (i.e., when referring to emotion that is not currently being experienced).

Voluntary production of emotional expression is usually studied by asking subjects to deliberately produce facial expressions for specific emotions. Although no exemplars are provided, subjects may be allowed to "practice" with a mirror until they feel they have successfully produced the requested expression. Using this technique, we compared the posing abilities of our matched samples of maltreating and nonmaltreating mothers and their 3- to 7-year-old children (Camras et al., 1988). Subjects were asked to produce expressions for six emotions: happiness, surprise, anger, fear, sadness, and disgust.

Results showed that both maltreating mothers and their children produced expressions that were less easily identified by observers than were the expressions of their nonmaltreatment counterparts. Furthermore, when data from the maltreatment and nonmaltreatment groups were combined, a significant positive correlation was found between mothers' posing abilities and their children's expression recognition scores. These findings suggest that mothers' capacity to deliberately produce emotional facial expressions contributes to their children's development of emotion recognition skills.

MOTHERS' SPONTANEOUS EXPRESSIVE BEHAVIOR

In a further effort to investigate the expressive environments that maltreating and nonmaltreating mothers provide for their children, we examined mother–child interactions in both laboratory and natural settings (Camras, et al., 1990). In the laboratory, the children and their mothers were videotaped while playing with several toys selected by the experimenters to elicit a variety of emotional responses. In addition, two research assistants visited each mother–child pair at home for seven 1-hour observation sessions.

The mothers' and children's facial expressions were coded using several systems. The videotaped laboratory behavior was scored using Ekman and Friesen's (1978) Facial Action Coding System (FACS), a fine-grained, anatomically based system for comprehensive coding of all facial movements. Subsequently, coders utilized Friesen and Ekman's (1984) Emotion Facial Action Coding System (EMFACS) to identify patterns of facial muscle actions hypothesized to be expressions of happiness, surprise, anger, disgust, fear, and sadness. Facial behavior during the home observation sessions was coded by hand using a simplified system involving three non-mutually exclusive categories: smile (i.e., facial movement produced by the action of m. zygomatic major), negative upper face actions (i.e., facial movements of the brows that are components of the emotional expressions of anger, fear, or sadness), and negative lower face actions (i.e., facial movements of the nose or mouth that are components of the emotional expressions of anger, disgust, fear, sadness, and contempt). To compare expressive behavior produced at home to that produced in the laboratory, the videorecorded laboratory facial behavior was also recoded using the simplified three-category system. Finally, portions of both the laboratory play session and the videorecorded home observation sessions were rated on a set of emotion scales (i.e., happiness, anger/disgust/contempt, sadness, positive expressiveness, negative expressiveness, general expressiveness) by observers who made intuitive judgments based on facial, postural, vocal, and verbal emotion cues (Widlansky, 1994).

Given the significant difference between maltreating and nonmaltreating mothers in their expression posing skill, it was surprised to find that the facial movement coding showed no differences in their spontaneous facial behavior. Maltreating and nonmaltreating mothers also did not receive significantly different observer ratings of emotion except on a single scale—sadness—where maltreating mothers received higher ratings than nonmaltreating mothers. However, the higher sadness ratings received by the maltreating mothers appeared more attributable to postural cues and lack of facial muscle tonus than to production of sadness-relevant facial muscle movements. These findings thus indicate that maltreating and nonmaltreating mothers do not differ in the facial movements they produce during some spontaneous social interactions. However, they may differ in other interactional contexts that were not observed in this study (e.g., more highly charged emotional situations).

Despite our failure to find group differences between maltreating and nonmaltreating mothers, regression analyses indicated that maternal facial behavior is related to children's expression recognition skills. These analyses showed that children's recognition scores were predicted by both maltreatment status and mother's use of negative lower face actions in both the laboratory play session and the home observations. The negative lower face actions observed were primarily lip presses, which may be an expressive indicator of concentration, determination, frustration, mild anger, or regulated anger (Darwin 1872/1965; Ekman & Friesen, 1975). These affective responses might be expected to commonly occur in the type of interactions observed.

These findings indicated that mothers who showed more expressive signs of concentration, determination, or mild anger had children who were better at recognizing emotional expression. Thus, maternal modeling of such low intensity emotional expressions may enhance the development of children's expression recognition skills.

At the same time, Camras et al. (1990) also found evidence that maternal modeling of more intense negative emotional expressions may have the opposite effect on development. That is, mothers who produced more intense negative affect during the home observations (i.e., involving negative upper face as well as negative lower face components) had children who were less able to recognize emotional expressions. This finding is consistent with results reported in several studies of nonmaltreated children. For example, Denham et al. (1994) found that mothers who produced more full-face anger expressions in the laboratory had children who scored lower on her test of general emotion knowledge. Similarly, Dunn and Brown (1994) reported that higher levels of negative expression in the home were related to lower aggregate emotion knowledge test scores. As indicated earlier, these findings suggest that maternal displays of intense negative emotion may adversely affect the development of emotion knowledge despite the child's increased exposure to natural exemplars of negative emotion test items. If maltreating and nonmaltreating mothers differ in the expression of intense negative emotion outside the confines of our study, this difference might similarly contribute to differences in their children's expression recognition skill.

Why should exposure to intense negative expressiveness be inversely related to children's expression recognition skill? Camras et al. (1990) proposed that this relationship reflects the influence of strongly negative maternal affect on children's "effectance motivation." Aber and Allen (1987) reported that maltreated children demonstrate less effectance motivation (i.e., "secure readiness to learn") than do nonmaltreated children, presumably due to their experiencing a more punishing and less rewarding environment. Among other things, this lesser learning readiness would make maltreated children less able to learn about emotional facial expressions irrespective of whether maltreating and nonmaltreating mothers differ in their production of facial expressions. Effectance motivation might also explain the inverse relationship found between family negativity and nonmaltreated children's general emotion knowledge (Denham et al., 1994, Dunn & Brown, 1994).

CONTEXTUAL USE OF FACIAL EXPRESSIONS

To explore further possible differences between maltreating and nonmaltreating mothers' facial behavior, Sachs-Alter (1989) assessed the contexts in which the mothers in Camras' study produced emotion expressions while interacting with their young children. A sample of each mother's positive expressions (e.g., smiles), negative upper face movements (e.g., lowered brows), and negative lower face movements (e.g., lip presses) was systematically selected from the data. Sachs-Alter developed an empirically driven coding system in which each facial expression was categorized into 1 of 14 situational contexts (e.g., mother demonstrated competence; child displays positive behavior or affect). Sachs-Alter then compared the distribution of maltreating mothers' and nonmaltreating mothers' facial expressions across the contexts.

Results showed that control mothers produced significantly more of their positive expressions in response to their child displaying positive affect or behavior than did maltreating mothers (39% of control mothers' positive expressions vs. 15% of maltreating mothers' positive expressions). In contrast, maltreating mothers produced more positive expressions than control mothers when they: (a) demonstrated competence in a task (13% vs. 2% of positive expressions); (b) had difficulty with a task (16% vs. 7% of positive expressions); and (c) directed or instructed their children (18% vs. 10% of positive expressions).

The results also showed differences between maltreating and nonmaltreating mothers' contextual use of negative facial expressions of emotion, or components of such expressions (e.g., lip presses or lowered brows). Control mothers produced significantly more of these expressions when instructing or directing their children than did maltreating mothers (26% of control mothers' negative expressions vs. 14% of maltreating mothers' negative expressions). Maltreating mothers produced more negative, or partially negative, facial expressions than control mothers when children: (a) demonstrated difficulty accomplishing a task (34% vs. 20% of negative expressions); (b) displayed positive behavior or affect (8% vs. 0% of negative expressions); and (c) displayed negative behavior or affect (5% vs. 1% of negative expressions).

Thus, when responding to their young children's positive affect or behavior, control mothers used more positive facial expressions than maltreating mothers. Control mothers' positive facial expressions in response to their children's positive affect or behavior may contribute to an emotional environment that promotes the child's effectance motivation in the emotion-learning domain. Maltreating mothers, on the other hand, seemed to use negative facial expressions in a range of child-centered situations, presumably communicating negativity or dissatisfaction with their children, which would be likely to diminish the children's motivational level. In contrast, control mothers produced more of their negative expressions to punctuate the seriousness of their instruction to their children, not in response to their children per se.

Findings also suggested that the valence (positive or negative) of control mothers' facial expressions more often matched the contextual valence than did maltreating mothers' expressions. Mismatches between an expressed emotion and the context in which it is produced may create a conflicting, confusing expressive environment that in turn detracts from the maltreated child's growing understanding of emotion.

BEYOND THE FACE: CHILDREN'S UNDERSTANDING OF EMOTION SITUATIONS

Facial expressions are a valuable source of information about another person's emotion state. Understanding other people's emotions, however, involves more than reading facial expressions. Additional information about other people's emotions, for example, comes from one's appraisal of the situation at hand. By about 4 years of age, children's predictions of the emotion that would be elicited by many situations (e.g., a birthday party or a funeral) match those of adults. This is especially true if the situations are familiar and elicit simple emotions such as happiness, sadness, and fear, and often anger and disgust (Gnepp, 1983; Harris, 1983; Wiggers & van Lieshout, 1985). Young children also seem to understand that positive emotions are generally associated with goal achievement and that negative emotions may result from failing to achieve a goal (Stein & Levine, 1989).

Gnepp and colleagues (Gnepp & Chilamkurti, 1988; Gnepp & Gould, 1985; Gnepp, Klayman, & Trabasso, 1982; Gnepp, McKee, & Domanic, 1987) examined children's understanding that a single situation can elicit different emotions in different people due to unique previous experiences, personality characteristics, or group membership (e.g., age, gender, ethnic background). Results from these studies reveal a developmental progression in complex emotion understanding. Preschoolers understand that situational cues do not always elicit the same emotion responses in all people. Young school-aged children (5- to 8-year-olds) can predict an individual's atypical response to an emotion situation when they are given direct information about the individual's previous emotional responses in similar situations (e.g., Sarah likes tigers, therefore she will be happy if she sees a tiger). Older children can often make accurate inferences about another person's emotion response based on more subtle or indirect information about that person (e.g., Sarah was bitten by the class gerbil, therefore, now she is afraid of gerbils).

CHILDREN'S INFERENCES ABOUT OTHERS' FEELINGS BASED ON MULTIPLE SOURCES OF INFORMATION

When multiple cues represent the same emotion, children's emotion inferences are highly accurate across age groups (Gnepp, 1983; Reichenbach & Masters, 1983; Wiggers & van Lieshout, 1985). Not surprisingly, congruent messages conveyed facially and situationally are easily understood by younger and older children alike, and enhance clear communication. Emotion messages are not always congruent, however, resulting in greater ambiguity in emotion interpretation.

Considerable research has examined children's resolutions of apparent facial and situational cue conflicts (e.g., a picture of a smiling child about to receive a shot at a doctor's office). Some studies (Gnepp, 1983; Kurdek & Rodgon, 1975; Reichenbach & Masters, 1983) report that when presented with conflicting emotion cues, younger children's emotion interpretations are more biased toward the facial cue (in the example about Sarah, concluding that the child feels happy). Other studies (Burns & Cavey, 1957; Gove & Keating, 1979; Iannotti, 1975) report precisely the opposite finding, that young children tend to be more influenced by situational cues (in the same example, concluding that the child feels afraid despite the smiling face).

Such inconsistencies across studies may be due to differences in the nature of the conflict between the facial and situational cues. Some apparent conflicts between facial and situational cues are due to masking true emotion, a concept well understood by 10-year-olds; less so by younger children (Saarni, 1979). In other cases, facial and situational cue conflicts may be due to a unique set of circumstances that could genuinely produce an atypical emotion response (e.g., having a toothache and responding with a fearful expression when offered an ice cream cone).

MALTREATED AND NONMALTREATED CHILDREN'S RESPONSES TO MULTIPLE EMOTION CUES

Sachs-Alter (1993) compared maltreated and nonmaltreated peers in their ability to use information about another person's previous experience ("personal information") as a cue when making inferences about that person's emotion responses, and compared maltreated and control children's ability to use previous experience information to justify apparent discrepancies between facial and situational emotion cues. The subjects were 82 urban children between the ages of 5 and 10, equally divided into a younger and older age group. Half of the children in each age group had a documented history of physical maltreatment. Control children were matched to maltreated children by gender, age, race, and SES.

The experimenter presented each child with six two-part vignettes about children in familiar emotion-eliciting situations. The first part of each story was designed to evoke a negative emotion in the story protagonist and the second part described a situation that usually evokes a positive response (e.g., Part 1: Pat's coach didn't let Pat play in his/her soccer game today; Part 2: Pat's team won today's game.). Thus, an emotion conflict was built into each vignette. Children were asked to choose the protagonist's emotion response to each complete story (happy, sad, mad, or scared) and to explain how they made their emotion choice.

Results revealed that younger children and maltreated children were significantly more likely than older and nonmaltreated children to ignore information about the protagonist's prior experience when identifying the emotional response to the complete story. For example, in response to the soccer story, younger and maltreated children were more likely to say that the protagonist felt happy despite the fact that the child was forbidden to participate in the game.

Another part of Sachs-Alter's study examined children's use of information about a previous experience to help reconcile descrepant facial and situational cues. The authors predicted that when children were given a justification for a protagonist's atypical facial expression, they would conclude that the facial expression accurately represented the protagonist's emotion state. Subjects were again presented with the two-part stories just described. These vignettes had been pretested to determine the specific negative emotion predicted by most children to be elicited by Part 1 of the story (e.g., sadness for the soccer story). Some subjects (Condition 1) were presented with these stories accompanied by illustrations depicting a plausible, but not typically predicted, negative emotional facial expression (e.g., anger in the soccer story). The other subjects (Condition 2) were presented with identical stories and illustrations except that the illustrations were void of facial cues.

Results showed that children presented with atypical, negative facial expressions chose that atypical emotion as representing the protagonist's feeling state significantly more often than children who were not shown any facial cues (69% of Condition 1 subjects' emotion choices vs. 26% of Condition 2 subjects' emotion choices). Thus, children will utilize atypical facial cues when making their emotion judgments as long as the atypical reaction is justified.

Results also revealed some maltreatment-related differences in this area of emotion information processing. Maltreated females in this study were significantly less likely than nonmaltreated females to make emotion inferences that demonstrated use of the previous experience information provided. That is, even when presented with a justification for the atypical facial expression (e.g., the relevant previous experience information), maltreated females selected the emotion depicted facially less often than nonmaltreated females. Further research is needed to replicate these findings with respect to age, gender, and maltreatment differences. However, Sachs-Alter's study suggests that some maltreated children may be less able than their peers to: (a) process and remember multiple pieces of conflicting information; (b) recognize that information about one's previous experiences would affect emotion reactions at a later point in time; and ultimately, (c) integrate and interpret complex emotion messages.

QUALITATIVE DIFFERENCES IN MALTREATED AND NONMALTREATED CHILDREN'S UNDERSTANDING OF OTHERS' EMOTIONS

Beyond the previously described differences between maltreated and nonmaltreated children in their use of emotion cues, Sachs-Alter's study revealed several striking qualitative differences in the children's responses.

Most children in this study used projection extensively to guide their emotion interpretations. The familiarity of the situations described in the vignettes, and the age and gender similarities between the subjects and protagonists, often prompted explicit self-referencing as in the following response to a story in which a child's sibling took his favorite toy without permission and broke it:

Q: How do you know that Alan feels mad?
A: Because his brother broke his earphones and if my brother broke my earphones I'd be mad (younger, nonmaltreated male).

Although most children made emotion choices based on projection, the experiences and frames of references of maltreated children often seemed to lead them to draw conclusions about other people's emotional reactions that differed from those of nonmaltreated children. Consider, for example, the following response to the vignette in which a child spills juice on the protagonist's new sweater on purpose:

Q: How do you know that Mark feels scared?
A: He scared because it was a new sweater and he gonna get whooped when he get home (older, maltreated male).

This child's use of self directed his focus away from the perpetrator of the offending action (i.e., the child who intentionally spilled juice on him) and instead led him to focus on what was more salient from his experience (i.e., the protagonist's emotional reaction to anticipated punishment).

As illustrated by this child's response, maltreated children also tended to distort the emotion script by adding elements to the stimulus story that reflected the projective process. For example, in response to a vignette about a child who had been previously bitten by a gerbil and whose teacher chose her to feed their class gerbil, a younger, maltreated female reasoned that the protagonist felt sad "because it (the gerbil) already bit her hand and the teacher said I don't give a care." Similarly, in response to a story in which a child who has a toothache is given an ice cream cone, a younger maltreated male concluded that the protagonist felt mad "because he didn't want to eat it [the ice cream] and his mama made him eat it and she want it to hurt." In these cases, the child elaborated on the original story by interjecting elements (e.g., teacher does not care about child's feelings; mother wants child to hurt) and drew emotion conclusions based on this projective material.

Children's responses in this study made it abundantly clear that their interpretations of cues to others' emotions are inextricably linked to their own experiences and their unique psychological organization. Self-referencing when judging another person's emotion response is common among both maltreated and nonmaltreated children. However, the outcome of self-referencing seems to vary with each child's own experiences and sense of self. To the extent that maltreated and nonmaltreated children differ in their experiences of the world and their senses of self (Aber, Allen, Carlson, & Cicchetti, 1989; Erickson, Egeland, & Pianta, 1989), they would be expected to differ in their interpretations, and perhaps more frequently misattribute the causation, of others' emotion responses.

Sachs-Alter also observed that maltreated children often became overwhelmed by the emotional stimulus, their responses at times reflecting substantial disorganization in thinking. The disorganizing effects of childhood maltreatment resonate on cognitive and affective levels, which in turn impact relational and behavioral domains (Cicchetti, 1989). Among the affective consequences of maltreatment is a tendency to become overwhelmed by emotionally arousing stimuli (Aber & Cicchetti, 1984; Mueller & Silverman, 1989) that can be manifested by underresponding or overresponding to stimuli. Either of these response sets is likely to result in decreased understanding of emotion messages.

The following responses to a story about a child who was the star in the school play but whose father forgot to come to the play illustrate the disorganizing effects of poor affective regulation on children's understanding of other people's emotions:

Q: How do you know that Sam feels mad?
A: Cuz everybody laughing at him and he want to kick everybody and he didn't even want his dad to come (to the play) and he didn't want everybody to laugh at him so he kick the door and he kick the windows. He hate everybody. He want to kick everybody and everybody want to kick his butt and everybody enjoyed the show (younger, maltreated male).

Q: How do you know that Sue feels sad?
A: Sad because her father didn't come and he might have forgot or he might have gone to see his other daughter and she might feel real sad and she might cry because everybody else's mother and father came except hers. But her mother probably came, but maybe her father is in the bathroom now or at McDonald's getting a happy meal (older, maltreated female).

In these examples, the child seemed to overrespond to the emotional content in the stimulus vignette, producing loose and disorganized thinking. Accurate interpretation of another person's emotional state requires some degree of organization in cognitive and affective domains. To the extent that intrapsychic disorganization is a developmental consequence of maltreatment, maltreated children would be more likely to misinterpret another person's emotion state than nonmaltreated peers.

SUMMARY AND CONCLUSION

As reviewed in this chapter, our research identified several aspects of emotion understanding that were problematic for maltreated children. Maltreated children were significantly less accurate in recognizing prototypic emotional facial expressions than were their nonmaltreated peers. Some maltreated children were also less able to utilize information about a story character's past experience to accurately understand the protagonist's current emotional response to a situation or to resolve apparent discrepancies between facial and situational emotion cues. Finally, in explaining story characters' emotional reactions, maltreated children tended to distort the story by adding extraneous material that appeared to be particularly related to their own maltreatment experience.

Our investigation suggested several factors that might contribute to maltreated children's difficulties in recognizing emotional facial expressions. Although we found no quantitative differences in expressiveness between maltreating and nonmaltreating mothers, we did find an overall relationship between children's recognition scores and mothers' production of negative lower facial expressions (e.g., lip presses representing concentration, determination, or mild anger). If maltreating mothers use fewer of these expressions during interactions not observed in our study, this might contribute to maltreated children's lesser recognition skills. In addition, our results showed that maltreating and nonmaltreating mothers differed in the contexts in which their expressions were produced. Some of these differences (e.g., in contexts for smiling) may reflect a tendency for maltreating mothers to mismatch facial and nonfacial emotion cues, making it more difficult for their children to learn the normative meaning of facial expressions.

Our review of the maltreatment literature and the emotion socialization literature also suggested other possible factors that might contribute to maltreated children's lesser emotion understanding. In particular, we suggested that high levels of intense negative emotion in the family might be detrimental to the child's effectance motivation and thus detract from his or her development in both emotion and nonemotion domains. Within our study, we found that intense negative expressiveness was in fact related to lesser recognition skill. If maltreating and nonmaltreating mothers differ in such expressiveness during highly charged emotion situations (not observed in our study), this might also contribute to the differences in their children's expression recognition abilities. In this case, maternal expressiveness would negatively influence children's learning disposition in general, and their expression recognition skill in particular.

One limitation of our study points to an important direction for future research. As in many investigations of maltreatment, physical abuse and physical/emotional neglect were confounded. Future investigations using larger sample sizes might attempt to distinguish between the effects of physical abuse and physical/emotional neglect on children's emotion recognition skills. Similarly, investigating differences in their mothers' expressive behavior might provide further information regarding the development of emotion recognition both in both maltreated and nonmaltreated populations.

REFERENCES

Aber, J.L., & Allen, J.P. (1987). The effects of maltreatment on young children's socioemotional development: An attachment theory perspective. *Developmental Psychology, 23*, 406–414.

Aber, J.L., Allen, J.P., Carlson, V., & Cicchetti, D. (1989). The effects of maltreatment on development during early childhood: Recent studies and their theoretical, clinical, and policy implications. In D. Cicchetti & V. Carlson (Eds.), *Child maltreatment: Theory and research on the causes and consequences of child abuse and neglect* (pp. 579–619). Cambridge: Cambridge University Press.

Aber, J.L., & Cicchetti, D. (1984). The socioemotional development of maltreated children. In H.E. Fitzgerald, B.M. Lester, & M.W. Yogman (Eds.), *Theory and research in behavioral pediatrics* (Vol. 2, pp. 147–205). New York: Plenum Press.

Barahal, R., Waterman, J., & Martin, H. (1981). The social-cognitive development of abused children. *Journal of Consulting and Clinical Psychology, 49*, 508–516.

Bousha, D., & Twentyman, C. (1984). Mother–child interactional style in abuse, neglect, and control groups: Naturalistic observations in the home. *Journal of Abnormal Psychology, 93*, 106–114.

Bugental, D., Blue, J., & Lewis, J. (1990). Caregiver beliefs and dysphoric affect directed to difficult children. *Developmental Psychology, 26*(4), 631–638.

Burgess, R., & Conger, R. (1978). Family interaction in abusive, neglectful and normal families. *Child Development, 49*, 1163–1173.

Burns, N., & Cavey, L. (1957). Age differences in empathic ability among children. *Canadian Journal of Psychology, 11*, 227–230.

Camras, L.A., & Allison, K. (1985). Children's understanding of emotional facial expressions and verbal labels. *Journal of Nonverbal Behavior, 9*(2), 84–94.

Camras, L.A., Grow, G., & Ribordy, S. (1983). Recognition of emotional expressions by abused children. *Journal of Clinical Child Psychology, 12*(3), 325–328.

Camras, L., Ribordy, S., Hill, J., Martino, S., Sachs, V., Spaccarelli, S., & Stefani, R. (1990). Maternal facial behavior and the recognition and production of emotional expression by maltreated and nonmaltreated children. *Developmental Psychology, 26*(2), 304–312.

Camras, L., Ribordy, S., Hill, J., Martino, S., Spaccarelli, S., & Stefani, R. (1988). Recognition and posing of emotional expressions by abused children and their mothers. *Developmental Psychology, 24*, 776–781.

Carlson, V., Cicchetti, D., Barnett, D., & Braunwald, K. (1989). Finding order in disorganization. In D. Cicchetti & V. Carlson (Eds.), *Child maltreatment: Research and theory on the cause and consequences of child abuse and neglect* (pp. 494–528). New York: Cambridge University Press.

Caron, R., Caron, A., & Myers, R. (1982). Abstraction of invariant facial expressions in infancy. *Child Development, 53,* 1008–1015.

Cassidy, J., Parke, R., Butkovsky, L., & Braungart, J. (1992). Family–peer connections: The roles of emotional expressiveness within the family and children's understanding of emotion. *Child Development, 63,* 603–618.

Cicchetti, D. (1989). How research on child maltreatment has informed the study of child development: Perspectives from developmental psychopathology. In D. Cicchetti & V. Carlson (Eds.), *Child maltreatment: Theory and research on the causes and consequences of child abuse and neglect* (pp. 377–431). Cambridge: Cambridge University Press.

Cicchetti, D. (1993). Developmental psychopathology: Reactions, reflections, projections. *Developmental Review, 13,* 471–502.

Cicchetti, D., & Beeghly, M. (1987). Symbolic development in maltreated youngsters: An organizational perspective. In D. Cicchetti & M. Beeghly (Eds.), *New Directions for Child Development* (Vol. 36, pp. 47–67). San Francisco: Josey-Bass.

Crittenden, P. (1981). Abusing, neglecting, problematic, and adequate dyads: Differentiating by patterns of interaction. *Merrill-Palmer Quarterly, 27*(3), 201–218.

Daly, E., Abramovitch, R., & Pliner, P. (1980) The relationship between mother's encoding and their children's decoding of facial expressions of emotion. *Merrill-Palmer Quarterly, 26*(1), 25–33.

Darwin, C. (1965). *The expression of the emotions in man and animals.* Chicago: University of Chicago Press. (Original work published 1872)

Denham, S. (1986). Social cognition, social behavior and emotion in preschoolers: Contextual validation. *Child Development, 57,* 194–201.

Denham, S., & Couchard, E. (1988, March). *Knowledge about emotions: Relations with socialization and social behavior.* Paper presented at meeting of the Conference on Human Development, Charleston, SC.

Denham, S., Zoller, D., & Couchard, E. (1994). Socialization of preschoolers emotion understanding. *Developmental Psychology, 30*(6), 928–936.

Dodge, K., Pettit, G., McClaskey, C., & Brown, M. (1987). Social competence in children. *Monographs of the Society for Research in Child Development, 51*(2), 1–85.

Dunn, J., & Brown, J. (1994). Affect expression in the family, children's understanding of emotions, and their interactions with others. *Merrill-Palmer Quarterly, 40*(1), 120–137.

Dunn, J., Brown, J., & Beardsall, L. (1991). Family talk about feeling states and children's later understanding of others' emotions. *Developmental Psychology, 27,* 448–455.

During, S., & McMahon, R. (1991). Recognition of emotional facial expressions by abusive mothers and their children. *Journal of Clinical Child Psychology, 20*(2), 132–139.

Egeland, B. (1991). A longitudinal study of high-risk families. In R. Starr & D. Wolfe (Eds.), *The effects of child abuse and neglect* (pp. 33–56). New York: Guilford Press.

Ekman, P. (1984). Expression and the nature of emotion. In K. Scherer & P. Ekman (Eds.), *Approaches to emotion* (pp. 319–344). Hillsdale, NJ: Lawrence Erlbaum Associates.

Ekman, P. (1994). Strong evidence for universals in facial expressions: A reply to Russell's mistaken critique. *Psychological Bulletin, 115,* 268–287.

Ekman, P., & Friesen, W.V. (1975). *Unmasking the face.* Englewood Cliffs, NJ: Prentice-Hall.

Ekman, P., & Friesen, W. (1978). *The facial action coding system.* Palo Alto: Consulting Psychologists Press.

Erickson, M.F., Egeland, B., & Pianta, R. (1989). The effects of maltreatment on the development of young children. In D. Cicchetti & V. Carlson (Eds.), *Child maltreatment: Theory and research on the causes and consequences of child abuse and neglect* (pp. 647–684). Cambridge: Cambridge University Press.

Friesen, W., & Ekman, P. (1984). *EMFACS: Emotion Facial Action Coding System* (Available from W. Friesen, Department of Psychiatry, University of California, San Francisco).

Freud, A. (1965). *Normality and pathology in childhood.* New York: International Universities Press.

Freud, S. (1955). An outline of psycho-analysis. In J. Strachey (Ed.), *The standard edition of the complete works of Sigmund Freud* (Vol. 23). London: Hogarth. (Original work published 1940)

Frodi, A., & Smetana, J. (1984). Abused, neglected and normal preschoolers ability to discriminate emotions in others: The effects of IQ. *Child Abuse and Neglect, 8,* 459–465.

George, C., & Main, M. (1979). Social interactions of young abused children: Approach, avoidance and aggression. *Child Development, 50,* 306–318.

Gnepp, J. (1983). Children's social sensitivity: Inferring emotions from conflicting cues. *Developmental Psychology, 19*(6), 805–814.

Gnepp, J., & Chilamkurti, C. (1988). Children's use of personality attributions to predict other people's emotional and behavioral reactions. *Child Development, 59,* 743–754.

Gnepp, J., & Gould, M.E. (1985). The development of personalized inferences: Understanding other people's emotional reactions in light of their prior experiences. *Child Development, 56,* 1455–1464.

Gnepp, J., Klayman, J., & Trabasso, T. (1982). A hierarchy of information sources for inferring emotional reactions. *Journal of Experimental Child Psychology, 33,* 111–123.

Gnepp, J., McKee, E., & Domanic, J.A. (1987). Children's use of situational information to infer emotion: Understanding emotionally equivocal situations. *Developmental Psychology, 23*(1), 114–123.

Gordon, S. (1989). The socialization of children's emotions: Emotional culture, competence and exposure. In C. Saarni & P. Harris (Eds.), *Children's understanding of emotion.* New York: Cambridge University Press.

Gove, F.L., & Keating, D.P. (1979). Empathic role-taking precursors. *Developmental Psychology, 15*(6), 594–600.

Halberstadt, A. (1986). Family socialization of emotional expression and nonverbal communication styles and skills. *Journal of Personality and Social Psychology, 51*(41), 827–836.

Halberstadt, A. (1991). Toward an ecology of expressiveness. In R. Feldman & B. Rime (Eds.), *Fundamentals of nonverbal behavior* (pp. 106–160). New York: Cambridge University Press.

Harris, P.L. (1983). Children's understanding of the link between situation and emotion. *Journal of Experimental Child Psychology, 36*, 490–509.

Haskett, M., & Kistner, J. (1991). Social interactions & peer perceptions of young physically abused children. *Child Development, 62*, 979–990.

Haviland, J., & Lelwica, M. (1987). The induced affect response: 10-week-old infants' responses to three emotion expressions. *Developmental Psychology, 23*(1), 97–104.

Herrenkohl, R., Herrenkohl, E., Egolf, B., & Wu, P. (1991). The developmental consequences of child abuse. In R. Starr & D. Wolfe (Eds.), *The effects of child abuse and neglect* (pp. 57–81). New York: Guilford Press.

Hoffman-Plotkin, D., & Twentyman, C. (1984). A multimodal assessment of behavioral and cognitive deficits in abused and nonabused children. *Child Development, 55*(3), 794–802.

Howes, C., & Eldredge, R. (1985). Response of abused, neglected and nonmaltreated children to the behaviors of their peers. *Journal Applied Development Psychology, 6*, 261–270.

Howes, C., & Espinosa, M. (1985). The consequences of child abuse for the formation of relationships with peers. *Child Abuse and Neglect, 9*, 397–404.

Iannotti, R.J. (1975). The nature and measurement of empathy in children. *The Counseling Psychologist, 5*(2), 21–25.

Izard, C.E. (1971). *The face of emotion.* New York: Appleton-Century-Crofts.

Jacobson, R., & Straker, G. (1982). Peer group interaction of physically abused children. *Child Abuse and Neglect, 6*, 321–327.

Kaufman, J., & Cicchetti, D. (1989). Effects of maltreatment on school-age children's socioemotional development: Assessments in a day-camp setting. *Developmental Psychology, 25*(4), 516–524.

Kavanaugh, K., Youngblade, L., Reid, J., & Fagot, B. (1988). Interactions between children and abusive vs. control parents. *Journal of Clinical Child Psychology, 17*(2), 137–142.

Klimes-Dougan, B., & Kistner, J. (1990). Physically abused preschoolers' responses to peers' distress. *Developmental Psychology, 26*(4), 599–602.

Kurdek, L.A., & Rodgon, M. (1975). Perceptual, cognitive and affective perspective taking in kindergarten through sixth grade children. *Developmental Psychology, 11*, 643–650.

Lewis, M., & Saarni, C. (1985). Culture and emotions. In M. Lewis & C. Saarni (Eds.), *The socialization of emotions* (pp. 1–17). New York: Plenum Press.

Lyons-Ruth, K., Connell, D., Zoll, D., & Stahl, J. (1987). Infants at social risk: Relations among infant maltreatment, maternal behavior and infant attachment behavior. *Developmental Psychology, 23*(2), 223–232.

Main, M., & George, C. (1985). Responses of abused and disadvantaged toddlers to distress in agemates. *Developmental Psychology, 21*(3), 407–412.

Mash, E., Johnston, C., & Kovitz, K. (1983). A comparison of the mother–child interactions of physically abused and nonabused children during play and task situations. *Journal of Clinical Child Psychology, 12*(3), 337–346.

Miller, P. (1986). Teasing as language socialization and play in a white working-class community. In B.B. Schieffelin & E. Ochs (Eds.), *Language socialization across cultures* (pp. 129–212). Cambridge: Cambridge University Press.

Miller, P., & Sperry, L. (1987). The socialization of anger and aggression. *Merrill-Palmer Quarterly, 33*(1), 1–31.

Mueller, E., & Silverman, N. (1989) Peer relations in maltreated children. In D. Cicchetti & V. Carlson (Eds.), *Child maltreatment* (pp. 529–578). Cambridge: Cambridge University Press.

Nelson, C. (1987). The recognition of facial expressions in the first two years of life: Mechanisms of development. *Child Development, 58*(4), 889–909.

Reichenbach, L., & Masters, J.C. (1983). Children's use of expressive and contextual cues in judgments of emotion. *Child Development, 54*, 993–1004.

Rogosch, F., & Cicchetti, D. (1994). Illustrating the interface of family and peer relations through the study of child maltreatment. *Social Development, 3*(3), 291–308.

Saarni, C. (1979). Children's understanding of display rules for expressive behavior. *Developmental Psychology, 15*(4), 424–429.

Saarni, C., & Harris, P. (Eds.). (1989). *Children's understanding of emotion.* New York: Cambridge University Press.

Sachs-Alter, E. (1989). *The contextual use of facial expressions by maltreating and nonmaltreating mothers.* Unpublished master's thesis, DePaul University, Chicago, IL.

Sachs-Alter, E. (1993). *Maltreated and nonmaltreated children's use of cues in understanding the emotions of others.* Unpublished doctoral dissertation, DePaul University, Chicago, IL.

Salzinger, S., Feldman, R., Hammer, M., & Rosario, M. (1993). The effects of physical abuse on children's social relationships. *Child Development, 64*, 169–187.

Shallice, T. (1988). *From neuropsychology to mental structure.* New York: Cambridge University Press.

Stein, N., & Levine, L. (1989). The causal organization of emotion knowledge. *Cognition and Emotion, 3*(4), 343–378.

Tomkins, S.S. (1962). *Affect, imagery, and consciousness* (Vol. 1). New York: Springer.

Trickett, P., Aber, J., Carlson, V., & Cicchetti, D. (1991). The relationship of sociometric status to the etiology and developmental sequelae of physical child abuse. *Developmental Psychology, 27*, 148–158.

Waldren, T., & Ogan, T. (1988). The development of social referencing. *Child Development, 59*, 1230–1240.

Widlansky, H. (1994). *Children's gaze and mother's intonation: Possible mediators of children's expression recognition learning.* Unpublished masters thesis, DePaul University, Chicago, IL.

Wiggers, M., & van Lieshout, C. (1985). Development of recognition of emotions: Children's reliance on situational and facial expressive cues. *Developmental Psychology, 21*(2), 338–349.

– 12 –

Socioemotional Assessment for Atypical Infants and Preschoolers

Susanne A. Denham
Susan Lydick
Jennifer Mitchell-Copeland
Katherine Sawyer
George Mason University

Consider the following: A 3-month-old infant shows up at the pediatrician's office difficult to soothe, exhibiting feeding and/or sleeping problems, irritable, not engaging in eye contact, not cuddling, and/or not seeming to use caregiver for distress relief. An 18-month-old toddler enters day care for the first time and cries stormily day after day when her parents drop her off; she stares into space much of the rest of the day and avoids contact with caregivers even though she appears miserable. A 3-year-old child consistently bites, kicks, and clutches at peers whenever his desires are thwarted. What can we do to ameliorate the socioemotional development of these children? How do these children's pediatricians, day-care providers, preschool/early childhood special education teachers, and parents decide whether these socioemotional difficulties are within normal developmental limits or whether further assessment and intervention are required? These are indeed difficult and pressing problems. DeGangi, Poisson, Sickel, and Weiner (1994) cogently stated that "professionals too often overlook precursors of emotional difficulties in infants and toddlers because they lack sufficient screening tools. . . . Concerns . . . which parents often report, are too frequently dismissed by professionals until more serious, long-term difficulties become apparent. Putting off the problem has its price" (p. 5).

So, despite Public Law 99-457's mandate for the integrated assessment of infants and young children's cognitive, social, and emotional status (Drotar & Sturm, 1989), and the concomitant pressing need for instruments, applied socioemotional assessment measures for infants and young children remain scarce (Lewis, 1985; Rossetti, 1990; Sattler, 1990). This dearth of assessment tools, and lack of integration among measures which do exist, create major problems in identifying and serving infants and preschoolers.[1]

First, it is difficult to screen infants and preschoolers potentially in need of diagnostic assessment in the socioemotional domain. Second, pinpointing diagnoses (i.e., determination of existence of delay or disability, identifying child and family strengths and needs). Third, creation of individual planning programs (i.e., creation of individual/family services plan, program placement, intervention goals, and remedial activities) is compromised for children found to be delayed in this area. Finally, evaluating a child's individual progress in a program and overall program efficacy are both hindered.

Such multistep assessment of socioemotional development has been hampered in two ways. The first problem is the widespread perception that early childhood intervention programs primarily serve to enhance cognitive abilities and improve later school performance. Likewise, the thrust of Public Laws 94-142 and 99-457 has often been interpreted as a focus on maximizing the cognitive and functional abilities of special needs infants, toddlers, and preschoolers, leaving socioemotional goals implicit rather than explicit. But, directly assessing socioemotional status and change is as vital as assessing other domains of development. For example, socioemotional variables are at times related to cognitive changes (Lewis, Sullivan, & Michalson, 1984), and are often more sensitive than cognitive variables to the effects of intervention (see Lazar & Darlington, 1982). Further, socioemotional variables are important in their own right as indices of adjustment that may predict later happiness and success (Lewis, 1985; Sroufe, Schork, Motti, Lawroski, & LaFreniere, 1984). Second, even though many developmentalists now agree on the importance of capturing the nature of and changes in socioemotional competence, instruments measuring this domain have often been less refined, valid, and/or reliable than those evaluating cognitive development.

To evaluate socioemotional assessment tools for screening, diagnosis, program planning, and evaluation, and to make decisions on what refinements are needed, we must carefully define what we mean by competence in

---

[1] We maintain that cognitive, language, sensory, and motor measures are necessary to evaluate any infant or young child's socioemotional development in perspective. Each child is a whole person with a unique pattern of strengths and challenges, not just a particular domain of development.

social and emotional domains. It is well documented that the conceptualization of these areas is problematic (e.g., see Waters & Sroufe, 1983). We generally espouse the view that competence, be it emotional or social, "refers broadly to an ability to generate and coordinate flexible, adaptive responses to demands and to generate and capitalize on opportunities in the environment" (p. 80). But, when viewing social or emotional competence from this level of abstraction, specific implications for assessment are not forthcoming. Conversely, defining social and emotional competence solely in terms of specific skills or lack thereof (as is often done) solves assessment problems at the expense of a developmental perspective.

Accordingly, we would argue that an organizational perspective will illuminate the common core features of the child's abilities to use inner and outer social and emotional resources to effect good outcomes in their social and emotional transactions with the world. Similarly, such a perspective can also point to assessment procedures appropriate to each age period. That is, each age period has salient issues, central developmental tasks in the social and emotional domains (Howes, 1987; Saarni, 1990; Waters & Sroufe, 1983; see Table 12.1).[2] We examine these central tasks closely at each age level; age-appropriate socioemotional tasks should be included in any socioemotional assessment.

It is important that this organizational perspective highlights each of the varied subdomains of socioemotional development that we need to consider for assessment. For example, many assessment tools that purport to pinpoint a child's functioning with the socioemotional domain, although psychometrically adequate, examine limited subdomains. In contrast, the organizational perspective, with its focus on developmental tasks at each age period, underscores that there are many other socioemotional skills that infants and preschoolers are gaining (e.g., attachment/separation/autonomy, development of self, expression of emotions and feelings, learning rules and expectations, social interactions, and play). Many such elements of appropriate socioemotional development are underrepresented in assessment.

In this chapter, then, we provide a guided tour of extant assessment tools within this framework and a discussion of where we need to go from here. The structure for the chapter is as follows: Starting with the infancy period and working forward throughout toddlerhood and preschool age, we reiterate age-related socioemotional developmental tasks. Within each period, we inspect extant measures that come closest to answering needs of screening,

---

[2] The existence of a salient issue specific to a particular age level, for example attachment, at 6 to 12 months, does not imply the nonexistence of development in this area before the most crucial age range. Further, it is not asserted that development of these milestones ceases after a crucial age range.

TABLE 12.1
Developmental Perspective: Socioemotional Competence From Birth to 5 Years

Age Range	Developmental Issues for Socioemotional Competence[a]
0–3 months	Physiological regulation
3–6 months	Management of tension
7–12 months	Establishing an effective attachment relationship with caregiver(s); recognition of peer as social partner
13–18 months	Exploration and mastery; complementary and reciprocal play structures; stable friendships
19–30 months	Individuation; communication of meaning (cognitive and socioemotional); flexibility of friendship
31–54 months	Management of impulses; social knowledge of peer group, differentiation of friends from playmates; consolidation of emotional competence skills (i.e., regulating expressiveness, understanding emotions of self and others, reaction to others' emotions); sex-role identification

[a]Incorporating material from Howes (1987), Saarni (1990), and Waters and Sroufe (1983).

diagnosis, program planning, and evaluation.[3] Finally, we attempt to synthesize the current state of socioemotional assessment for atypical infants and preschoolers, integrate a best practices approach to such assessment (cf. Bagnato & Neisworth, 1991), and point toward plans for the future.

EARLY INFANCY PERIOD: RESOURCES THAT WOULD PREDICT POSITIVE SOCIOEMOTIONAL DEVELOPMENT

During the first 3 months of life, the major question with regard to the assessment of socioemotional competence of the infant is whether he or she has the ability to adequately modulate physiologic states and sleep/wake cycles. This crucial ability is thought to determine, to a large extent, how predictable and readable the baby is, and thus how likely the caregiver is to

---

[3] Measures that could arguably be included as socioemotional assessments during infancy, toddlerhood, and preschool age range, such as the Conners Scales (Conners, 1985), the Preschool Problem Behavior Questionnaire (Behar & Stringfield, 1974), the Child Personality Inventory, the Vineland Adaptive Behavior Scale (Sparrow, Balla, & Cicchetti, 1984), the Eyberg Inventory (Boggs, Eyberg, & Reynolds, 1990), and certain observational systems, are not included because of one or more of the following reasons: First, they are redundant of a measure already included that is considered more comprehensive. Second, they lack specificity and/or comprehensiveness of coverage of developmentally appropriate socioemotional skills. Finally, they require too much time and expense to use.

be able to respond appropriately. Development of physiological regulation is thought to determine the likelihood of feeding success, success of caregiver efforts at consoling, and contingent responsiveness in infant–caregiver face-to-face interaction.

When state control is accomplished, new motor and cognitive skills lead the baby into frustrating circumstances. So, from 3 to 6 months, management of tension is the socioemotional developmental task to be accomplished. Now socioemotional competence involves a balance between development of infant internal mechanisms and self-comforting skills that allow the child to begin to wait for help from his or her caregiver when he or she is mildly distressed (e.g., hungry or tired), and the ability to get the caregiver to respond appropriately and provide comfort when distress levels are too high. These experiences are important because the infant's experiences of successes or failures with getting the comfort he or she needs from adults as well as sharing in pleasure during the first few months of life determine whether the child expects his or her caregiver to provide what he or she needs. These foundations of physiological regulation and management of tension in turn are theorized to relate to the development of the attachment relationship, a key socioemotional developmental task during the next period.

Infants who were sick at birth and thus spent the neonatal period in the neonatal intensive care unit (NICU; e.g., due to preterm birth, small size for gestational age, prenatal drug exposure, or severe birth asphyxia for full terms) often appear less likely to make smooth, predictable transitions. Furthermore, they often have more difficulty, later, with the development of tension regulation. These difficulties may have to do with damage to central nervous system (CNS) or sensory organs prenatally or during the birth process, side effects of life-sustaining medical interventions, and/or simply differences in early physiological organization as a result of infant sensory experiences in the NICU. For example, he or she may have less opportunity for practice of self-quieting skills that promote the development of state control, such as snuggling on the tummy or hand-to-mouth activity, if he or she must be placed on his or her back or have hands restrained in the isolette for medical reasons. As a consequence, there may be a very disorganized, unpredictable quality to such a baby's state transitions and emotion regulation through the first half year. It can be very difficult for caregivers to get to know these babies and how best to comfort them. Furthermore, if the infant has a delayed or atypical capacity to sustain a quiet alert state, the infant is likely to have reduced opportunity for attending to sensory stimuli from caregivers, and perhaps less ability to integrate these stimuli in early interaction and regulation of emotion (see Field, 1980).

EARLY INFANCY PERIOD: ASSESSMENT TOOLS

The issue then arises of how to assess physiological regulation and tension regulation during these periods (0–3 months, 3–6 months), and what to do with the information gathered. NICU graduates are likely to be assessed on a regular basis in a high-risk developmental clinic, and thus their behavioral style as well as the caregiver's comes to be known to the infant specialist or developmental team during the first 6 months of life. Socioemotional assessment in such settings is likely to consist primarily of nonstandardized interview data and behavioral observations noted incidentally during standardized mental or motor assessment. Such data do give an indication of infant physiological regulatory capacity as well as a good sense of how well the caregiver meets the infant's unique behavioral style. For example, interview data about infant sleep patterns provides important information about the development of physical regulation, and an observation of an infant feeding that happens to occur during the assessment gives important clues as to the fit between the baby and his social environment, without the caregiver feeling as if he or she is being tested. However, similar procedures at this and later age periods are certainly unstandardized, vulnerable to the individual practices of the clinic, pediatrician, or early childhood educator. Even though we acknowledge that observing incidental occurrences of developmental tasks during infant–parent play sessions is not only appropriate, but vital (Bagnato & Neisworth, 1991), we ask: Can we do better than this status quo?

Screening Measures.[4] Screening alerts us to the existence of deficits in age-appropriate socioemotional competence; they may or may not be standardized. For years, the Denver Developmental Screening Test (DDST) has been used to screen for the presence of developmental delays in children from birth to 6 years (Frankenburg, Camp, & Van Natta, 1971; Frankenburg, & Coons, 1983; Frankenburg, Dodds, Fandal, Kazuk, & Cohrs, 1975); it is standardized with norms for each activity indicating when 25%, 50%, and 90% of children pass. Scoring is categorical; an infant receives either "normal," "questionable," or "delayed" status; within this framework, adequate psychometric properties have been reported (Frankenburg et al., 1971). However, the DDST has few truly socioemotional items in its personal social domain. Within the age range from birth to 6 months, only "regards face," two items referring to smiling, playing peek-a-boo, resisting the pulling away of a toy, and initial shyness with strangers are assessed

---

[4] Many of the measures subsequently reviewed overlap more than one of the developmental age ranges listed here. Our convention is to introduce the measure and evaluate it at the earliest age at which it can be used, but to describe pertinent items and subscales at later ages if appropriate.

(actually, after this age range there are even fewer socioemotional items on the DDST). Nonetheless, failure of a sufficient number of these items to render the infant's developmental profile as either questionable or abnormal would certainly alert practitioners that further diagnosis was necessary.

To home in on age-specific socioemotional abilities more pointedly, Field's Interaction Rating Scales (IRS, see Table 12.2; Field, 1980) could be useful to evaluate the socioemotional status of young infants. Devised as an applied research tool, the IRS evaluates infant state, amount of physical activity, head orientation (i.e., head aversion), gaze behavior, facial expressions, fussiness, and vocalizations, during face-to-face interaction with the caregiver and feeding (the feeding scales also include a rating of feeding persistence). As seen in Table 12.2, these behaviors rated on 3-point scales are critical markers of the young infant's capacity for social interaction. Some reliability and validity data have been reported for the IRS (Field, 1980); refinement could render this promising screening tool an important tool in the assessment of young infants socioemotional status. The IRS is an example of a judgment-based measure appropriate to sample ambiguous characteristics and response classes that are not discrete (see Bagnato & Neisworth, 1991, who state that "Ratings from professionals, parents, and other caregivers are valuable for appraising the child's perceived strengths and weaknesses," p. 65). Many of the assessment tools that follow are judgment-based measures, and our caveat would be that these measures are only equal to the judge's acumen.

Diagnostic Assessment. Hopefully, use of diagnostic assessment after screening will allow us to find out the reason(s) why an infant is not showing skills that make up socioemotional competence for the age. We often use judgment-based or standardized, norm-referenced measures to make a diagnostic statement. Norm-referenced assessment tools generally provide summary scores that indicate how the infant or child compares to others his or her age on the selected abilities. For norm-referenced assessment tools useful during this age range and later ones, we examine those that cover specific skills or broad socioemotional deficits, as well as those that address more comprehensive age-appropriate developmental tasks.

The Neonatal Behavior Assessment Scale (NBAS; Brazelton, 1984; see Crowell & Fleischmann, 1993, for a summary of extant psychometric data, especially predictive validity) appears to be an excellent method for diagnostic assessment of socioemotional milestones for the birth to 1-month age period. This is a standardized 20 to 30 minute interaction designed to assess the baby's ability to respond to both the examiner and objects, including both positive and aversive stimuli; a broad range of neonatal behaviors (e.g., state control, reflexive/elicited responses, temperament, and social behaviors) are assessed. Brazelton reported that the greatest benefit of this assess-

TABLE 12.2
Interaction Rating Scales

Face-to-Face Interactions

Infant Ratings

A. State rating (.91)
 1. predominantly drowsy
 2. somewhat drowsy
 3. predominantly alert
B. Physical activity (.82)
 1. frequent squirming/arching of back
 2. occasional squirming/arching of back
 3. relaxed body with cycling of limbs toward mother
C. Head orientation (.96)
 1. frequent head aversion
 2. occasional head aversion
 3. rare head aversion
D. Gaze behavior (.85)
 1. seldom looks at mother
 2. sometimes looks at mother
 3. frequently looks at mother
E. Facial expressions (.84)
 1. frequent pouting or cry face
 2. bland expression
 3. occasional smiling or "contented" expression
F. Fussiness (.96)
 1. frequent fussing or crying
 2. occasional fussing
 3. no fussing
G. Vocalization (.82)
 1. no vocalizations
 2. a few vocalizations
 3. several vocalizations

INFANT FACE-TO-FACE RATING = TOTAL/7

Mother Ratings

A. State rating (.83)
 1. predominantly depressed or anxious looking
 2. somewhat depressed or anxious looking
 3. alert and attentive
B. Physical activity (.63)
 1. minimal activity or overly active
 2. moderate activity
 3. some activity
C. Head orientation (.96)
 1. frequent head aversion
 2. occasional head aversion
 3. infrequent head aversion

Mother Ratings (continued)

D. Gaze behavior (.92)
 1. seldom looks at infant
 2. sometimes looks at infant
 3. constantly looks at infant
E. Silence during infant gaze aversion (.82)
 1. rarely quiet when infant looking away
 2. sometimes quiet when infant looking away
 3. usually quiet when infant looking away
F. Facial expressions (.83)
 1. flat or tense expressions
 2. alternately flat or tense and contented
 3. frequent smiling or "contented" expression
G. Vocalization (.92)
 1. constant, non-contingent talking or no talking
 2. moderate amount of talking and somewhat contingent
 3. contingent talking and sensitive pacing of vocalizations
H. Infantized behaviors (.91)
 1. never imitative of infant or no simplified behaviors
 2. sometimes imitative and some simplified behaviors
 3. frequent imitative and simplified behaviors
I. Contingent responsivity (.82)
 1. rarely responds in kind or with short latency to infant behaviors
 2. sometimes responds in kind or with short latency to infant behaviors
 3. often responds in kind or with short latency to infant behaviors
J. Gameplaying (.98)
 1. rarely plays infant, age-appropriate games
 2. sometimes plays infant, age-appropriate games
 3. often plays infant, age-appropriate games

MOTHER FACE-TO-FACE RATING = TOTAL/10

Source: Field (1980). Reprinted by permission.

ment can be achieved if conducted in the presence of the parents so that the parents can see and hear about their baby's individual response style. This assessment then provides both baseline data for follow-up assessment of socioemotional development, as well as an excellent opportunity for the examiner to model optimal caregiver response for the particular baby's style.

Another tool that may be used to assess very young infants' regulatory readiness for social interaction is the Nursing Child Assessment Satellite Training (NCAST), which includes the Nursing Child Assessment Feeding Scale (NCAFS), and the Nursing Child Assessment Teaching Scale (NCATS). These scales can be used to assess clarity of infant cues and responsiveness to the parent (Barnard, Eyres, Lobo, & Snyder, 1983; Barnard & Kelly, 1990). The Feeding Scale is normed for birth to 12 months, with the Teaching Scale normed for the birth to age 3; validity data for both are excellent. For example, clarity of infant cues on the NCAFS correlates with concurrent HOME data and with later security of attachment. Barnard et al. gave numerous examples of discriminant validity. As expected, test–retest reliability for infant scales is only moderate, given that infants are constantly developing. Internal consistency of NCATS and NCAFS infant scales' range from the .50s for separate scales to the .70s for total scores. The advantage of this tool over the NBAS is that it covers a much broader age range. Furthermore, it provides an assessment of parent sensitivity to cues, response to distress, and socioemotional growth fostering (see later).

The advantage of either of these systems over informal observation of infant regulatory behaviors, cues, and parent responsivity is that the behaviors are clearly defined; thus, professionals from a variety of disciplines can communicate. But, there is a problem if examiners become so immersed in a system that they fail to use their knowledge of development to understand the infant's socioemotional behavior in perspective. Another disadvantage of these systems is the hours of rather costly training required.

The Behavior Rating Scales (BRS) of the Bayley Scales of Infant Development (BSID-II; Bayley, 1993) are norm-referenced scales that cover an even broader age range, but they were not necessarily developed specifically for socioemotional assessment. They were more narrowly developed to ". . . measure dimensions of the child's behavior that are relevant to an assessment setting," but, conversely, are also seen as useful for describing ". . . qualitative differences often found in children with a clinical diagnosis" (Bayley, 1993, p. 21). In contrast with the BSID Infant Behavior Record (IBR; Bayley, 1969), the changes in the BSID–II BRS include a 5-point scoring system for all items (with good behavioral descriptors; see, e.g., Table 12.3) which increase reliability, via increased variance, and ease of scoring. Another useful aspect of the BRS items is their grouping by age; only items relevant for the age of the child being tested are actually scored.

TABLE 12.3
Behavior Rating Scales: Sample Items

Item	Rating (Circle)
5. Positive Affect 1–42 months	
No positive affect displayed	1
One or two brief displays of positive affect	2
Three or more brief displays of positive affect	3
One or two intense, heightened, or prolonged displays of positive affect	4
Three or more intense, heightened, or prolonged displays of positive affect	5
6. Negative Affect 1–42 months	
Three or more intense, heightened, or prolonged displays of negative affect	1
One or two intense, heightened, or prolonged displays of negative affect	2
Three or more brief displays of negative affect	3
One or two brief displays of negative affect	4
No negative affect displayed	5
7. Soothability When Upset 1–42 months	
Cannot be soothed	1
Soothed only by being physically comforted (e.g., held, patted)	2
Soothed by being given a desired toy or object	3
Soothed by being spoken to	4
Does not need external assistance to be soothed	5
8. Hypersensitivity to Test Materials and Stimuli 1–42 months	
Constantly hypersensitive disrupts testing	1
Typically hypersensitive: Returns to test activity in one or two instances	2
Occasionally hypersensitive	3
Typically reacts appropriately: Hypersensitive in a few instances	4
Constantly responds appropriately	5

In contrast, on the IBR the rater was required to score nonrelevant items; such a practice can make the rater doubt the validity of the instrument, thus feeling less invested in rating.

More specifically, the BRS provides an Attention/Arousal Factor for 1- to 5-month-olds assessed. There are nine rating scale items measuring state of arousal, affect, interest, orientation to the examiner, and energy level. The Bayley manual says that scores for this factor in the nonoptimal range (i.e., less than the 11th percentile for all BRS scores; "questionable" scores are in the 11th to 25th percentile range, with "normal" scores above the 25th percentile) denote inability to remain aroused and a low degree of interaction with the environment. Such scores should alert the professional to possible difficulties with physiological regulation, and suggest need for more detailed interviews with parents about state control and sleep patterns.

The Orientation/Engagement Factor (6–42 months) measures approach–avoidance of environmental interactions that are task-related or social (e.g., positive affect, predominant state, lability of state, interest in test stimuli, energy, initiative with tasks, enthusiasm toward tasks, fearfulness, social engagement). Nonoptimal scores indicate low initiative and involvement with task and social partners. The Emotional Regulation Factor (6–42 months) measures the child's activity, adaptability, affect, cooperation, persistence, and frustration tolerance. In short, this factor highlights the toddler's ability to cope with heightened levels of both positive and negative emotions. Nonoptimal scores denote negative and irritable emotional tone, poor adaptability, and irregular or unstable self-regulation, with a tendency to diminished sociability and higher levels of distress.

Content validity of the BRS appears adequate; regarding construct validity, factor analyses of normal and clinical standardization groups showed three factors (motor quality, orientation/engagement, and emotional regulation) for 6- to 12- and 13- to 42-month-old groups. The BRS also differentiate children with significant impairments, such as Down syndrome and autistic children, from normal children.

Furthermore, a "Social Facet" score or factor score can be derived from the BSID–II Mental Development Index. For example, the items that load on this factor at a developmental age of 1 month include regards person, responds to voice, eyes follow, becomes excited in anticipation, adjusts in anticipation of being picked up; at a developmental age of 2 months, the additional items include visually recognizes caregiver, smiles when examiner speaks, smiles when examiner smiles; at 3 months there is one additional item, reacts to disappearance of face. At 4 months' developmental age, additional items include vocalizing when the examiner smiles and mirror approach; finally, at 6 months' developmental age, the item "cooperates in game" is included in the Social Facet (only two items, pats toy in imitation, and understands perspective of another, load on the Social Facet at later developmental ages). It is very important to remember that the facet score needs to be interpreted in terms of consistency of the score relative to the mental age of the child. A social facet score that is low relative to the mental age of the child suggests that socioemotional development is atypical for the cognitive level of the child. In this case, it is the task of the professional to further assess whether the caregiving environment might be failing to provide the appropriate social interaction that the baby needs, or whether the infant might have some visual or auditory deficit, or whether nonoptimal state control (BRS Attention/Arousal score) seems to be prohibiting social skill.

Working from a slightly different perspective, the Early Coping Inventory (ECI; Zeitlin, Williamson, & Szczepanski, 1988) is described as an observation instrument, having a 5-point scale to measure "coping related behaviors that a child uses to manage routine opportunities, challenges, and frustrations encountered in daily living" (Zeitlin et al., 1988, p. 2). Given that the inventory covers the age range from 4 to 36 months, it appears likely to be an excellent tool for assessment of coping behaviors, particularly those that are related to level of tolerance for frustration. In order to complete the ECI, the child is observed in a variety of situations over a period of time. Effectiveness of coping scores for three scales, Sensorimotor Organization, Reactive Behavior, and Self-Initiated Behavior, as well as average Adaptive Behavior indexes, are obtained from the ratings, and the infant's most and least effective coping behaviors are listed. The Adaptive Behavior Index typifies the child's overall coping and helps to determine the type and intensity of intervention required. Content validity and interrater reliability reported in the manual are excellent; less clear is construct validity, and no internal consistency measures are reported.

Consistent with our developmental perspective, the specific behaviors used to demonstrate most items will vary with the child's developmental age. For example, a 4-month-old, rated on "Child uses a variety of behaviors in responding to others" may demonstrate smiling, looking, head turning, or simple vocalizations. The same 4-month-old can shake an object in anticipation of an event, noise, or modify a reach pattern to touch or grasp objects. Even a young infant can show reactions to the feelings and moods of others, and express a range of emotions. The ECI manual offers examples of the developmental progression of later meanings for several items. Overall, the ECI appears to objectively capture the essence of critical markers of socioemotional development, those contributing to resiliency in a social setting.

Greenspan's (1992) Functional Emotional Assessment Scale for Infancy and Early Childhood (FEASIE) represents a more clinical viewpoint because it "emphasizes understanding the infant and young child's emotional and social functioning in the context of relationships with his or her caregivers and family" (p. 381), and is tied to Greenspan's theory of emotional development. It is Greenspan's notion that an "overall clinical functional assessment" minimizes errors in service recommendations that can be made when more structured tests are used. Accordingly, free, unstructured interaction between the infant or child and his or her caregiver, as well as the clinician, is the setting for the assessment. Quantitative (but not standardized) scores at each level are used as summaries for the Primary Emotional Capacities and Emotional Range (Sensorimotor and Affective). Although because of the issue of nonstandardization Greenspan asserted that these scores should be used only for descriptive purposes, the categories used in the scale can be rated reliably and do discriminate between clinical and nonclinical groups. Furthermore, related motor, sensory, language, and cognitive capacities are evaluated at every age level (see footnote 1), as well as general infant and caregiver tendencies. The assessor using the FEASIE would begin by examining age-expected capacities, and then prior capacities. For the early infancy period, primary emotional capacities and range can be summarized to include the following (see Table 12.4 for an example of the rating sheet for this age range):

1. By 3 months, the infant can be calm; recovers from crying with comforting; is able to be alert; looks at one when talked to; and brightens up when provided with appropriate visual, auditory, and/or tactile experiences (Greenspan, 1992, p. 389); Greenspan (1994) called this overall ability "mutual attention" (p. 39).
2. By 5 months, the infant evidences positive loving affect toward key caregivers; looks and/or smiles spontaneously and responds to their facial expressions, voices, or touch with signs of pleasure (Greenspan, 1992, p. 393). Greenspan (1994) called this ability "mutual engagement" (p. 39).

TABLE 12.4
Functional Emotional Assessment Scale for Infancy and Early Childhood:
Early Infancy

Rating Sheet

Rating Scale: 0 = Capacity not present
     1 = Capacity fleetingly present
     2 = Capacity intermittently present
     3 = Capacity present most of the time
     4 = Capacity present all the time in all circumstances
   N/A = Not Applicable, because there was no opportunity to
        observe the presence or absence of this capacity

(Continued)

TABLE 12.4
(Continued)

| REGULATION AND INTEREST IN THE WORLD (3 MONTHS) | Rating |

REGULATION AND INTEREST IN THE WORLD   *Rating*
(3 MONTHS)

Primary Emotional:
1. Shows interest in different sensations for 3+ seconds _____
2. Remains calm and focused for 2+ minutes _____

Emotional Range—Sensorimotor:
1. Looks at sights for 3+ seconds _____
2. Listens to sounds for 3+ seconds _____
3. Relaxes, smiles, vocalizes, or looks in response to light or firm touch _____
4. Relaxes, smiles, vocalizes, or looks in response to moving of limbs _____
5. Tolerates/shows pleasure in gentle movement in space _____
6. Tolerates/shows pleasure in smells _____
7. Relaxes/shows pleasure when held firmly _____
8. Relaxes/shows pleasure when rocked rhythmically _____
9. Recovers from distress within 20 minutes, with help from caregiver _____

Emotional Range—Affective:
1. Shows interest in caregiver _____
2. Shows interest in happy caregiver _____
3. Shows interest in assertive caregiver _____

Selected Capacities:
1. *Motor:*
    a. Holds head upright on own _____
    b. Lifts head by leaning on elbows _____
    c. Hands open 75% of the time _____
    d. Rolls side to back/stomach to back _____
    e. Reaches for toy _____
    f. Manipulates toy _____

2. *Sensory:*
    a. Follows objects in horizontal plane _____
    b. Follows objects in vertical plane _____
    c. Responds to a variety of sounds _____
    d. Tolerates deep pressure-type touch _____

3. *Language:*
    a. Vocalizes with at least one sound type _____

4. *Cognitive:* (Same as Sensory and Language) _____

Clearly, the FEASIE is a judgment-based socioemotional assessment. Its goal is to "assist the clinician in systematizing and fine-tuning clinical judgments" (Greenspan, 1992, p. 388), yielding a profile that alerts early childhood clinicians and educators to explore the infant's strengths and weaknesses in greater depth, creating direct links to intervention. Complex clinical judgments are operationalized, but the FEASIE does not go so far as to tie them to specific intervention objectives. This work remains to be done, but our outlook is optimistic.

Some of our cautious optimism derives from the fact that the FEASIE is actually a component of a larger, developmentally based diagnostic classification system of mental health and developmental disorders of infancy and early childhood (Emde, Bingham, & Harmon, 1993; Greenspan, 1994; National Center for Clinical Infant Programs [NCCIP], 1993). The axes of this diagnostic classification system include the following: (a) Axis I: primary diagnosis—traumatic stress disorder, disorders of affect, adjustment disorder, regulatory disorder, sleep behavior disorder, eating disorder, or disorders of relating and communicating; (b) Axis II: Relationship disorder; (c) Axis III: medical and developmental disorders and conditions; (d) Axis IV psychosocial stressors; and (e) Axis V: functional emotional developmental level (assessable by the FEASIE). Hence, this system represents the culmination of the efforts of a multidisciplinary Task Force of the National Center for Clinical Infant Programs to build a database about infants and toddlers with socioemotional problems requiring diagnosis and intervention, identify recurring patterns of behavioral problems, and develop refined descriptive categories.

According to NCCIP (1993), evaluation within this framework should lead to preliminary notions about nature of an infant's difficulties, strengths, adaptive capacity, function in major areas of development, the relative contribution of the areas assessed, and, finally, a treatment or intervention plan. Although the need to evaluate this new system's reliability, validity, coverage, and feasibility is mandatory, it is particularly promising as a comprehensive means to address diagnosis of disordered socioemotional status.

Program Planning and Evaluation. Diagnosis without treatment is useless. Often we use criterion-referenced measurement techniques to create individual goals for children whose needs have been diagnosed. Criterion-referenced tests provide information about specifically what a child can do, whereas norm-referenced interpretations provide information about how a child performs in relation to others the same age.

The precision of behavioral definitions in most criterion-referenced assessments, as well as their specificity of criteria and conditions for performance (i.e., the "who, what, when, where, and how" of performance; Cohen & Gross, 1979), make these important tools in our repertoire.

Popham (1978) reported several possible psychometric attributes to report in order to maximize faith in criterion-referenced assessment. First, content validity should be detailed. That is, a panel of expert judges should judge each item in a scale for appropriateness, and the percent of the total pool of items that are appropriate should be reported. If these indices fall below a preestablished cutoff, assessment tool creators must "go back to the drawing board" to eliminate and/or add items. Once a suitable pool of items is established, an internal consistency statistic can be utilized to convey the extent to which the assessment tool reflects the domain of interest. For reliability, Popham suggested an ingenious decision-consistency measure. Because qualitative descriptions from such measures lead to placement decisions, one way to determine reliability would be to examine the relation between decisions made across raters or occasions.

The Hawaii Early Learning Profile Strands (HELP; Parks, 1992a) are an excellent example of criterion-referenced tools that can enable us to plan for socioemotional intervention, beginning in this period (birth) and remaining pertinent until 3 years of age. They are used by interdisciplinary teams that are involved in the assessment and planning of comprehensive services for children birth to 3 years and their families. HELP strands are designed to be used with young children who are delayed, have disabilities, or are considered at risk. One of HELP's most applauded features is its high number of specific skills and intervention strategies in sensory organization, cognitive, language (receptive and expressive), gross motor, fine motor, self-help, and socioemotional areas. The HELP Strands report qualitative descriptions of behaviors within these major domains of development, along with approximate developmental age levels. This developmental age level obtained can be utilized to substantiate need for intervention, but is not equivalent to a score on a norm-referenced scale. However, many professionals assert that descriptions of the child's behaviors and skills are more important than age levels for determining next steps in intervention. Their density helps families and clinicians with curriculum planning, enables identification of strengths and needs, and facilitates monitoring of the child's progress in small incremental steps.

In terms of administration, the examiner (who may be a teacher, infant specialist, or other professional) begins with a free-play warm-up period, followed by structured facilitation of 5 to 10 preselected play and daily living activities observed by an entire assessment team, a period of movement or motor activity, snack, and additional or closing activities. For administration of this criterion-referenced tool, and others to be discussed, assessors are encouraged to capitalize on the infant or child's spontaneous behavior, such as (but not limited to) reactions to a new place and new people, parent–infant interaction during diaper changes, self-help during toileting for older children, tantruming/upset, climbing steps, and transitions between activities. *Inside Help* also provides excellent adaptations for disabled infants and preschoolers. In terms of scoring, two activities in a row passed with good quality constitutes the basal level of development, with two activities in a row failed corresponding to the ceiling level of development. Thus, "the highest skill in the strand for which the child receives full credit after passing more than two consecutive skills is the approximate [beginning] age range level of the child for that strand of development" (Parks, 1992b, p. xviii). It also is important to note that HELP credit codes are well differentiated. Not only are clear passes and failures noted, but emerging skills are indicated, and atypical or dysfunctional skills and behaviors are identified according to specific criteria. Last, it is noted when a skill's presence or absence is compromised by some behavior of the caregiver (e.g., a caregiver may strenuously hinder autonomy).

The results of such an assessment period or periods would be much information on the child's developmental level, style, ability to interact, and customary behaviors, leading to a unique description of the child and program planning objectives. In HELP's socioemotional strand, attachment/separation/autonomy, development of self, expression of emotions and feelings, learning rules and expectations, and social interactions and play are assessed. Each of these strand concepts is assessed via items appropriate from birth to age 3. For the birth to 6 months period, the following items are included:

- *Attachment/Separation/Autonomy:* Enjoys and needs a great deal of physical contact and tactile stimulation; establishes eye contact, draws attention to self when in distress; awakens of quiets to parent's voice; socializes with strangers/anyone; discriminates strangers; recognizes parent visually (4–8 months); lifts arms to parent (5–9 months); explores adult features (5–7 months); displays stranger anxiety (5–8 months).
- *Development of Self:* Inspects own hands; plays with own hands, feet, fingers, toes; makes approach movements to mirror; looks and vocalizes to own name (5–7 months); smiles at mirror image (5.5–8.5 months).
- *Expression of Emotions and Feelings:* Cries when hungry or uncomfortable; smiles reflexively; responds with a smile when socially approached; laughs, squeals, vocalizes attitudes (pleasure and displeasure); responds to facial expression (6–7 months); may show fear and insecurity with previously accepted situations (6–18 months).
- *Learning Rules and Expectations:* Shows anticipatory excitement; becomes aware of strange situations; distinguishes between friendly and angry voices.
- *Social Interactions and Play:* Regards face; establishes eye contact; molds and relaxes body when held; cuddles; responds to smile when socially

approached; vocalizes in response to adult talk and smile; laughs when head is covered with a cloth; demands social attention (3–8 months); enjoys social play (3–6 months); hand regard no longer present; repeats enjoyable activities (4–8 months); plays peek-a-boo (6–10 months); cooperates in games (6–10 months). [Note that even HELP omits mention of peers as social objects.]

These items are closely imbedded within an actual curriculum, and are followed chronologically by HELP For Special Preschoolers (HELP–SP; Foruno et al., 1985). Hence, assessment leads directly to behavioral objectives of what to do with infants who have specific needs in the socioemotional area. This is a major strength of HELP and HELP–SP.

The Early Learning Accomplishment Profile (ELAP; Glover, Preminger, & Sanford, 1978) is another criterion-referenced tool for assessing development in infancy and early childhood. Like the HELP, it has basal and ceiling rules, and gives information that it is tied directly to a curriculum. Its major disadvantage, in our view, is that it is not at all comprehensive, with only 37 items through preschool.

MID-INFANCY (7–18 MONTHS): RESOURCES THAT WOULD PREDICT POSITIVE SOCIOEMOTIONAL DEVELOPMENT

Interest in people and the world burgeon during this period, with cognitive advances such as the development of a sense of self and basic notions about causality supporting socioemotional advancement. From 6 to 12 months, the infant begins to have a set of expectancies about his or her caregiver's responsiveness in distress relief and positive affect sharing contexts. During the period of consolidation of these expectancies, the infant may demonstrate marked separation anxiety and fear of strangers, but these too are evidence of a clearcut attachment to these caregivers, the infant's sense of "this is my person." But, on a more positive note, the caregiver is also used as a base for exploration of the complex material and social world, a source of "emotional refueling" (Fraiberg, 1980), and peers are becoming a source of interest.

The infant–caregiver system is often compromised, however. The infant may lack affective involvement, seem incapable of wide-ranging contingent interactions with others. Or, the caregiver's abilities to read and respond contingently and multimodally to the infant may be impaired (whether by ignoring or misreading the infants cues, by being overly intrusive, preoccupied, or depressed; Greenspan, 1992). Such difficulties are seen in a variety of contexts (e.g., the infant was born preterm, the caregiver is depressed;

Field, 1980). These risks need to be assessed to understand an infant's socioemotional competence.

"The competent 12-month-old is the infant who can separate from the caregiver to explore novel aspects of the surround when stress is minimal, but seeks contact when distressed, readily derives comfort from the contact, and can thus return to play" (Waters & Sroufe, 1983, p. 93). We have a picture of an explorer hurtling toward autonomy, curious about how the world works, wanting to new things. He or she still wants closeness with the caregiver, and to please, but "me-ness" can be a higher priority!

Again, this move toward even more complex socioemotional development may be jeopardized. The toddler may exhibit withdrawn, overly compliant, or hyperaggressive, disorganized behavior. Or, instead of admiring the toddler's initiative and autonomy, tolerantly following his or her lead but supplying firm limits when necessary, the caregiver may be overly intrusive, controlling, or fearful (Greenspan, 1992). This is a pivotal point in socioemotional development, which we need to be able to sensitively assess.

MID-INFANCY (7–18 MONTHS): ASSESSMENT TOOLS

Unfortunately, however, very few period-specific assessment tools exist for this age range. And, the informal observation pursued in pediatric well-baby visits, developmental follow-up clinics, and large-scale developmental screening programs is particularly risky for pinpointing these important developmental issues. For example, it is unlikely that an opportunity for assessing difficulties of attachment would be especially created. And, it would be all too easy in a brief interaction to entirely miss, or misread as normally developing, the toddler who isn't saying "No," or who, given a novel environment offered an interesting array of toys merely clings to the caregiver, uneasy about anything out of the ordinary.

Screening. No DDST items assess the foregoing abilities of this age range. Moreover, regarding attachment, Crowell and Fleischmann (1993) discussed the infeasibility of using the Strange Situation as a diagnostic measure. However, they do suggest using Gaensbauer and Harmon's (1981) Structured Playroom measure. In this observational system, infant and caregiver are observed for episodes of longer duration (free play, caregiver–stranger–infant interaction, and a separation–reunion), in order to rate the 12- to 18-month-old infant's emotional responsiveness, ability to organize social behaviors and cooperate in play, and the dyadic interaction between caregiver and infant. Gaensbauer and Harmon reported concurrent validity indices. Although clinical experience and training are important in learning to use and applying it, this procedure appears promising.

TABLE 12.5
Lewis and Michalson System: Exemplary Scale Descriptions

LM Scale	Behaviors Scored 1[a]	Behaviors Scored 5
Happiness	Relax	Laugh, giggle
	Slight smile	Squeal
Positive affiliation	Slight smile at other	Follow other
	Lean toward	Hug/kiss
Fear	Sober	Grasp/cling
	Decreased activity	Scream
Anger	Look hard at	Stomp
	Frown	Yell
Negative affiliation[b]	Suck thumb	Search for mother
	Sober	Fret/cry
Competence	Vocalize	Initiate activity
	Look around alertly	Create an activity

[a]Two examplars for scores of 1 and 5 are given for each scale; most scale points included more exemplars.
[b]In this study, this scale was scored for toddlers' reactions directed toward the absent mother.
Source: Lewis and Michalson (1983). *Children's emotions and moods*. New York: Plenum Press. Reprinted by permission.

Another potential assessment tool, Lewis and Michalson's observational technique for assessing emotions (LM; Lewis & Michalson, 1983) could prove quite useful in screening during this and the following age period. This is an observational system in which individual differences in the emotional states of happiness, fear, anger, affiliation, and competence, are coded according to behavioral definitions and rank ordered on an intensity dimension. The system was originally validated by assessing these states across a number of specific eliciting contexts, and both interobserver reliability and concurrent validity have been established (Denham & Mitchell-Copeland, 1993; Lewis & Michalson, 1983; see Table 12.5 for exemplars of each scale).

Professionals like pediatricians and/or pediatric nurses could be educated about assessing socioemotional milestones of this age range; for example, the pediatric visit seems like a very rich opportunity for eliciting emotions and social affiliative behaviors. In such a setting there would be great potential for picking up atypical interaction patterns. Contexts include the low stress affiliation situation of the doctor or nurse in the room, but not looking at or touching the baby, with caregiver holding baby, or the more high stress affiliation elicitors of doctor/nurse approach, examining baby, and administering noxious stimuli such as immunization. The wide range of sensitive ratings made using the LM system could lead to judgments regarding need for further diagnostic work.

Sometimes the line between screening and diagnosis is blurry. DeGangi et al. (1994) created the Infant/Toddler Screening Checklist (I/TSC). There are five forms of this checklist, beginning with age 7 months and ranging to 30 months, and one form that can quickly screen the entire age range. Parents complete items (with or without an interviewer's assistance) on subscales including self-regulation of arousal and physiological state, attention, sleep, sensory integration (e.g., eating/feeding, dressing, bathing, and touch), movement and sensory-based motor planning, listening and language, looking and sight, and attachment/emotional functioning. They mark items *never or sometimes, most times,* or *past.* The total score is then compared to a cutoff score derived for each age range.

DeGangi et al. suggested that screening is most effective when the I/TSC is administered in conjunction with observation of the child's ability to self-regulate in action, as well as parent–child interaction, for example. They further asserted that the I/TSC can be used as a diagnostic tool, especially if also used together with traditional developmental tests such as the BSID–II or the aforementioned observational tools. In terms of psychometric adequacy, relatively few regulatory disordered infants and toddlers were included at each age level for the norming sample. Nonetheless, accuracy for cutoff scores is relatively good, with false-delayed and false-normal rates ranging from 0 to 14% across age levels. DeGangi et al. reported good concurrent validity, but we suggest ongoing efforts with larger samples are needed.

Diagnosis. There is a similar lack of comprehensive diagnostic assessment tools for socioemotional development specifically during this age period. Larzelere's Toddler Behavior Checklist (TBC; Larzelere, Amberson, & Martin, 1992; Larzelere, Martin, & Amberson, 1989) is, however, available. The TBC is a 103-item norm-referenced parent-completed checklist of problem behaviors for 9- to 48-month-olds. Its scoring is broken down into five areas of concern: oppositional, immaturity, emotional instability, physical aggression, and shyness. Each area of concern is evaluated by parents with regard to both frequency of occurrences by the child and how often it has been considered a discipline problem. Parents are asked to rate on 4-point scales how often their children have behaved in this way within the past month, and on 3-point scales how often they have considered the behavior a discipline problem in the past month (see Table 12.6 for an example). Thus, there are 10 normed scales; coefficient alphas of .67 to .91 suggest that their internal consistency is good. Moreover, Larzelere et al. (1992) created a normed "discipline–behavior ratio" that is a rough index of how often a given behavior is considered discipline problems.

A toddler who scores 1 standard deviation above the mean for other children in the age range, for any of these factors, may be developing maladap-

TABLE 12.6
Larzelere Toddler Behavior Checklist: Sample Items

Please give us the following information about the child you are describing (your cover letter specifies which child you should describe on this checklist):

Age: _____ years and _____ months
Sex: Male Female (Circle correct answer)
Order of birth: First-born Second Third Other: _____

Directions: Behaviors typical of young children are listed below. Please tell us two things about each item: 1) How often has your child behaved in this way in the past month, and 2) Have you considered this behavior a discipline problem in the past month?

Definitions: A child's behavior is considered a *discipline problem* when you feel a need to take some specific corrective action to discourage it (such as verbal correction, removing the child from the situation, spanking, or sending the child to his or her room.)

A behavior is *not* a discipline problem if you consider it to be:
a) appropriate for the situation and age of the child
b) something the child will grow out of without correction by you, or
c) an indication mainly that the child has some other need, such as more sleep or attention, and for that reason does not require *specific* action to correct the behavior, but only requires action to meet the more general need.

Circle the most appropriate answer to both questions for each item.

How often has your child done this in the past month?	ANSWERS: N Never R Rarely S Sometimes F Frequently	Have you considered this a discipline problem this last month?	ANSWERS: N NEVER S SOMETIMES F FREQUENTLY
N R S F	1. Dawdles and wastes time (for example, at meal time).		N S F
N R S F	2. Refuses to eat food served.		N S F
N R S F	3. Refuses to go to bed when asked.-------------		N S F
N R S F	4. Gets angry when he/she does not get his/her way.		N S F
N R S F	5. Disobedient at home.		N S F
N R S F	6. Has temper tantrums. -------------------------		N S F
N R S F	7. Whining.		N S F
N R S F	8. Cries without reason.		N S F

Source: R. E. Larzelere. Reproduced by permission.

tive social behavior patterns, perhaps as a result of lack of negotiation of the previous socioemotional developmental task. The TBC highlights just which behaviors are of concern. Given that research suggests that oppositional and aggressive styles begin to show stability as early as 2 years of age (Campbell, 1988; Campbell & Ewing, 1990), a standardized measure of these styles seems particularly important for assessing need for intervention as well as a means for tracking success of intervention on follow-up assessments. Larzerlere et al. (1992) also showed evidence of a developmental progression in the normative incidence of these behavior problems across a relatively broad age span. This quality is useful in terms of pinpointing children with more than the usual "growing pains." Furthermore, a significant discrepancy between number and level of toddler problem behaviors endorsed versus the number and level of the behaviors viewed as discipline problems provides useful information about actual child behavior versus appropriateness of parental expectations. Knowing that such a discrepancy exists provides potentially very useful information with regard to material for parent teaching.

The FEASIE also continues to be a useful diagnostic tool for this age range. It includes the following important skills for this age range:

1. By 9 months the infant is able to interact in a purposeful (i.e., intentional, reciprocal, cause-and-effect) manner; is able to initiate signals and respond purposefully to another person's signals. Gestures are used to initiate closeness, pleasure, excitement, exploratory behavior, protest/anger, and fear (Greenspan, 1992, pp. 395–396). Greenspan (1994) called this ability "interactive intentionality and reciprocity" (p. 39).
2. By 13 months, the infant begins to develop a complex sense of self by organizing behavior and emotion. The toddler sequences a number of gestures together and responds consistently to caregivers' gestures, thereby forming chains of interaction. The toddler also manifests a wide range of organized, socially meaningful behaviors and feelings dealing with warmth, pleasure, assertion, exploration, protest, and anger (Greenspan, 1992, pp. 398–399). Greenspan (1994) called this constellation of abilities "representational/affective communication" (p. 39).

If these abilities are adequately assessed by very well-trained developmental clinicians, especially if included within the NCCIP multisystem classification, then professionals should move with confidence toward specifying objectives for intervention.

Program Planning and Evaluation. Despite our hopes for the FEASIE, at this point the HELP is much more directly related to specific behavioral objectives for children. For this age range, the HELP Strands include the following assessment items/behavioral objectives:

- *Attachment/Separation/Autonomy:* Lets only parent meet needs; explores environment enthusiastically—safety precautions important; likes to be in constant sight and hearing of adult; attempts self-direction, resists adult control.
- *Development of Self:* Shows like/dislike for certain people, objects, places; displays independent behavior; is difficult to discipline—the "no" stage; shows toy preferences; enjoys being the center of attention; recognizes several people in addition to immediate family; identifies self in mirror.
- *Expression of Emotions and Feelings:* Displays frequent tantrum behaviors; hugs and kisses parents.
- *Learning Rules and Expectations:* Acts impulsively, unable to recognize rules; hands toy back to adult; needs and expects rituals and routines; begins to show a sense of humor—laughs at incongruities; displays distractible behavior; tends to be quite messy.
- *Social Interactions and Play:* Extends toy to show others, not for release; repeats sounds or gestures if laughed at; gives toy to familiar adult spontaneously and on request; plays ball cooperatively. [Again peers are not mentioned, even though Table 12.1 indicates that friendships may begin during this period.]

Another criterion-referenced assessment leading relatively directly to intervention, which is also family and child friendly, is the Transdisciplinary Play-Based Assessment (TPBA; Linder, 1990) used from 6 to 72 months. For this assessment system, children are observed by parents and an assessment team, in unstructured and structured situations, to elicit the abilities of infants, toddlers, and preschoolers. Assessed are temperament, mastery motivation, social interactions with parent, social interaction with facilitator, characteristics of dramatic play in relation to emotional development, humor and social conventions, and social interactions with peers.

Elements of temperament include activity level, adaptability to new people, situations, and objects, reactivity, goal direction, persistence, and the quality of exploration, rather than just its amount. In social interaction with parent, the TPBA assesses initiation of interactions, turn-taking, reaction to adult emotion and authority, reaction to parent's absence and reunion, and use of parent as a secure base. Social interactions with the facilitator parallel those with the parent so comparisons can be made. Illogical or dysfluent thought processes during dramatic play can be highlighted, as well as play themes of dependency, loss, control, fear. Emotional competence issues such as difficulty expressing or regulating, or labeling, certain emotions, may come to light. Social interactions with peers in dyads and in groups also are gauged.

There are many advantages of TPBA. First, assessment of socioemotional development using this perspective is incredibly comprehensive and flexible in permitting individualization, much more so than most other socioemotional assessments. Because it is broken down into subdomains, TPBA allows examination of qualitatively different aspects of socioemotional competence. Moreover, TPBA provides a very thick description of a child's socioemotional development. It is a qualitative description, describing how a child does something, not just that he or she does it. Finally, based naturalistically as it is, TPBA has tremendous face validity. That is, delays and deviations in socioemotional development are reflected in play assessed in the child's natural environment, probably tapping his or her highest level of performance. Such assessment is less stressful on the child than other means of testing, is not culturally biased, and can be used with children with disabilities. Given that TPBA determines specific strengths and weaknesses, it flows well into intervention.

However, there are distinct disadvantages. There is no quantitative means of summarizing findings from the measure. Standardization is not accomplished—different materials, means of administration, for example, are used across children. Because of these limitations, there are no conventional psychometric data on TPBA, and therefore it would be difficult to use to compare children or determine intervention outcomes.

LATE INFANCY/TODDLERHOOD (19–36 MONTHS): RESOURCES THAT WOULD PREDICT POSITIVE SOCIOEMOTIONAL DEVELOPMENT

During this age period, the task of individuation is continuing with a vengeance. Controlling behavior, and who does that controlling, is very important to the child. The stage is set for a pendulum swinging from pitched battles to the charm and pride of a little person who begins to perform complex tasks, such as dressing, independently. Mood is stabilizing, and peers begin to assume real importance as attachment to nonadults consolidates.

This toddler period is a particularly difficult period in terms of socioemotional assessment. Child behavior during this period is typically extremely confusing because the continuing task of individuation causes a conflict within the child as to the need to test the limits of his or her autonomy, while needing to find how to remain attached to the parent. Therefore, it can be very difficult for even the experienced clinician to assess whether, for example, a particular toddler's level of negativism (or, conversely, clinginess) is developmentally appropriate and thus likely to be leading to a healthy individuation, or whether the behavior pattern is outside the limits of what is considered normal. Even though adequate assessment of individuation is difficult to achieve, it is especially important for atypical children at this developmental level. Such children are likely to have experienced serious medical interventions and health problems that often encourage an overprotective parenting style. Child overdependence on the parent is often not recognized by professionals until the child begins school, is forced to separate from the parent, and is expected to exhibit a high degree of self-reliance, making the school experience very stressful for the child.

LATE INFANCY/TODDLERHOOD (19–36 MONTHS): ASSESSMENT TOOLS

Screening. Two socioemotional items appear on the DDST for this age range—playing interactive games and separating easily from the mother. According to DDST scoring conventions, however, failure of these two items at this point would not be considered as problematic for this domain of development unless earlier milestones were also failed. But, it is encouraging to note that two major socioemotional tasks of the period are in fact covered by the DDST. A research task could be used in an ecologically valid manner to capture many of the important aspects of socioemotional development during this period. Matas, Arend, and Sroufe (1978) developed a judgment-based measure, the Tool Use Problem-Solving Task (TUT), that assesses the child's capacity to exercise self-reliance. Faced with four difficult problems after free-play and clean-up periods, the competent child is seen as enthusiastic and persistent, and seems to have an "I can do it myself" attitude. However, the other equally important component of competence is the child's knowing that he or she can turn to an adult when faced with a difficult problem. Symbolic play, oppositionality, compliance, active noncompliance and ignoring, verbal negativism, frustration behavior, aggression, whining/crying, help-seeking, enthusiasm, positive–negative affect, and nontask-related behavior are rated. Moreover, maternal supportive presence and quality of assistance also are rated. Concurrent and predictive validity, as well as interrater and internal consistency reliability for some of these scales are shown in Denham, Renwick, and Holt (1991), as well as in Matas et al. (1978). The procedure is not difficult to stage or to score.

Meier (1993) created a screening instrument with a socioemotional scale that includes the following items: separates easily, shares toys, puts toys away, plays cooperatively or dramatically with other children, takes turns, plays in group games, plays independently, tries out new social or group experiences, is friendly, talks easily with others. At last, peer-related skills are assessed! Items are rated 0 to 2 with respect to how well they describe the child's socioemotional status, and Meier asserted that these total scores also can be utilized for pre-, mid-, and postintervention evaluation. He argued for a simple instrument such as this to guard against what he called the "paralysis of analysis" (p. 25) of more complex assessments.

Meier also included the following items on emotional/behavior disorders: hits, damages, tantrums, not follow rules, teases/threatens/swears, lies/cheats, yells, interrupts, rude, clings to, withdraw, soils, sex play, restless, clumsy, sad, strange sounds, distracted, cruel/angry/fights, argues with adult, annoys others. In general, both the development and disorder items are developmentally appropriate, with a range of difficulty sensitive to differentiating this age group's developmental trajectories. The screening instrument is economical in material and professional time, but Meier does not provide cutoff scores.

Zabel (1982) also created a teacher screening tool for identifying young children at risk for socioemotional developmental deficits. The tool focused on the presence or absence of the following major areas (with examples of specific items included in parentheses):

1. Short attention span (e.g., unable to concentrate: not able to pay attention long enough to finish an activity).
2. Restless or hyperactive (e.g., moves around constantly, fidgets).
3. Does not seem to move with a purpose in mind.
4. Picks on other children.
5. Does not complete tasks (e.g., careless, unorganized approach to activities).
6. Listening difficulties (e.g., does not seem to understand).
7. Avoids participation with other children or only knows how to play by hurting others.
8. Avoids adults.
9. Repetitive behavior.
10. Ritualistic or unusual behavior.
11. Resistant to discipline or direction (e.g., impertinent, defiant, resentful, destructive).
12. Unusual language content; echolalic.
13. Speech problems (rate, articulation, stuttering, voice).
14. Lack of self-help skills.
15. Self-aggressive or self-derogatory.
16. Temperamental (e.g., overly sensitive, sad, irritable).

It would seem that this instrument would be useful in a day-care or preschool setting, to pinpoint the difficulties that a teacher/caregiver noted in a child's socioemotional development, but again no cutoff score is given for the need for intervention. Note, moreover, that positive developmental milestones are not included. We argue for the necessity of knowing the presence of both deficits and strengths in socioemotional competence.

Diagnosis. The Child Behavior Checklist for 2- and 3-Year-Olds (CBCL/2–3) was designed to extend previously developed empirically based assessment procedures (Achenbach, Edelbrock, & Howell, 1987). The measure is completed by parents; in the norming sample, results for 398 children were factor analyzed, yielding six syndromes having at least eight items loading at .30 or above: social withdrawal, depressed, sleep problems, somatic problems, aggressive, and destructive (items contributing to each factors can be seen in Table 12.7). Further, second-order analyses showed that there was a broadband internalizing grouping (i.e., the first two syndromes in the previous list) and a broadband externalizing grouping (i.e., the last two syndromes). Psychometric properties of the CBCL/2–3 are excellent, in the tradition of these empirically based measures. Mean test–retest reliability was reported as .87 (.69 at 1 year). Prediction of CBCL/4–16 scores at 4 was .63 (.55 for 2 years). Children referred for services scored significantly higher than those nonreferred on all scales. Moreover, there was a lack of association between these scores and the Bayley Scales of Infant Intelligence or the McCarthy Scales of Children's Abilities, demonstrating that the CBCL/2–3 taps behavioral/emotional problems independent of cognitive ability.

But this measure, like others of its ilk, is good for gross screening of pathology but not for pinpointing socioemotional developmental processes. Second, the measure is less comprehensive than the CBCL/4–16. Hence, given these strengths and weaknesses, we recommend it for evaluation of programs, initial gross diagnosis, and initial phases of treatment plans.

The FEASIE, still appropriate for this age period, specifies the following objectives:

1. By 18 months, the infant elaborates complex, lengthy sequences of interaction that convey basic emotional themes, such as those outlined for the earlier age range, but now including limit-setting. Imitation and

TABLE 12.7
Loadings of Items on Syndrome Scales
Derived From Principal Components/Varimax Analyses

Internalizing Scales			Neither Internalizing nor Externalizing		
I. Anxious/Depressed			III. Sleep Problems		
68.	Self-conscious	.60	38.	Trouble getting to sleep	.60
10.	Clings to adults	.58	94.	Wakes often at night	.60

(Continued)

TABLE 12.7
(Continued)

Internalizing Scales			Neither Internalizing nor Externalizing		
13.	Looks unhappy w.o. reason	.58	64.	Resists going to bed	.56
33.	Feelings easily hurt	.55	48.	Nightmares	.55
37.	Upset when separated	.49	22.	Doesn't want to sleep alone	.55
87.	Too fearful or anxious	.47	84.	Talks, cries out in sleep	.53
50.	Overtired	.47	74.	Sleeps less than most children	.44
47.	Nervous, highstrung, tense	.36		Eigenvalue	3.39
90.	Unhappy, sad, depressed	.32	IV.	Somatic Problems	
96.	Wants attention	.30	45.	Nausea	.62
73.	Shy or timid	.30	39.	Headaches	.61
	Eigenvalue	3.56	1.	Aches	.60
			86.	Overconcern w. neatness	.60
II.	Withdrawn		61.	Refuses to eat	.60
70.	Little affection	.57	24.	Doesn't eat well	.56
98.	Withdrawn	.56	93.	Vomiting	.47
67.	Unresponsive to affection	.44	78.	Stomachaches	.45
71.	Little interest	.44	19.	Diarrhea	.43
26.	No fun	.44	65.	Resists toilet training	.37
23.	Doesn't answer	.41	52.	Painful bowel movements	.37
27.	Lacks guilt	.40	7.	Can't stand things out of place	.34
62.	Refuses active games	.40	12.	Constipated	.33
88.	Uncooperative	.39	41.	Holds breath	.31
89.	Underactive	.38		Eigenvalue	3.16
2.	Acts too young	.37			
4.	Avoids eye contact	.37			
81.	Stubborn	.31			
25.	Doesn't get along w. other children	.30			
	Eigenvalue	4.68			

Externalizing Scales

V.	Aggressive Behavior		VI.	Destructive Behavior	
40.	Hits others	.60	42.	Hurts w.o. meaning to	.52
85.	Temper	.59	9.	Chews nonfood	.44
35.	Fights	.53	18.	Destroys others' things	.43
20.	Disobedient	.53	17.	Destroys own things	.41
58.	Punishment doesn't change behavior	.52	63.	Rocks head or body	.41
44.	Angry moods	.50	75.	Smears bowel movements	.39
16.	Demands must be met	.48	36.	Gets into things	.39
66.	Screams	.47	5.	Can't concentrate	.36
91.	Loud	.47	59.	Quickly shifts activity	.35
69.	Selfish	.45	31.	Eats nonfood	.34
97.	Whining	.44	14.	Cruel to animals	.30
15.	Defiant	.43		Eigenvalue	2.82
30.	Jealous	.42			
82.	Sudden mood changes	.42			
29.	Easily frustrated	.41			
	Eigenvalue	7.24			

Source: Achenbach (1992). Copyright T.M. Achenbach. Reproduced by permission.

humor are also used in elaborating on these themes (Greenspan, 1992, pp. 400–402). Greenspan (1994) called this ability "representational/affective communication" (p. 39).

2. By 24 months, the child creates mental representations of feelings and ideas that can be expressed symbolically (e.g., pretend play and words to convey) emotional themes, and to communicate about intentions wishes, needs, or feelings (Greenspan, 1992, pp. 403–404).

3. By 30 months, the child can elaborate a number of ideas, using symbolic communication and make-believe play, that go beyond basic needs and deal with more complex intentions, wishes, or feelings (early themes, as well as showing off; Greenspan, 1992, p. 406). Greenspan (1994) called this ability "representational elaboration" (p. 39).

Planning and Program Evaluation. At this age range, both the HELP and TPBA are appropriate. The HELP assessment items and objectives include:

- *Attachment/Separation/Autonomy:* Displays dependent behavior, clings/whines; feels strongly possessive of loved ones; separates easily in familiar surroundings; shows independence; insists on doing things independently.

- *Development of Self:* Uses own name to refer to self; experiences a strong sense of self-importance; recognizes self in photographs; uses "self-centered" pronouns; values own property, uses word "mine"; takes pride in clothing; becoming aware of gender differences; distinguishes self as a separate person, contrasts self with others; knows own sex or sex of others; takes pride in achievements, resists help.

- *Expression of Emotions and Feelings:* Expresses affection; shows jealousy at attention given to others, especially other family members; shows a wide variety of emotions (e.g., fear, anger, sympathy, modesty, guilty, joy); feels easily frustrated; attempts to comfort others in distress; frustration tantrums peak; dramatizes (feelings) using a doll; fatigues easily; may develop sudden fears, especially of large animals; demonstrates extreme emotional shifts and paradoxical responses.

- *Learning Rules and Expectations:* Desires control of others—orders, fights, resists; remembers where objects belong; demonstrates awareness of class routines; holds parent's hand outdoors; Says "no," but submits anyway; dawdles and procrastinates; begins to obey and respect simple rules; resists change, is extremely ritualistic; experiences difficulty with transitions.

- *Social Interactions and Play:* Interacts with peers using gestures; engages in parallel play; defends possessions; displays shyness with strangers and in outside situations; tends to be physically aggressive; enjoys a wide range of relationships, meets more people; relates best to one familiar adult at a time; engages best in peer interaction with just one older child, not a sibling; initiates own play, but requires supervision to carry out ideas; tends to be dictatorial and demanding; talks with a loud, urgent voice; participates in interactive games. [The HELP integrates peer skills at this point in time.]

We continue to assert that HELP and TPBA tap the important socioemotional skills to attained by children with this age range.

PRESCHOOL (37–60 MONTHS): RESOURCES THAT WOULD PREDICT POSITIVE SOCIOEMOTIONAL DEVELOPMENT

During the preschool period, socioemotional competence takes on even greater importance because of the child's experience in the expanding peer arena. Management of impulses and peer relations, along with consolidation of emotional competence skills, including regulating one's own expressiveness, understanding the emotions of self and others, and reacting appropriately to others emotions (Saarni, 1990), take precedence. These skills allow emotion to be moderated by the use of higher order interaction skills or symbolic abilities, not merely impulsively expressed as felt. With such ability, the child has a vehicle with which to regulate emotions; he or she has experience in attaching labels to inner feelings and therefore can bring them to consciousness. Understanding and regulating affect are also important contributors to success in social relationships (Denham, McKinley, Couchoud, & Holt, 1990; Sroufe et al., 1984), because these abilities enhance the child's ability to solve social problems.

Such problem-solving ability constitutes another critical milestone that fosters adaptive socioemotional development during the preschool years. For example, the child who can consider alternative solutions to problems is less likely to take a toy out of the hands of another without consideration for the other person's desires. After considering the consequences of an act, he or she may be less likely to push another child away simply because that child is in the way of a desired goal. Further, if he or she can recognize feelings in him or herself, the child also can begin to empathize with feelings seen in others. Given the complexity of emerging skills in emotion, social cognition, and also specific peer interaction behaviors, there are a multitude of factors that can thwart the development of emotional competence for the at-risk preschooler who lives in an environment that is chaotic and stressful. Stability of behavior problems from this point, often emotion-related (Campbell, 1988), suggests that socioemotional assessment and intervention are increasingly crucial.

PRESCHOOL (37–60 MONTHS): ASSESSMENT TOOLS

Screening. No new items appear on the DDST at this age range. However, the earlier cited ones remain important; failure of them could, depending on the child's age, render their DDST score as questionable even without failures in other domains. In the research-based tradition, Crowell and Feldman (1988) developed a judgment-based Problem-Solving Task to extend the use of the Matas et al. (1978) TUT to the 24- to 54-month age group. Tasks involve common toys and activities, ranked by difficulty, and a separation–reunion sequence is added to the general procedures of Matas et al. The session is videotaped for scoring on scales also similar to those of Matas et al. Indices of discriminant validity have been reported for this age range, so that this type of procedure could continue being useful in early stages of screening.

Where more time is available to observe the child within the peer social milieu, the Minnesota Preschool Affect Checklist (MPAC; Sroufe et al., 1984) would be useful to summarize aspects of affect and social interaction that have been identified as particularly salient or germane for this period of development. These developmental tasks include the expression and regulation of positive and negative affect, productive involvement in purposeful activity, impulse control and management of frustration, interaction with peers, and ability to respond prosocially to the needs of others. For each observation period, observers note the presence or absence of items included with these overarching developmental tasks, which sample well the domain of skills for this age period. The MPAC has demonstrated reliability and validity for this age level (see also Denham, Zahn-Waxler, Cummings, & Iannotti, 1990).

Diagnosis. Although within this age range the CBCL 4–16 becomes appropriate (Achenbach & Edelbrock, 1986), it is so similar to the CBCL 2–3 in strengths and weaknesses that we do not discuss it further. For diagnostic coverage of both positive and negative socioemotional milestones during the preschool period, we prefer the Preschool Socioaffective Profile (PSP; Dumas & Serketich, 1993; LaFreniere, Dumas, Capuano, Coutu, & Giuliani, 1993; LaFreniere, Dumas, Capuano, & Dubeau, 1992). It is a norm-referenced test which was developed from a developmental adaptational perspective; it targets behaviors reflecting emotional expression in social interaction with peers and adults, along with characteristic emotion in a nonsocial context. There have been three standardization samples, all showing good to excellent interrater, internal consistency, and test–retest reliability. Three factors have been isolated from the PSP's items: social competence, externalizing, and internalizing behavior (see Table 12.8 for items contributing to these factors). Concurrent validation exists with both

TABLE 12.8
Preschool Socioaffective Profile: Factors and Items

	Quebec (N = 910)	Indiana (N = 960)	Colorado (N = 439)
Angry–Aggressive		1st Factor	
1. Irritable, gets mad easily	.84	.80	.82
2. Easily frustrated	.78	.62	.63
3. Defiant when reprimanded	.77	.79	.78
4. Gets into conflicts with other children	.76	.77	.76
5. Screams or yells easily	.76	.71	.67
6. Gets angry when interrupted	.71	.79	.75
7. Hits, bites or kicks other children	.71	.74	.72
8. Hits teacher when angry	.66	.62	.63
9. Forces other children to do things	.65	.77	.71
10. Opposes the teacher	.58	.72	.69
Social–Competence		2nd Factor	
1. Negotiates solution to conflicts	.73	.67	.53
2. Comforts or assists children in difficulty	.72	.70	.72
3. Takes other children's viewpoint into account	.69	.66	.74
4. Works easily in a group	.68	.60	.66
5. Cooperates with other children	.66	.61	.73
6. Takes pleasures in own accomplishments	.65	.45	.60
7. Accepts compromises	.65	.49	.60
8. Attentive toward younger children	.63	.55	.68
9. Takes care of toys	.58	.63	.58
10. Helps with everyday tasks	.57	.53	.65
Anxious–Withdrawn		3rd Factor	
1. Remains apart, isolated from the group	.70	.78	.70
2. Inactive, watches others play	.69	.80	.60
3. Sad, unhappy, or depressed	.67	.67	.67
4. Inhibited or uneasy in the group	.66	.75	.69
5. Doesn't talk or interact during group activities	.64	.66	.51
6. Timid, afraid, avoids new situations	.62	.74	.75
7. Goes unnoticed in a group	.54	.67	.57
8. Worries	.50	.50	.57
9. Tired	.49	.53	.35
10. Neutral expression, doesn't smile or laugh	.49	.63	.45

Source: LaFreniere et al., 1993. Reproduced by permission.

broad and narrow band measures of the CBCL/4–16, as well as with observations of social behavior and peer sociometrics. Because this measure provides a picture of specific types of problems as well as positive social adaptation, it assists teachers and parents in understanding the child's strengths and weaknesses. Moreover, it is sensitive to behavioral change over time in order to evaluate intervention outcomes.

The FEASIE is still appropriate at this age range. Skills it now taps include:

1. By 36 months, ideas dealing with complex intentions, wishing, and feelings in pretend play or other types of symbolic communication are now logically tied to one another. The child can distinguish what is real from the unreal, and switches back and forth between fantasy and reality with little difficulty (Greenspan, 1992, p. 408). Greenspan (1994) called this the first level of representational differentiation.

2. After 42 months, the child is capable of even more elaborate complex pretend play and symbolic communication dealing with complex intentions, wishes, or feelings. The play or direct communication is characterized by three or more ideas that are logically connected and informed by concepts involving causality, time, and space (Greenspan, 1992, p. 411). Emotional themes now include separation and loss. This is the second, more mature, level of representational differentiation.

It becomes clearer that as a diagnostic tool, the FEASIE richly plumbs elements of emotional competence. It does not, however, directly examine aspects of the peer arena.

Program Planning and Evaluation. The TPBA is still appropriate at this age range. Further, the HELP–SP picks up at this range, continuing the HELP tradition of adherence to a developmental perspective.

ONGOING TRANSACTIONAL ASSESSMENT

We now have reviewed the measures at each age level with which we can screen, diagnose, or plan interventions for socioemotional difficulties in infancy and preschool. These measures do not tell a complete story, however. As Greenspan (1994) has strongly asserted, "Assessment and diagnosis must be guided by the awareness that all [children] are participants in [family] relationships" (p. 34). Transactional assessment is needed (Parks, 1992b). That is, both the physical and parent-interactional environments in which the child functions should be described by interactive and ecological measures (Bagnato & Neisworth, 1991). The space, routine, and play materials available to the infant or child on a regular basis, as well as their parents' or caregivers' abilities to read, interpret, and respond to their cues, need to be detailed. In general, these goals are met by different means for infants as opposed to toddlers and preschoolers. NCATS and NCAFS scales measure parent sensitivity to infant cues, response to distress, socioemotional growth fostering and cognitive growth fostering. In general, psychometric data are even better than for NCAST infant scales. The IRS includes ratings of caregiver state (e.g., depressed, anxious, alert), physical activity, head orientation, gaze behavior, silence during gaze aversion, facial expressions, vocalizations, infantilized behaviors (i.e., imitation of infant), contingent responsivity, and game playing.

Greenspan–Lieberman Observation System for Assessment of Caregiver–Infant Interaction during Semi-Structured Play (GLOS; Clark, Paulson, & Conlin, 1993; Greenspan, 1983; Greenspan & Lieberman, 1989) consists of 53 parent and 43 child variables rated every 15 seconds from a 10-minute video of free play. Parent behaviors include interaction with the infant, including pleasurable, neutral, or aversive tactile experiences and contingent responses to the infant's behavior. Infants from newborn to toddler age are rated on their response to physical contact with caregivers and responses to caregiver behavior. All ratings are subjective. In terms of validity, the GLOS distinguishes between the caregiving of adolescent and young adult mothers (Clark et al., 1993). Similarly, caregiver tendencies on the FEASIE include information gleaned by history-taking or direct observation: The caregiver is comforting, finds appropriate levels of stimulation, pleasurably engages the infant/child, reads and responds to emotional signals and needs, encourages forward development. If there is reason to believe that caregiver patterns are suboptimal, Greenspan suggested examining overstimulation, unavailability, rigidity, randomness or overconcreteness, illogicality in reading or responding to signals, and avoidance of selected emotional themes or instability in the face of intense emotion. Although the behaviors appear relevant for the assessment purposes detailed here, there are some problems in performing and interpreting either measure.

The Parent–Child Early Relational Assessment (PCERA; Clark, 1985) assesses the quality of parent–child relationships through "parental affect and behavior [which] provide a regulatory or organizing function" (Clark, et al., 1993, p. 203). Four 5-minute periods, free play, structured task, feeding, and separation–reunion are rated. The ratings focus on both dyad members' positive and negative affect and responsiveness. Further, there are several ratings of the dyad's functioning overall, and caregivers' perceptions are sought. Discriminant validity has been shown through demonstration of differences between a variety of high-risk and well-functioning groups of parents and infants; associations with security of attachment have also been found (Clark et al., 1993). This is a comprehensive evaluation of parent–child interaction and relationship quality, obtaining data on several developmentally important milestones, but much training and experience are needed to use the PCERA.

TABLE 12.9
Home Observation for Measurement of the Environment

Subscale Items (0–3 years)	Subscale Items (3–6 years)
Mother's emotional and verbal responsivity	Stimulation through toys, games, and reading materials
Avoidance of restriction and punishment	Positive social responsiveness
Organization of physical and temporal environment	Physical environment: safe, clean, and conducive to development
Provision of appropriate play materials	Pride, affection, warmth
Maternal involvement with child	Stimulation of academic behavior
Opportunities for variety in daily stimulation	Modeling and encouragement of social maturity
	Variety of stimulation
	Physical punishment

Reproduced by permission of R. S. Bradley.

The Home Observation for Measurement of the Environment (HOME; Caldwell & Bradley, 1978) was designed to assess the qualities of person–person and person–object interactions that comprise the infant or young child's learning environment (Calloway, 1982). It samples aspects of the quantity and quality of social, emotional, and cognitive support available within the child's home (see Table 12.9). Information is gained through observation and interview, by a person who observes the child in the home; only presence or absence of behaviors is noted. Calloway (1982) provided estimates of validity.

The Parent Behavior Progression (PBP; Bromwich, 1983) taps behaviors that reflect attitudes and feelings of parents. It was designed to be part of an ongoing parent–staff relationships rather than an initial diagnostic tool. It is a checklist of 17 reported or observed parent behaviors at each of six levels, with the goal of aiding in formulation of short-term goals for families and improving parent–child interaction. The PBP is associated with HOME scores, and has the added information of parents' perceptions.

INTEGRATION AND SUGGESTIONS

Given the relative shortage of developmentally based, psychometrically excellent, ecologically and clinically valid socioemotional assessment tools, the decision for how to proceed at any given age level could be difficult. We can make a start, however. First, to what overall course would we adhere? In their guidelines for the assessment of social competence from an organizational perspective, Waters and Sroufe (1983) called for broadband, multi-method assessments that are tied to real-life adaptational problems, call for the coordination of affect, cognition, and behavior, and tax the integrative capacities of the child. It would be our recommendation, too, to create a flexible battery of socioemotional assessment techniques at each age level during this period. Choosing the best extant measures of developmentally salient issues, using as much naturalistic data as possible, and gathering information from multiple sources, occasions, and settings in order to obtain converging views allows for errors of measurement to be minimized. Thus, our assessments of current socioemotional functioning are more believable, because we can average across testing environment, instrumentation, representativeness of behaviors, and biases of varying raters (Martin, 1986).

Following such recommendations is also appropriate in following PL 99-457's implications for assessment that assists in the team decision–making of early educators (Bagnato & Neisworth, 1991). Functional rather than categorical assessment, assessing for instruction, is vital. Hence, our general conclusions from this extensive review of socioemotional assessment tools would be as follows:

1. Take time to listen to the parent (see Brazelton, 1992; Parks, 1992b). Collect a complete developmental history and social history, because parents' perceptions of their infants are crucial information. You need to know if they are misperceiving, and, if they are, help them find social support or parent education. If they are accurate, recommendations for infant/child programming can be made. We feel that this recommendation is critical to adequate socioemotional assessment

   And, over and above interviewing the parents for background, parental participation in the actual assessment process is not only required by PL 99-457, but it just makes good sense: These are the people who are most expert about the child in question. In order to be successful in meeting this goal, however, we must enable parents to transmit information productively; we must allow parental anxiety, sadness, guilt, or anger at having an infant or child with a problem to be expressed. An excellent working alliance can be formed with parents and child when appropriate assessment tools and techniques are utilized.

   What assessment procedures of those reviewed garner parent information? The DDST takes some parent report, the ECI could conceivably be completed by parents, the I/TSC explicitly calls for parent completion, and TPBA requires the parent to participate as a full team member. Among transactional assessments, the PBP gleans important parental perceptions. Although not asking for parent input, the NBAS is quite useful to demonstrate to parents, and all the transactional assessments include information about parenting that could be discussed with parents for their perspective. On balance, however, these measures, like most in childhood assessment, do not make full use of parents' store of information.

2. Observe the infant/child interaction with a variety of persons, including parents, peers, and, where applicable, other caregivers/teachers. How children play and work alone or with others, act/react, speak/remain silent, express/inhibit feelings, is central to socioemotional development, and there is no substitute for direct observation. Observation, as well as embedding queries about socioemotional development within age-appropriate play, loom particularly important to our goals here. Direct assessment can be problematic due to lack of verbal, visuomotor, and complex information-processing skills, and inability to cope with its demand characteristics (Martin, 1986). Measures that make good use of observation or embedding within ecologically valid play procedures include the IRS, NCAST, BSID social facet, FEASIE, HELP, Structured Playroom, LM, TPBA, TUT, MPAC, GLOS, and PCERA (see Table 12.10).

3. Choice of setting is crucial. The place(s) of assessment should be as free of stress as possible for both the infant/child and parents. Illness, fatigue, fear, anxiety, excitement, or upset can influence socioemotional behavior and render our assessment invalid. Assessors must also learn to be "preschool" psychologists, not merely "developmental" or "school" psychologists (Bagnato & Neisworth, 1991), in order to gain and maintain the rapport so important at this age range.

4. Given the proliferation of criterion-referenced and judgment-based measures that we have reported here, as well as the few norm-referenced tools mentioned, decision rules for screening and diagnosis are also vital. For norm-referenced tests, Bagnato and Neisworth (1991) suggested a principle of 1 standard deviation below average for eligibility for special concern and services. The problem can be solved for criterion-referenced measures by adopting a rule of 25% delay in age functioning. For transactional measures, a consensus as to a cutoff for environmental risk for socioemotional difficulties would have to be decided on; for most of the measures included here, that task has yet to be completed.

But, for judgment-based measures, Bagnato and Neisworth (1990) asserted that a team consensus is really critical. Their System to Plan Early Childhood Services (SPECS) is an excellent example of a totally seamless assessment-planning system in which professionals and parents provide information on all areas of development, and then rate the child on a 5-point scale regarding the child's level of development in each domain. The next consensus reached is regarding level of intervention. SPECS or a system modeled on it would seem extremely promising particularly for the socioemotional domain.

TABLE 12.10
Assessment Measures Reviewed

Early Infancy (0–6 mos)

Screening

DDST (0–72 months)
IRS (0–4 months)

Diagnosis

NBAS (0–1 month)
NCAFS (0–12 months) and NCATS (0–36 months)
BRS (0–42 months)
ECI (4–36 months)
FEASIE (0–72 months)

Program Planning and Evaluation

HELP (0 to 36 months)
E-LAP (0–36 months; too sparse to be mentioned further)

Mid-Infancy (7–18 months)

Screening

DDST
I/TSC (7–30 months)
Structured Playroom (7–18 months)
LM (3–30 months)

Diagnosis

NCAFS, NCATS
BRS
ECI
FEASIE
TBC (9–48 months)

Program Planning and Evaluation

HELP
TPBA (7–72 months)

Late Infancy/Toddlerhood (19–36 months)

Screening

DDST
I/TSC
LM
TUT (19–54 months)
Meier's Developmental Checklist
Zabel's Teacher Screening Measure

(Continued)

TABLE 12.10
(Continued)

Diagnosis

NCATS
BRS
ECI
TBC
CBCL 2–3 (24–36 months)

Program Planning and Evaluation

HELP
TPBA

Preschool (37–60 months)

Screening

DDST
Problem-Solving Task
Meier's Developmental Checklist
Zabel's Teacher Screening Measure
MPAC

Diagnosis

BRS through 42 months
CBCL 2–3, then CBCL 4–16
PSP

Program Planning and Evaluation

TPBA
HELP-SP (37–60 months)

Transactional Assessment

NCATS and NCAFS
GLOS
PCERA
PBP
HOME

Are we any closer now to making decisions about what are the best techniques (technically, ecologically, and practically) to choose for socioemotional assessment? For early infancy, we would recommend both the DDST and IRS for screening (given a means of a consensus for the IRS). Parent-child observation should always be part of socioemotional screening, despite its cost. For diagnosis, the BRS seems the most useful, especially as it would already routinely be given. With slightly longer observation, the ECI could be completed (or possibly could be completed by the parent). The HELP would be the best planning measure. It is encouraging that many organizational developmental milestones are picked up here.

For middle infancy, we recommend the I/TSC (especially because it gives the parent's perspective, and as it continues to be refined) and either the Structured Playroom or the LM system for screening, the BRS and ECI for diagnosis, and either the HELP of TPBA for program planning. For late infancy, we would use the I/TSC and TUT for screening (and add either Meier or Zabel if the child is in day care). The same diagnostic and planning tools can be used as in middle infancy. The TPBA would be much more useful if there were direct ties to intervention curriculum objectives, and if a developmental age were obtainable. Clearly, shortcomings abound for measures in age ranges regarding coverage of developmental milestones.

For the preschool period, we would recommend the same measures for screening, with the BRS or PSP for diagnosis and the HELP–SP or TPBA for planning. We would like to see even better coverage of developmental milestones in our measures at this age level, although the problem is not as severe as for the two preceding age periods. As for transactional measures, where at all feasible, the PBP and the HOME are recommended for all ages at which they are appropriate.

Basically, we have not recommended the NBAS or NCAST only because of their expense and the necessity of extensive training. They are excellent tools to be included when deemed possible or necessary. As for the FEASIE and the NCCIP diagnostic system, we feel that clinical training is of paramount importance. Applied developmental psychologists who can sensitively and accurately make judgments regarding emotional development are crucially needed.

In short, there is much work to be done to unite a developmental perspective with the practical issue of assessment. We would encourage psychologists and psychologists-in-training to take the recommendations made here seriously; perhaps a more unified approach can yet be found.

REFERENCES

Achenbach, T. M. (1992). *Manual for the CBCL/2-3 and 1992 Profile*. Burlington: University of Vermont Department of Psychiatry.
Achenbach, T. M., & Edelbrock, C. S. (1986). *Child Behavior Checklist and Youth Self-Report*. Burlington, VT: Author.

Achenbach, T. M., Edelbrock, C. S., & Howell, C. T. (1987). Empirically based assessment of the behavioral/emotional problems of 2- and 3-year-old children. *Journal of Abnormal Child Psychology, 15,* 629-650.

Bagnato, S., & Neisworth, J. (1990). *System to Plan early Childhood Services* (SPECS). Circle Pines, MN: American Guidance Service.

Bagnato, S., & Neisworth, J. (1991). *Assessment for early intervention: Best practices for professionals.* New York: Guilford.

Barnard, K. E., Eyres, S., Lobo, M., & Snyder, C. (1983). An ecological paradigm for assessment & intervention. In T. B. Brazelton & B. M. Lester (Eds.), *New approaches to developmental screening of infants* (pp. 199–218). New York: Elsevier.

Barnard, K. E., & Kelly, J. (1990). Assessment of parent–child interaction. In S. J. Meisels & J. P. Shonkoff (Eds.), *Handbook of early childhood intervention* (pp. 278–302). New York: Cambridge University Press.

Bayley, N. (1969). *Bayley Scales of Infant Development.* New York: Psychological Corporation.

Bayley, N. (1993). *Bayley Scales of Infant Development.* San Antonio, TX: Psychological Corporation.

Behar, L., & Stringfield. (1974). A behavior rating scale for the preschool child. *Developmental Psychology, 10,* 601–610.

Boggs, S. R., Eyberg, S., & Reynolds, L. A. (1990). Concurrent validity of the Eyberg Child Behavior Inventory. *Journal of Clinical Child Psychology, 19,* 75–78.

Brazelton, T. B. (1984). *Neonatal Behavioral Assessment Scale.* Philadelphia: J. B. Lippincott.

Bromwich, R. (1983). *Parent Behavior Progression: Manual and 1983 supplement.* Northridge: Center for Research Development and Services, Department of Educational Psychology, California State University.

Caldwell, B., & Bradley, R. (1978). *Manual for the Home Observation for Measurement of the Environment.* Little Rock: University of Arkansas.

Campbell, S. (1988). *Behavior problems in preschool children: Clinical and developmental issues.* New York: Guilford.

Campbell, S., & Ewing, L. J. (1990). Follow-up of hard-to-manage preschoolers: Adjustment at age 9 and predictors of continuing symptoms. *Journal of Child Psychology and Psychiatry, 31,* 871-889.

Clark, R. (1985). *The Parent-Child Early Relational Assessment.* Unpublished manuscript, University of Wisconsin, Madison, WI.

Clark, R., Paulson, A., & Conlin, S. (1993). Assessment of developmental status and parent-infant relationships: The therapeutic process of evaluation. In C. H. Zeanah (Ed.), *Handbook of infant mental health* (pp. 191–209). New York: Guilford.

Cohen, M. A., & Gross, P. J. (1979). *The developmental resource: Behavioral sequences for assessment and program planning.* New York: Grune & Stratton.

Conners, C. K. (1985). *The Conners Ratings Scales: Instruments for the assessment of childhood psychopathology.* Unpublished manuscript, Children's Hospital National Medical Center, Washington, DC.

Crowell, J. A., & Feldman, S. S. (1988). Mothers' internal working models of relationships and children's behavioral and developmental status: A study of mother–child interaction. *Child Development, 59* 1273–1285.

Crowell, J. A., & Fleischmann, M. A. (1993). Use of structured research procedures in clinical assessments of infants. In C. H. Zeanah (Ed.), *Handbook of infant mental health* (pp. 210–222). New York: Guilford.

DeGangi, G. A., Poisson, Sickel, R. Z., & Weiner, A. S. (1994). *Infant/Toddler Screening Checklist: A screening tool for parents*. Tucson, AZ: Therapy Skill Builders, Psychological Corporation.

Denham, S. A., McKinley, M., Couchoud, E. A., & Holt, R. (1990). Emotional and behavioral predictors of preschool peer ratings. *Child Development, 61,* 1145–1152.

Denham, S. A., & Mitchell-Copeland, J. (1993). Multivariate cross-validation of Lewis and Michalson's system for assessing socioemotional competence. *Infant Mental Health Journal, 14,* 133–146.

Denham, S. A., Renwick, S., & Holt, R. (1991). Working and playing together: Prediction of preschool socioemotional competence from mother–child interaction. *Child Development, 62,* 242–249.

Denham, S. A., Zahn-Waxler, C., Cummings, E. M., & Iannotti, R. J. (1990). Social competence in young children's peer relations: Patterns of development and change. *Child Psychiatry and Human Development, 22,* 29–44.

Drotar, D., & Sturm, L. (1989). Training psychologists as infant specialists. *Infants and Young Children, 2,* 58–66.

Dumas, J. E., & Serketich, W. J. (1993, November). *The Preschool Socioaffective Profile (PSP): Its application to a Head Start population.* Poster presented at the second national Head Start Research Conference, Washington, DC.

Emde, R. N., Bingham, R. D., & Harmon, R. J. (1993). Classification and the diagnostic process in infancy. In C. H. Zeanah (Ed.), *Handbook of infant mental health* (pp. 225–235). New York: Guilford.

Field, T. (1980). Interactions of preterm and term infants with their lower- and middle-class teenage and adult mothers. In T. Field, S. Goldberg, D. Stern, & A. Sostek (Eds.), *High-risk infants and children: Adult and peer interactions* (pp. 113–132). New York: Academic Press.

Foruno, S., O Reilly, A., Hoska, C. M., Instauka, T. T., Allman, T. L., & Zeisloft, B. (1985). *Help for special preschoolers.* Palo Alto, CA: VORT Corporation.

Fraiberg, S. (1980). *Clinical studies in infant mental health: The first year of life.* New York: Basic Books.

Frankenburg, W. K., Camp, B. W., & Van Natta, P. A. (1971). Validity of the Denver Developmental Screening Test. *Child Development, 42,* 475–485.

Frankenburg, W. K., & Coons, C. E. (1983). Early identification of at risk children. In T. B. Brazelton & B. M. Lester (Eds.), *New approaches to developmental screening of infants* (pp. 137–152). New York: Elsevier.

Frankenburg, W. K., Dodds, J. B., Fandal, A. W., Kazuk, E., & Cohrs, M. (1975). *Denver Developmental Screening Test.* Denver, CO: Denver Developmental Materials.

Gaensbauer, T. J., & Harmon, R. J. (1981). Clinical assessment in infancy utilizing structured playroom situations. *Journal of the American Academy of Child Psychiatry, 20,* 264–280.

Glover, M. E., Preminger, J. L., & Sanford, A. R. (1978). *The Early Learning Accomplishment Profile for developmentally young children: Birth to 36 months*. Chapel Hill, NC: Chapel Hill Training-Outreach Project.

Greenspan, S. (1983). Parenting in infancy and early childhood: A developmental structuralist approach to delineating adaptive and maladaptive patterns. In J. Sasserath & R. Hoekelman (Eds.), *Minimizing high risk parenting* (pp. 79–86). Skillman, NJ: Johnson & Johnson Baby Products.

Greenspan, S. (1992). *Infancy and early childhood: The practice of clinical assessment and intervention with emotional and developmental challenges*. Madison, CT: International Universities Press.

Greenspan, S. (1994). Diagnostic classification of mental health and developmental disorders of infancy and early childhood. *Zero to Three, 14*, 34–41.

Greenspan, S., & Lieberman, A. F. (1989). Infants, mothers, and their interaction: A quantitative clinical approach to developmental assessment. In S. I. Greenspan & G. H. Pollock (Eds.), *The course of life, Vol. I: Infancy* (pp. 503–560). Madison, CT: International Universities Press.

Howes, C. (1987). Social competence with peers in young children: Developmental sequences. *Developmental Review, 7*, 252–272.

LaFreniere, P. J., Dumas, J. E., Capuano, F., & Dubeau, D. (1992). Development and validation of the Preschool Socioaffective Profile. *Psychological Assessment, 4*, 442–450.

LaFreniere, P. J., Dumas, J. E., Capuano, F., Coutu, D., & Giuliani, L. (1993, March). *The revised Preschool Socio-affective Profile*. Paper presented at the biennial meeting of the Society for Research in Child Development, New Orleans, LA.

Larzelere, R. E., Amberson, T. G., & Martin, J. A. (1992). Age differences in perceived discipline problems for 9 to 48 months. *Family Relations, 41*, 192–199.

Larzelere, R. E., Martin, J. A., & Amberson, T. G. (1989). The Toddler Behavior Checklist: A parent-completed assessment of socioemotional characteristics of young preschoolers. *Family Relations, 38*, 418–425.

Lazar, I., & Darlington, R. (1982). Lasting effects of early education: A report from the Consortium of Longitudinal Studies. *Monograph of the Society for Research in Child Development, 47*(2–3), Serial No. 195.

Lewis, M. (1985). The role of emotion in development. *Journal of Children in Contemporary Society, 17*, 7–22.

Lewis, M., & Michalson, L. (1983). *Children's emotions and moods: Developmental theory and measurement*. New York: Plenum.

Lewis, M., Sullivan, M. W., & Michalson, L. (1984). The cognitive-emotional fugue. In C. E. Izard, J. Kagan, & R. B. Zajonc (Eds.), *Emotions, cognition, and behavior* (pp. 264–288). New York: Cambridge University Press.

Linder, T. (1990). *Transdisciplinary play-based assessment: A functional approach to working with children*. Baltimore: P. H. Brookes.

Martin, R. P. (1986). Assessment of the social and emotional functioning of preschool children. *School Psychology Review, 15*, 216–232.

Matas, L, Arend, R. A., & Sroufe, L. A. (1978). Continuity of adaptation in the second year: The relationship between quality of attachment and later competence. *Child Development, 49*, 547–556.

Meier, J. H. (1993, November). *Developmental screening and assessment.* Poster presented at the second National Head Start Research Conference, Washington, DC.

National Center for Clinical Infant Programs (NCCIP). (1993). *Classification of mental health and developmental disorders of infancy and early childhood.* Arlington, VA: Author.

Parks, S. (1992a). *HELP strands: Curriculum-based developmental assessment birth to three years.* Palo Alto, CA: VORT Corporation.

Parks, S. (1992b). *Inside HELP--Hawaii Early Learning Profile administration and reference manual.* Palo Alto, CA: VORT Corporation.

Popham, W. J. (1978). Well-crafted criterion-referenced tests. *Educational Leadership, 36,* 91–95.

Rossetti, L. M. (1990). *Infant-toddler assessment: An interdisciplinary approach.* Boston: Little, Brown.

Saarni, C. (1990). Emotional competence. In R. Thompson (Ed.), *Nebraska symposium: Socioemotional development* (pp. 115–161). Lincoln: University of Nebraska Press.

Sattler, J. M. (1990). *Assessment of children* (3rd ed.). San Diego: Jerome Sattler.

Sparrow, S. S., Balla, D. A., & Cicchetti, D. V. (1984). *Vineland Adaptive Behavior Scales.* Circle Pines, MN: American Guidance Services.

Sroufe, L.A., Schork, E., Motti, F., Lawroski, N. & LaFreniere, P. (1984). The role of affect in social competence. In C. E. Izard, J. Kagan, & R. B. Zajonc (Eds.), *Emotions, cognition and behavior* (pp. 289–319). Cambridge: Cambridge University Press.

Waters, E., & Sroufe, L. A. (1983). Social competence as a developmental construct. *Developmental Review, 3,* 79–97.

Zabel, M. K. (1982). *Identification and programming for behaviorally impaired preschool children: Current procedures and programs.* Educational Research Information Clearinghouse, No. ED 243–258.

Zeitlin, S., Williamson, G. G., & Szczepanski, M. (1988). *Early Coping Inventory: A measure of adaptive behavior.* Bensenville, IL: Scholastic Testing Service.

Author Index

Subject Index